797,885 Books

are available to read at

www.ForgottenBooks.com

Forgotten Books' App
Available for mobile, tablet & eReader

ISBN 978-1-331-04895-4
PIBN 10138132

This book is a reproduction of an important historical work. Forgotten Books uses state-of-the-art technology to digitally reconstruct the work, preserving the original format whilst repairing imperfections present in the aged copy. In rare cases, an imperfection in the original, such as a blemish or missing page, may be replicated in our edition. We do, however, repair the vast majority of imperfections successfully; any imperfections that remain are intentionally left to preserve the state of such historical works.

Forgotten Books is a registered trademark of FB &c Ltd.
Copyright © 2015 FB &c Ltd.
FB &c Ltd, Dalton House, 60 Windsor Avenue, London, SW19 2RR.
Company number 08720141. Registered in England and Wales.

For support please visit www.forgottenbooks.com

A good deal of this book involved the financing of war and the issuing of paper money by the colonies

p 282 — 1st mention of Washington

English
Français
Deutsche
Italiano
Español
Português

www.forgottenbooks.com

Mythology Photography **Fiction** Fishing Christianity **Art** Cooking Essays Buddhism Freemasonry Medicine **Biology** Music **Ancient Egypt** Evolution Carpentry Physics Dance Geology **Mathematics** Fitness Shakespeare **Folklore** Yoga Marketing **Confidence** Immortality Biographies Poetry **Psychology** Witchcraft Electronics Chemistry History **Law** Accounting **Philosophy** Anthropology Alchemy Drama Quantum Mechanics Atheism Sexual Health **Ancient History** **Entrepreneurship** Languages Sport Paleontology Needlework Islam **Metaphysics** Investment Archaeology Parenting Statistics Criminology **Motivational**

A HISTORY

OF THE

COLONIES PLANTED BY THE ENGLISH

ON

THE CONTINENT OF

NORTH AMERICA,

FROM THEIR

SETTLEMENT, TO THE COMMENCEMENT OF THAT WAR WHICH TERMINATED IN THEIR

INDEPENDENCE.

BY JOHN MARSHALL.

PHILADELPHIA:
PUBLISHED BY ABRAHAM SMALL.

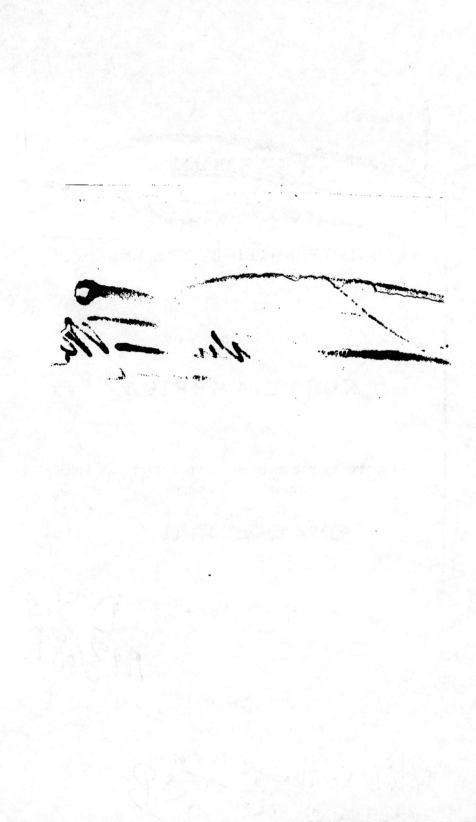

PREFACE.

So large a portion of the life of General Washington was devoted to the public, so elevated and important were the stations which he filled, that the history of his life is, at the same time, the history of his nation.

The part he took, while commander in chief, in the civil as well as military affairs of the United States, was so considerable, that few events of general interest occurred, which were not, in some degree, influenced by him. A detail of the transactions in which he was either immediately or remotely concerned, would comprehend so great a part of those which belong to general history, that the entire exclusion of the few in which he bore no part, while it would scarcely give to the work more of the peculiar character of biography, would expose it to the charge of being an incomplete history of the times.

His administration of the government while President of the United States, cannot be well understood without a full knowledge of the political measures of the day, and of the motives by which his own conduct was regulated.

These considerations appeared to require that his biography should present a general historical view of the transactions of the time, as well as a particular narrative of the part performed by himself.

Our ideas of America, of the character of our revolution, of those who engaged in it, and of the struggles by which it was accomplished, would be imperfect without some knowledge of our colonial history. No work had been published when this was undertaken, from which that knowledge could be collected. To have taken up the history of the United States when the command of the army was conferred on General Washington, would have been to introduce the reader abruptly into the midst of scenes and transactions, with the causes of which, and with the actors in them, he would naturally wish to be intimately acquainted. This was the apology of the author for the introductory volume to the Life of General Washing-

PREFACE. vii

ton. Had the essays since written towards a general history of the English colonies been then in possession of the public, this volume would not have appeared. But, although they might have prevented its appearance, they ought not to prevent its being corrected and offered to the public in a form less exceptionable than that which it originally bore. From the extreme, I may add unpardonable, precipitation with which it was hurried to the press, many errors were overlooked which, on a perusal of the book, were as apparent to the author as to others. He was desirous of correcting these errors, and of making the work more worthy of the public to which it was offered, as well as more satisfactory to himself. For this purpose he has given it, since the impressions under which it was compiled have worn off, more than one attentive reading; has made several alterations in th language; and has expunged much of the less essential matter with which the narrative was burthened. He dares not flatter himself that he has succeeded completely in his attempt to entitle this work to the approbation of the literary public of America; but hopes that its claims to that approbation are stronger than in its original form.

Believing that motives no longer exist for connecting the History of the English Colonies in North America with the Life of Washington, the author has obtained the permission of the proprietor of the copy-right to separate the Introduction from the other volumes, and to publish it as a distinct work.

CONTENTS.

CHAPTER I.

Commission of Cabot.—His voyage to America.—Views of discovery relinquished by Henry VII.—Resumed by Elizabeth.—Letters patent to Sir Humphry Gilbert.—His voyages and death.—Patent to Sir Walter Raleigh.—Voyage of Sir Richard Grenville.—Colonists carried back to England by Drake.—Grenville arrives with other colonists.—They are left on Roanoke Island.—Are destroyed by the Indians—Arrival of John White.—He returns to England for succour.—Raleigh assigns his patent.—Patent to Sir Thomas Gates and others—Code of laws for the proposed colony drawn up by the King. - - - - *Page* 9

CHAPTER II.

Voyage of Newport.—Settlement at Jamestown.—Distress of colonists.—Smith.—He is captured by the Indians.—Condemned to death, saved by Pocahontas.—Returns to Jamestown.—Newport arrives with fresh settlers.—Smith explores the Chesapeake.—Is chosen president.—New charter.—Third voyage of Newport.—Smith sails for Europe.—Condition of the colony.—Colonists determine to abandon the country.—Are stopped by Lord Delaware.—Sir Thomas Dale.—New charter.—Captain Argal seizes Pocahontas.—She marries Mr. Rolf.—Separate property in lands and labour.—Expedition against Port Royal.—Against Manhadoes.—Fifty acres of

CONTENTS.

land for each settler.—Tobacco.—Sir Thomas Dale.—Mr. Yeardley.—First assembly.—First arrival of females.—Of convicts.—Of African slaves.—Two councils established.—Prosperity of the colony.—Indians attempt to massacre the whites.—General war.—Dissolution of the company.—Arbitrary measures of the crown.—Sir John Harvey.—Sir William Berkeley.—Provincial assembly restored.—Virginia declares in favour of Charles II —Grant to Lord Baltimore.—Arrival of a colony in Maryland.—Assembly composed of freemen.—William Claybourne.—Assembly composed of representatives.—Divided into two branches.—Tyrannical proceedings.
Page 29

CHAPTER III.

First ineffectual attempts of the Plymouth company to settle the country.—Settlement at New Plymouth.—Sir Henry Rosewell and company.—New charter.—Settlements prosecuted vigorously.—Government transferred to the colonists.—Boston founded.—Religious intolerance.—General court established.—Royal commission for the government of the plantations.—Contest with the French colony of Acadié.—Hugh Peters.—Henry Vane.—Mrs. Hutchison.—Maine granted to Gorges.—Quo warranto against the patent of the colony.—Religious dissentions —Providence settled.—Rhode Island settled.—Connecticut settled.—War with the Pequods.—New Haven settled. - - - - 73

CHAPTER IV.

Massachusetts claims New Hampshire and part of Maine.—Dissentions among the inhabitants.—Confederation of the New England colonies.—Rhode Island excluded from it.—Separate chambers provided for the two branches of the Legislature.—New England takes part with Parliament.—Treaty with Acadié.—Petition of the non-conformists.—Disputes between Massachusetts and Connecticut.—War between England and Holland.—Machinations of the Dutch at Manhadoes among the Indians.—Massachusetts refuses to join the united colonies in the war.—Application of New Haven to Cromwell for assistance.—Peace with the Dutch.—Expedition of Sedgewic against Acadié.—Religious intolerance. *Page* 108

CHAPTER V.

Transactions succeeding the restoration of Charles II.—Contests between Connecticut and New Haven.—Discontents in Virginia.—Grant to the duke of York.—Commissioners appointed by the crown.—Conquest of the Dutch settlements.—Conduct of Massachusetts to the royal commissioners —Their recall. Massachusetts evades a summons to appear before the King and council.—Settlement of Carolina —Form of government.—Constitution of Mr. Locke.—Discontents in the county of Albemarle.—Invasion from Florida.—Abolition of the constitution of Mr. Locke.—Bacon's rebellion.—His death.—Assembly deprived of judicial power.—Discontents in Virginia.—Population of the colony. - 130

CHAPTER VI.

Prosperity of New England.—War with Philip.—Edward Randolph arrives in Boston.—Maine adjudged to Gorges.—Purchased by Massachusetts.—Royal government erected in New Hampshire.—Complaints against Massachusetts.—Their letters patent cancelled.—Death of Charles II.—James II. proclaimed.—New commission for the government of New England.—Sir Edmond Andros.—The charter of Rhode Island abrogated.—Odious measures of the new government.—Andros deposed.—William and Mary proclaimed.—Review of proceedings in New York and the Jerseys.—Pennsylvania granted to William Penn.—Frame of government —Foundation of Philadelphia laid.—Assembly convened.—First acts of the Legislature.—Boundary line with lord Baltimore settled. 165

CONTENTS.

CHAPTER VII.

New charter of Massachusetts.—Affairs of New York.—War with France.—Schenectady destroyed.—Expedition against Port Royal.—Against Quebec.—Acadié recovered by France.—Pemaquid taken.—Attempt on St. Johns.—Peace.—Affairs of New York.—Of Virginia.—Disputes between England and France respecting boundary in America.—Re-commencement of hostilities.—Quotas of the respective colonies.—Treaty of neutrality between France and the five nations.—Expedition against Port Royal—Incursion into Massachusetts.—Plan for the invasion of Canada.—Port Royal taken.—Expedition against Quebec.—Treaty of Utrecht.—Affairs of New York. —Of Carolina.—Expedition against St. Augustine.—Attempt to establish the Episcopal church.—Invasion of the colony.—Bills of credit issued.—Legislature continues itself.—Massacre in North Carolina by the Indians.—Tuscaroras defeated.—Scheme of a Bank. - - *Page* 186

CHAPTER VIII.

Proceedings of the legislature of Massachusetts.—Intrigues of the French among the Indians.—War with the savages.—Peace.—Controversy with the governor.—Decided in England.---Contests concerning the governor's salary.---The assembly adjourned to Salem.---Contest concerning the salary terminated.---Great depreciation of the paper currency.---Scheme of a land bank.---Company dissolved by act of Parliament.---Governor Shirley arrives.---Review of transactions in New York. - - - - - 215

CHAPTER IX.

War with the southern Indians.—Dissatisfaction of Carolina with the proprietors.---Rupture with Spain.---Combination to subvert the proprietary government.---Revolution completed.---Expedition from the Havanna against Charleston.---Peace

CONTENTS.   xiii

with Spain.—The proprietors surrender their interest to the crown.—The province divided.—Georgia settled—Impolicy of the first regulations.—Intrigues of the Spaniards with the slaves of South Carolia.—Insurrection of the Slaves. *P.* 238

CHAPTER X.

War declared against Spain.—Expedition against St. Augustine.—Georgia invaded.—Spaniards land on an island in the Altamaha.—Appearance of a fleet from Charleston.—Spanish army re-embarks.—Hostilities with France.—Expedition against Louisbourg.—Louisbourg surrenders.—Great plans of the belligerent powers.—Misfortunes of the armament under the duke D'Anville.—The French fleet dispersed by a storm.—Expedition against Nova Scotia.—Treaty of Aix la Chapelle.—Paper money of Massachusetts redeemed.—Contests between the French and English respecting boundaries.—Statement respecting the discovery of the Mississippi.—Scheme for connecting Louisiana with Canada—Relative strength of the French and English colonies.—Defeat at the Little Meadows.—Convention at Albany.—Plan of union.—Objected to both in America and Great Britain.   -   -   253

CHAPTER XI.

General Braddock arrives.—Convention of governors and plan of the campaign.—French expelled from Nova Scotia, and inhabitants transplanted.—Expedition against fort Du Quêsne.—Battle of Monongahela.—Defeat and death of General Braddock.—Expedition against Crown Point.—Dieskan defeated.—Expedition against Niagara.—Frontiers distressed by the Indians.—Meeting of the governors at New York.—Plan for the campaign of 1756.—Lord Loudoun arrives.—Montcalm takes Oswego.—Lord Loudoun abandons offensive operations.—Small pox breaks out in Albany.—Campaign of 1757 opened.—Admiral Holbourne arrives at Halifax.—Is joined by the earl of Loudoun.—Expedition against Louisbourg relinquished.—Lord Loudoun returns to New York.—Fort William

Henry taken.—Controversy between Lord Loudoun and the assembly of Massachusetts - - *Page* 287

CHAPTER XII.

Preparations for the campaign of 1758.—Admiral Boscawen and general Amherst arrive at Halifax.—Plan of the campaign.—Expedition against Louisbourg, Ticonderoga, and Crown Point.—General Abercrombie repulsed under the walls of Ticonderoga.—Fort Frontignac taken.—Expedition against fort Du Quesne.—Preparations for the campaign of 1759.—General Amherst succeeds general Abercrombie.—Plan of the campaign.—Ticonderoga and Crown Point taken.—Army goes into winter quarters.—French repulsed at Oswego.—Defeated at Niagara.—Niagara taken.—Expedition against Quebec.—Check to the English army.—Battle on the Plains of Abraham.—Death of Wolf and Montcalm.—Quebec capitulates.—Garrisoned by the English under the command of general Murray.—Attempt to recover Quebec—Battle near Sillery.—Quebec besieged by Monsieur Levi.—Siege raised.—Montreal capitulates.—War with the southern Indians.—Battle near the town of Etchoe.—Grant defeats them and burns their towns.—Treaty with the Cherokees.—War with Spain.—Success of the English.—Peace. - 311

CHAPTER XIII.

Opinions on the supremacy of parliament, and its right to tax the colonies.—The stamp act.—Congress at New York.—Violence in the towns.—Change of administration.—Stamp act repealed.—Opposition to the mutiny act.—Act imposing duties on tea, &c. resisted in America.—Letters from the assembly of Massachusetts to members of the administration.—Petition to the King.—Circular letter to the colonial assemblies—Letter from the earl of Hillsborough.—Assembly of Massachusetts dissolved.—Seizure of the Sloop Liberty.—Convention at Fanueil Hall.—Moderation of its proceedings.—Two British regiments arrive at Boston.—Resolutions of the house of Burgesses of Virginia —Assembly dissolved.— The members form an association.—General measures against importation.—General court convened in Massachusetts.— Its proceedings.—Is prorogued.—Duties, except that on tea, repealed.—Circular letter of the earl of Hillsborough.—New York recedes from the non-importation agreement in part.— Her example followed.—Riot in Boston.—Trial and acquittal of Captain Preston. - - *Page* 350

CHAPTER XIV.

Insurrection in North Carolina —Dissatisfaction of Massachusetts.—Corresponding committees.—Governor Hutchinson's correspondence communicated by Dr. Franklin.—The assembly petition for his removal.—He is succeeded by general Gage.—Measures to enforce the act concerning duties.—Ferment in America.—The tea thrown into the sea at Boston.— Measures of Parliament.—General enthusiasm in America. —A general congress proposed.—General Gage arrives.— Troops stationed on Boston neck.—New counsellors and judges.—Obliged to resign.—Boston neck fortified.—Military stores seized by general Gage.—Preparations for defence.— King's speech.—Proceedings of Parliament.—Battle of Lexington.—Massachusetts raises men.—Meeting of Congress. —Proceedings of that body—Transactions in Virginia.— Provincial congress of South Carolina.—Battle of Breed's hill. - - - - - 395

A HISTORY

OF THE

AMERICAN COLONIES.

CHAPTER I.

Commission of Cabot.—His voyage to America.—Views of discovery relinquished by Henry VII.—Resumed by Elizabeth.—Letters patent to Sir Humphry Gilbert.—His voyages and death.—Patent to Sir Walter Raleigh.—Voyage of Sir Richard Grenville.—Colonists carried back to England by Drake.—Grenville arrives with other colonists.—They are left on Roanoke Island.—Are destroyed by the Indians.—Arrival of John White.—He returns to England for succour.—Raleigh assigns his patent.—Patent to Sir Thomas Gates and others.—Code of laws for the proposed colony drawn up by the King.

THE UNITED STATES OF AMERICA extend, on the Atlantic, from the bay of Passamaquoddi in the the 45th, to cape Florida in the 25th, degree of north latitude; and thence, on the gulph of Mexico, including the small adjacent islands, to the mouth of the Sabine, in the 17th degree of west longitude from Washington. From the mouth of the Sabine to the Rocky mountains, they are separated from Spanish America by a line which pursues an irregular north western direction to the 42d degree of north latitude, whence it proceeds west, to the Pacific. On the north they are bounded by the British provinces; from which, between the Lake of the Woods and the Rocky, or Stony mountains, they are separated by the 49th parallel of north latitude. Their northern boundary, west of these mountains, has not yet been adjusted.

The extent of this vast Republic, in consequence of its recent acquisition of almost unexplored territory, has not yet been accurately ascertained; but may be stated at two millions of square miles.

Its population, which began on the Atlantic, and is travelling rapidly westward, amounted in 1820, according to the census of that year, to nine millions six hundred and fifty four thousand four hundred and fifteen persons. The enumerations which have been made under the authority of government, show an augmentation of numbers at the rate of about thirty-four *per centum** in ten years; and it is probable, that for many years to come, this ratio will not be materially changed.

Public sentiment, to which the policy of the go-

---

* The general estimate in the United States is, that their population doubles in twenty-five years.

vernment conforms, is opposed to a large military establishment; and the distance of the United States from the great powers of the world, protects them from the danger to which this policy might otherwise expose them.

The navy has become an object of great interest to the nation, and may be expected to grow with its resources. In April 1816, Congress passed an act appropriating one million of dollars annually, to its gradual increase; and authorising the construction of nine ships, to rate not less than seventy-four guns each, and of twelve, to rate not less than forty-four guns each. The execution of this act is in rapid progress. Inconsiderable as the navy now is, with respect to the number and force of its ships, it is deemed inferior to none in existence for the bravery and skill of its officers and men. When we take into view the extensive sea coast of the United States, the magnificent lakes, or inland seas, which form a considerable part of their northern frontier, the abundance of their materials for ship building, and the genius of their population for maritime enterprise, it is not easy to resist the conviction that this bulwark of defence will, at no very distant period, attain a size and strength sufficient to ensure the safety of the nation and the respect of the world.

The net revenue of the United States amounted, in the year 1822, to considerably more than twenty millions of dollars; and, unless a course of legislation unfavourable to its augmentation be adopted, must grow with their population.

In arts, in arms, and in power, they have advanced, and are advancing, with unexampled rapidity.

The history of their progress, from the first feeble settlements made by Europeans on a savage coast, to their present state of greatness; while it has just claims to the attention of the curious of all nations, may be expected deeply to interest every American.

Soon after the return of Columbus from that memorable voyage which opened the vast regions of the west to civilised man, the maritime states of Europe manifested a desire to share with Spain, the glory, the wealth, and the dominion to be acquired in the new world. By no one of these states, was this desire carried into action more promptly than by England. Henry VII. had received communications from Columbus, during the tedious and uncertain negotiations of that great man, at the dilatory court of Ferdinand, which prepared him for the important discoveries afterwards made, and inclined him to countenance the propositions of his own subjects for engaging in similar adventures. On the 5th of March 1495, he granted a commission to John Cabot, an enterprising Venetian who had settled in Bristol, and to his three sons, Lewis, Sebastian, and Sanctius, empowering them, or either of them, to sail under the banner of England, towards the east, north, or west, in order to discover countries unoccupied by any christian state, and to take possession of them in his name.

Commission of Cabot.

It does not appear that the expedition contemplated at the date of this commission was prosecuted imme-

AMERICAN COLONIES. 13

diately; but in May 1496, Cabot, with his second son, Sebastian, sailed from Bristol in a small squadron, consisting of one ship furnished by the King, and four barks fitted out by merchants of that city; and, steering almost due west, discovered the islands of Newfoundland and St. Johns, and, soon afterward, reached the continent of North America, along which he sailed from the fifty sixth to the thirty eighth degree of north latitude, in the vain hope of discovering a passage into the Pacific. His voyage to America.

Thus, according to the English historians, was first discovered that immense continent which stretches from the gulph of Mexico as far north as has yet been explored; and to this voyage, the English trace their title to the country they afterwards acquired by settlement, and by arms.

France, which has since contested with Britain the possession of a considerable portion of this important territory, has also advanced claims to its discovery; but they seem not to be well founded.

The ardour which had been excited in the bosom of Henry for making acquisitions in the new world, expired with this first effort. Cabot, on his return, found that monarch entirely disinclined to the farther prosecution of a scheme in which he had engaged with some zeal, the commencement of which had been attended with encouraging appearances. The scheme of making settlements relinquished.

Several causes are supposed to have contributed to suspend the pursuits of the English in America. Previous to its discovery, the Portuguese had explored the Azores, or Western Islands; in consequence of which they claimed this continent, and contended for the exclusion of the Spaniards from the Western Ocean. The controversy was decided by the Pope, who, on the 7th of May 1493, of his own "mere liberality and certain knowledge, and the plenitude of apostolic authority," granted to Spain, the countries discovered or to be discovered by her, to the westward of a line to be drawn from pole to pole, a hundred leagues west of the Azores; (excepting such countries as might be in the possession of any other christian prince antecedent to the year 1493;) and to Portugal, her discoveries eastward of that line.

The validity of this grant was probably strengthened, in the opinion of Henry, by other circumstances. He set a high value on the friendship of the King of Spain, with whom he was then negotiating the marriage which afterwards took place between his eldest son and Catharine, the daughter of that monarch. Ferdinand was jealous to excess of all his rights; and Henry was not inclined to interrupt the harmony subsisting between the two crowns, by asserting claims to the country discovered by Cabot, which was obviously within the limits to which the pretensions of Spain extended.

The fisheries of Newfoundland were carried on by individuals, to a considerable extent, and a paltry traffic was continued with the natives; but no serious design of acquiring territory, and planting colonies in America was formed until the reign of Elizabeth,

Renewed by Elizabeth.

when a plan for making permanent settlements was proposed and patronised by several persons of rank and influence. To select a man qualified for this arduous task, and disposed to engage in it, was among the first objects to which their attention was directed. Sir Humphry Gilbert had rendered himself conspicuous by his military services, and by a treatise concerning the north-west passage, in which great ingenuity and learning, are stated by Dr. Robertson, to be mingled with the enthusiasm, the credulity, and sanguine expectation which incite men to new and hazardous undertakings. On this gentleman the adventurers turned their eyes, and he was placed at the head of the enterprise. On the 11th of June 1578, he obtained letters patent from the Queen, vesting in him the powers that were required; on receiving which, he, with the associates of his voyage, embarked for America. But his success did not equal his expectations. The various difficulties inseparable from the settlement of a distant, unexplored country, inhabited only by savages; the inadequacy of the supplies which could be furnished for a colony by the funds of a few private individuals; the misfortune of having approached the continent too far towards the north, where the cold barren coast of cape Breton was rather calculated to repel than invite a settlement; have been assigned as the probable causes of his failure.*

* Robertson. Chalmer

Two expeditions conducted by this gentleman ended disastrously. In the last, he himself perished; having done nothing farther in the execution of his patent, than taking possession of the island of Newfoundland, in the name of Elizabeth.

Sir Walter Raleigh, alike distinguished by his genius, his courage, and the severity of his fate, had been deeply interested in the adventures in which his half brother, Sir Humphry Gilbert, had wasted his fortune, and was not deterred by their failure, or by the difficulties attending such an enterprise, from prosecuting with vigour, a plan so well calculated to captivate his bold and romantic temper.

<small>1584
Patent to
Sir Walter
Raleigh.</small>

On the 26th of March, he obtained a patent from the Queen; and, on the 27th of April, dispatched two small vessels under the command of captains Amidas and Barlow for the purpose of visiting the country, and of acquiring some previous knowledge of those circumstances which might be essential to the welfare of the colony he was about to plant. To avoid the error of Gilbert in holding too far north, Amidas and Barlow took the route by the Canaries, and the West India islands, and approached the North American continent towards the gulph of Florida. On the 2d of July, they touched at a small island situate on the inlet into Pamplico sound, whence they proceeded to Roanoke, near the mouth of Albemarle sound.

After employing a few weeks in traffic with the Indians, from whom they collected some confused accounts respecting the neighbouring continent, they took with them two of the natives, who willingly accompanied them, and embarked for England, where they arrived on the 15th of September. The splendid description which they gave of the soil, the climate, and the productions of the country they had visited, so pleased Elizabeth, that she bestowed on it the name of Virginia, as a memorial that it had been discovered during the reign of a virgin Queen.* Raleigh, encouraged by their report to hasten his preparations for taking possession of the property, fitted out a squadron consisting of seven small ships, laden with arms, ammunition, provisions, and passengers, which sailed from Plymouth on the 9th of April, under the command of Sir Richard Grenville, who was his relation, and interested with him in the patent. Having taken the southern route, and wasted some time in cruising against the Spaniards, Sir Richard did not reach the coast of North America, until the close of the month of June. He touched at both the islands on which Amidas and Barlow had landed, and made some excursions into different parts of the continent around Pamplico, and Albemarle sounds.

1585
Voyage of Sir Richard Grenville.

Having established a colony, consisting of one hundred and eight persons, in the island of Roanoke, an incommodious station, without any safe harbour, he committed the government of it to Mr. Ralph Lane; and, on the 25th of August, sailed for England.†

First colony.

---

* Robertson. Chalmer. Stith. † Ibid.

An insatiate passion for gold, attended by an eager desire to find it in the bowels of the earth, for a long time the disease of Europeans in America, became the scourge of this feeble settlement. The English flattered themselves that the country they had discovered could not be destitute of those mines of the precious metals with which Spanish America abounded. The most diligent researches were made in quest of them; and the infatuating hope of finding them stimulated the colonists to the utmost exertions of which they were capable. The Indians soon discerned the object for which they searched with so much avidity, and amused them with tales of rich mines in countries they had not yet explored. Seduced by this information, they encountered incredible hardships, and, in this vain search wasted that time which ought to have been employed in providing the means of future subsistence. Mutual suspicion and disgust between them and the natives ripened into open hostility; and, the provisions brought from England being exhausted, they were under the necessity of resorting for food to the precarious supplies which could be drawn from the rivers and woods. In this state of distress, they were found, in June, by Sir Francis Drake, who was then returning from a successful expedition against the Spaniards in the West Indies. He agreed to supply them with about one hundred men, four months provisions, and a small vessel; but, before she could be brought into a place of security, and the men and stores disembarked, she was driven out to sea by a

1586

sudden and violent storm. Discouraged by this misfortune, and worn out with fatigue and famine, the colonists unanimously determined to abandon the colony, and were, at their own request, taken on board the fleet which sailed for England.* _{Colonists carried back to England by Drake.}

Thus terminated the first English colony planted in America. The only acquisition made by this expensive experiment, was a better knowledge of the country and its inhabitants.

A few days after the departure of Drake with Lane and his associates, a small vessel which had been dispatched by Raleigh with a supply of provisions, reached its place of destination. Not finding the colonists, this vessel returned to England. Soon after its departure, Sir Richard Grenville arrived with three ships and ample supplies. Having searched in vain for the colonists he had left, and being unable to conjecture their fate, he placed fifteen men in the island with provisions for two years, for the purpose of retaining possession of the country, and returned to England. This small party was soon destroyed by the Indians. _{Grenville plants a second colony.} _{Destroyed by the Indians.}

Not discouraged by the ill success which had thus far attended his efforts to make a settlement in America, Raleigh, in the following year, fitted out three ships under the command of captain John White, and, it is said, directed the colony to be removed to the waters of the Chesapeake, which bay had been ₁₅₈₇

* Robertson. Chalmer. Stith. Smith.

discovered by Lane in the preceding year. Instructed by calamity, he adopted more efficacious means for preserving and continuing the colony than had before been used. The number of men was greater; they were accompanied by some women, and their supply of provisions was more abundant. Mr. White was appointed their governor, twelve assistants were assigned him as a council, and a charter incorporating them by the name of the governor and assistants of the city of Raleigh in Virginia, was granted them.

<small>Third colony arrives.</small> Thus prepared for a permanent settlement, they arrived in July at Roanoke, where they received the melancholy intelligence of the loss of their countrymen who had been left there by Sir Richard Grenville. They determined, however, to remain at the same place, and began to make the necessary preparations for their accommodation. Aware of the danger to be apprehended from the hostile disposition of their neighbours, they endeavoured to effect a reconciliation with the natives, one of whom, who had accompanied Amidas and Barlow to England, and who was distinguished by his unshaken attachment to the English, was christened, and styled Lord of *Dassa Monpeake*, an Indian nation in the neighbourhood.*

About the same time the first child of English parentage was born in America. She was the daughter of Ananias Dare, and, after the place of her birth, was named *Virginia*.

<small>* Robertson, Chalmer. Stith. Smith</small>

Soon perceiving their want of many things essential to the preservation, and comfortable subsistence of a new settlement, the colonists, with one voice, deputed their governor, to solicit those specific aids which their situation particularly and essentially required. On his arrival in England, he found the whole nation alarmed at the formidable preparations for their invasion, made by Philip II. of Spain; and Raleigh, Grenville, and the other patrons of the colony, ardently engaged in those measures of defence which the public danger demanded. Mingling, however, with his exertions to defend his native country, some attention to the colony he had planted, Raleigh found leisure to fit out a small fleet for its relief, the command of which was given to Sir Richard Grenville; but, the apprehensions from the Spanish armament still increasing, the ships of force prepared by Raleigh were detained in port by order of the Queen, and Sir Richard Grenville was commanded not to leave Cornwall, where his services were deemed necessary. On the 22d of April, White put to sea with two small barks, but, instead of hastening to the relief of his distressed countrymen, wasted his time in cruising; and, being beaten by a superior force, was totally disabled from prosecuting his voyage.* [1588]

The attention of Raleigh being directed to other more splendid objects, he assigned his patent to Sir Thomas Smith and a company of merchants in London. [1589 Raleigh assigns his patent.]

* Robertson. Chalmer. Stith. Smith.

After this transfer, a year was permitted to elapse before any effort was made for the relief of the colony. In March, three ships fitted out by the company, in one of which Mr. White embarked, sailed from Plymouth; but, having cruelly and criminally wasted their time in plundering the Spaniards in the West Indies, they did not reach Hatteras until the month of August. They fired a gun to give notice of their arrival, and sent a party to the place where the colony had been left; but no vestige of their countrymen could be found. In attempting the next day to go to Roanoke, one of the boats, in passing a bar, was half filled with water, another was overset, and six men were drowned. Two other boats were fitted out with nineteen men to search the island thoroughly on which the colony had been left.

At the departure of Mr. White, it was in contemplation to remove about fifty miles into the country; and it had been agreed that, should the colonists leave the island, they would carve the name of the place to which they should remove, on some tree, door, or post; with the addition of a cross over it, as a signal of distress, if they should be really distressed at the time of changing their situation. After considerable search, the word CROATAN was found carved in fair capital letters on one of the chief posts, but unaccompanied by the sign of distress which had been agreed on.

Croatan was the name of an Indian town on the north side of Cape Lookout, and for that place, the fleet weighed anchor the next day. Meeting with a storm, and several accidents, they were discouraged from proceeding on their voyage, and, determining to suspend their search, returned to the West Indies.

The company made no farther attempt to find these lost colonists; nor has the time or the manner of their perishing ever been discovered.*

The subsequent voyages made by the English to North America were for the sole purpose of traffic, and were unimportant in their consequences, until the year 1602, when one was undertaken by Bartholomew Gosnald, which contributed greatly to the revival of the then dormant spirit of colonising in the new world. He sailed from Falmouth in a small bark with thirty two men; and steering nearly west, reached the American continent, on the 11th of May, in about forty three degrees of north latitude.

margin: 1602 Voyage of Gosnald.

Finding no good harbour at this place, Gosnald put to sea again and stood southward. The next morning, he descried a promontory which he called cape Cod, and, holding his course along the coast as it stretched to the south west, touched at two islands, the first of which he named Martha's Vineyard, and the second, Elizabeth's Island. Having passed some time at these places, examining the country, and trading with the natives, he returned to England.†

This voyage was completed in less than four months, and was attended with important consequen-

---

* Robertson. Chalmer. Stith. † Ibid.

ces. Gosnald had found a healthy climate, a rich soil, good harbours, and a route which shortened considerably the distance to the continent of North America. He had seen many of the fruits known and prised in Europe, blooming in the woods; and had planted European grain which grew rapidly. Encouraged by this experiment, and delighted with the country, he formed the resolution of transporting thither a colony, and of procuring the co-operation of others by whom his plan might be supported. So unfortunate however had been former attempts of this sort, that men of wealth and rank, though strongly impressed by his report of the country, were slow in giving full faith to his representations, and in entering completely into his views. One vessel was fitted out by the merchants of Bristol, and another by the earl of Southampton, and lord Arundel of Wardour, in order to learn whether Gosnald's account of the country was to be considered as a just representation of its state, or as the exaggerated description of a person fond of magnifying his own discoveries. Both returned with a full confirmation of his veracity, and with the addition of so many new circumstances in favour of the country, as greatly increased the desire of settling it.

Richard Hackluyt, prebendary of Westminster, a man of distinguished learning and intelligence, contributed more than any other by his judicious exertions, to form an association sufficiently extensive, powerful, and wealthy, to execute the often renewed, and often disappointed project of establishing colonies in America.

At length, such an association was formed; and a petition was presented to James I., who had succeeded to the crown of England, praying the royal sanction to the plan which was proposed. That pacific monarch was delighted with it, and immediately acceded to the wishes of its projectors. _{1606.}

On the 10th of April, letters patent were issued under the great seal of England, to the petitioners, Sir Thomas Gates and his associates, granting to them those territories in America, lying on the sea coast, between the 34th and 45th degrees of north latitude, and which either belonged to that monarch, or were not then possessed by any other Christian prince or people; and also the islands adjacent thereto, or within one hundred miles thereof. They were divided, at their own desire, into two companies. One, consisting of certain knights, gentlemen, merchants, and other adventurers of the city of London, and elsewhere, was called the first colony, and was required to settle between the 34th and 41st degrees of north latitude; the other, consisting of certain knights, gentlemen, merchants, and other adventurers of Bristol, Exeter, Plymouth, and elsewhere, was named the second colony, and was ordered to settle between the 38th and 45th degrees of north latitude; yet so that the colony last formed should not be planted within one hundred miles of the prior establishment.

The adventurers were empowered to transport so

many English subjects as should be willing to accompany them, who, with their descendants, were, at all times, to enjoy the same liberties, within any other dominions of the crown of England, as if they had remained, or were born, within the realm. A council consisting of thirteen, to be appointed and removed at the pleasure of the crown, was established for each colony, to govern it according to such laws as should be given under the sign manual and privy seal of England. Two other boards to consist also of thirteen persons each, and to be appointed by the King, were invested with the superior direction of the affairs of the colonies.

The adventurers were allowed to search for, and open mines of gold, silver, and copper, yielding one-fifth of the two former metals, and one-fifteenth of the last, to the King; and to make a coin which should be current both among the colonists and natives.

The president and council were authorised to repel those who should, without their authority, attempt to settle, or trade, within their jurisdiction, and to seize, and detain the persons, and effects, of such intruders, until they should pay a duty of two and one half *per centum ad valorem*, if subjects, but of five *per centum* if aliens. These taxes were to be applied, for twenty-one years, to the use of the adventurers, and were afterwards to be paid into the royal exchequer.

<small>Code of laws for the colony drawn up by the king.</small> While the council for the patentees were employed in making preparations to secure the benefits of their grant, James was assiduously engaged in the new,

and, to his vanity, the flattering task of framing a code of laws for the government of the colonies about to be planted. Having at length prepared this code, he issued it under the sign manual, and privy seal of England. By these regulations, he vested the general superintendence of the colonies, in a council in England, " composed of a few persons of consideration and talents." The church of England was established. The legislative and executive powers within the colonies, were vested in the president and councils; but their ordinances were not to touch life or member, were to continue in force only until made void by the King, or his council in England for Virginia, and were to be in substance, consonant to the laws of England. They were enjoined to permit none to withdraw the people from their allegiance to himself, and his successors; and to cause all persons so offending to be apprehended, and imprisoned until reformation; or, in cases highly offensive, to be sent to England to receive punishment. No person was to be permitted to remain in the colony without taking the oath of obedience. Tumults, mutiny, and rebellion, murder, and incest, were to be punished with death; and for these offences, the criminal was to be tried by a jury. Inferior crimes were to be punished in a summary way, at the discretion of the president and council.

Lands were to be holden within the colony as the same estates were enjoyed in England. Kindness towards the heathen was enjoined; and a power reserved to the King, and his successors to ordain farther laws, so that they were consonant to the jurisprudence of England.*

Under this charter, and these laws, which manifest, at the same time, a total disregard of all political liberty, and a total ignorance of the real advantages which a parent state may derive from its colonies; which vest the higher powers of legislation in persons residing out of the country, not chosen by the people, nor affected by the laws they make, and yet leave commerce unrestrained; the patentees proceeded to execute the arduous and almost untried task of peopling a strange, distant, and uncultivated land, covered with woods and marshes, and inhabited only by savages easily irritated, and when irritated, more fierce than the beasts they hunted.

* Robertson.

CHAPTER II.

Voyage of Newport.—Settlement at Jamestown.—Distress of colonists.—Smith.—He is captured by the Indians.—Condemned to death, saved by Pocahontas.—Returns to Jamestown.—Newport arrives with fresh settlers.—Smith explores the Chesapeake.—Is chosen president.—New charter.—Third voyage of Newport.—Smith sails for Europe.—Condition of the colony.—Colonists determine to abandon the country.—Are stopped by Lord Delaware.—Sir Thomas Dale.—New charter.—Capt. Argal seizes Pocahontas.—She marries Mr. Rolf.—Separate property in lands and labour.—Expedition against Port Royal.—Against Manhadoes.—Fifty acres of land for each settler.—Tobacco.—Sir Thomas Dale.—Mr. Yeardley.—First assembly.—First arrival of females.—Of convicts.—Of African slaves.—Two councils established.—Prosperity of the colony.—Indians attempt to massacre the whites.—General war.—Dissolution of the company.—Arbitrary measures of the crown.—Sir John Harvey.—Sir William Berkeley.—Provincial assembly restored.—Virginia declares in favour of Charles II.—Grant to Lord Baltimore.—Arrival of a colony in Maryland.—Assembly composed of freemen.—William Claybourne.—Assembly composed of representatives.—Divided into two branches.—Tyrannical proceedings.

1606.

THE funds immediately appropriated to the planting of colonies in America, were inconsiderable, and the early efforts to accomplish the object, were feeble.

The first expedition for the southern colony consisted of one vessel of a hundred tons, and two barks, carrying one hundred and five men, destined to remain in the country.

Voyage of Newport.

The command of this small squadron was given to captain Newport, who, on the 19th of December, sailed from the Thames. Three sealed packets were delivered to him, one addressed to himself, a second to captain Bartholomew Gosnald, and the third to captain John Radcliffe, containing the names of the council for this colony. These packets were accompanied with instructions directing that they should be opened, and the names of his Majesty's council proclaimed, within twenty-four hours after their arrival on the coast of Virginia, and not before. The council were then to proceed to the choice of a president, who was to have two votes. To this unaccountable concealment have those dissentions been attributed, which distracted the colonists on their passage, and which afterwards impeded the progress of their settlement.*

Newport, whose place of destination was Roanoke, took the circuitous route by the West India islands, and had a long passage of four months. The reckoning had been out for three days, and serious propo-

* Robertson. Chalmer. Stith.

sitions had been made for returning to England, when 1607. a fortunate storm drove him to the mouth of the Chesapeake. On the 26th of April, he descried cape Henry, and soon afterward cape Charles. A party of about thirty men, which went on shore at cape Henry, was immediately attacked by the natives, and, in the skirmish which ensued, several were wounded on both sides.

<small>Is driven in- to the Che- sapeake.</small>

The first act of the colonists was the selection of a spot for their settlement. They proceeded up a large river, called by the natives Powhatan, and agreed to make their first establishment upon a peninsula, on its northern side. In compliment to their sovereign, this place was named Jamestown, and the river was called James. Having disembarked, and opened the sealed packets brought from England, the members of the council proceeded to the election of a president, and Mr. Wingfield was chosen. But, under frivolous pretexts, they excluded from his seat among them, John Smith, one of the most extraordinary men of his age, whose courage and talents had excited their envy. During the passage, he had been imprisoned on the extravagant charge of intending to murder the council, usurp the government, and make himself king of Virginia.*

<small>May 13th.</small>

The first indications of a permanent settlement in their country, seem to have excited the jealousy of the natives. Displeased with the intrusion, or dissa-

---

* Robertson. Chalmer. Stith.

tisfied with the conduct of the intruders, they soon formed the design of expelling, or destroying, these unwelcome and formidable visitors. In execution of this intention, they attacked the colonists suddenly, while at work, and unsuspicious of their hostility; but were driven, terrified, into the woods by the fire from the ship. On the failure of this attempt, a temporary accommodation was effected.

Newport, though named of the council, had been ordered to return to England. As the time of his departure approached, the accusers of Smith, attempting to conceal their jealousy by the affectation of humanity, proposed that he also should return, instead of being prosecuted in Virginia; but, with the pride of conscious innocence, he demanded a trial; and, being honourably acquitted, took his seat in the council.

About the 15th of June, Newport sailed for England, leaving behind him one of the barks, and about one hundred colonists. While he remained, they had partaken of the food allowed the sailors; but after his departure, they were reduced to the necessity of subsisting on the distributions from the public stores, which had sustained great damage during their long passage. These were both scanty, and unwholesome; the allowance to each man, for a day, being only a pint of worm-eaten wheat and barley. This wretched food increased the malignity of the diseases generated by the climate, among men exposed to all its rigours. Before the month of September, fifty of the company were buried; among whom was Bartholomew Gosnald, who had planned the expedition, and had contributed greatly towards its prosecution. Their distress was increased by internal dissention. The president was charged with embezzling the best stores of the colony, and with feasting at his private table, on beef, bread, and *aqua vitæ*, while famine and death devoured his fellow adventurers. The odium against him was completed by the detection of an attempt to escape from them and their calamities, in the bark which had been left by Newport. In the burst of general indignation which followed the discovery of this meditated desertion, he was deposed, and Radcliffe chosen to succeed him.*

CHAP II.
1607.

As misfortune is not unfrequently, the parent of moderation and reflection, this state of misery produced a system of conduct towards the neighbouring Indians, which, for the moment, disarmed their resentments, and induced them to bring in such supplies as the country afforded at that season. It produced another effect of equal importance. A sense of imminent and common danger called forth those talents which were fitted to the exigency, and compelled submission to them. On captain Smith, who had preserved his health unimpaired, his spirits unbroken, and his judgment unclouded, amidst this general misery and dejection, all eyes were turned, and in him, all actual authority was placed by common consent. His example soon gave energy to others.

* Stith. Smith.

E.

He erected such rude fortifications as would resist the sudden attacks of the savages, and constructed such habitations as, by sheltering the survivors from the weather, contributed to restore and preserve their health, while his own accommodation gave place to that of all others. In the season of gathering corn, he penetrated into the country at the head of small parties, and by presents and caresses to those who were well disposed, and by attacking with open force, and defeating those who were hostile, he obtained abundant supplies.

While thus actively and usefully employed abroad, he was not permitted to withdraw his attention from the domestic concerns of the colony. Incapacity for command is seldom accompanied by a willingness to relinquish power; and it will excite no surprise that the late president saw, with regret, another placed above him. As unworthy minds most readily devise unworthy means, he sought, by intriguing with the factious, and fomenting their discontents, to regain his lost authority; and when these attempts were disconcerted, he formed a conspiracy with some of the principal persons in the colony, to escape in the bark, and thus to desert the country. The vigilance of Smith detected these machinations, and his vigour defeated them.*

The prospect which now presented itself of preserving the colony in quiet and plenty, until supplies could be received from England, was obscured by

* Stith.

an event which threatened, at first, the most disastrous consequences. In attempting to explore Chiccahomini river to its source, Smith was discovered and attacked by a numerous body of Indians; and in endeavouring, after a gallant defence, to make his escape, he sank up to his neck in a swamp, and was obliged to surrender. The wonder and veneration which he excited by the exhibition of a mariner's compass, saved him from immediate death. He was conducted in triumph, through several towns, to the palace of Powhatan, the most potent king in that part of the country, who doomed him to be put to death by placing his head upon a stone, and beating out his brains with a club. At the place of execution, with his head bowed down to receive the blow, he was rescued from a fate which appeared to be inevitable, by that enthusiastic and impassioned humanity which, in every climate, and in every state of society, finds its home in the female bosom. Pocahontas, the king's favourite daughter, then about thirteen years of age, whose entreaties for his life had been ineffectual, rushed between him and the executioner, and folding his head in her arms, and laying hers upon it, arrested the fatal blow. Her father was then prevailed upon to spare his life, and he was sent back to Jamestown.*

On arriving at that place, after an absence of seven weeks, he found the colony reduced to thirty-eight

* Stith.

CHAP. II.
1607.

persons, who seemed determined to abandon a country which appeared to them so unfavourable to human life. He came just in time to prevent the execution of this design. Alternately employing persuasion, threats, and even violence, he induced the majority to relinquish their intention; then turning the guns of the fort on the bark, on board which were the most determined, he compelled her to remain, or sink in the river.*

By a judicious regulation of intercourse with the Indians, over whom he had gained considerable influence, he restored plenty to the colony, and preserved it until the arrival of two vessels which had been dispatched from England under the command of captain Newport, with a supply of provisions and instruments of husbandry, and with a reinforcement of one hundred and twenty persons, composed of many gentlemen, several refiners, gold smiths, and jewellers, and a few labourers.

The influence of Smith disappeared with the danger which had produced it, and was succeeded by an improvident relaxation of discipline, productive of the most pernicious consequences.†

A glittering earth mistaken for gold dust.

About this time, a shining earth, mistaken by the colonists for gold dust, was found in a small stream of water near Jamestown. Their raging thirst for gold was re-excited by this incident. Stith, in his History of Virginia, describing the phrenzy of the

* Stith.   † Ibid.

moment, says, "there was no thought, no discourse, CHAP. II.
no hope, and no work, but to dig gold, wash gold, 1607.
refine gold, and load gold. And, notwithstanding
captain Smith's warm and judicious representations
how absurd it was to neglect other things of immediate use and necessity, to load such a drunken ship
with gilded dust, yet was he over-ruled, and her returns were made in a parcel of glittering dirt, which
is to be found in various parts of the country, and
which they, very sanguinely, concluded to be gold
dust."

The two vessels returned laden, one with this dirt, 1608.
and the other with cedar. This is the first remittance
ever made from America by an English colony.

The effects of this fatal delusion were soon felt, and
the colony again began to suffer that distress, from
scarcity of food, which had before brought it, more
than once, to the brink of ruin.

The researches of the English settlers had not yet
extended beyond the country adjacent to James river.
Smith had formed the bold design of exploring the Smith ex-
great bay of Chesapeake, examining the mighty rivers Chesa-
which empty into it, opening an intercourse with the peake.
nations inhabiting their borders, and acquiring a
knowledge of the state of their cultivation and population. Accompanied by Doctor Russel, he engaged
in this hardy enterprise in an open boat of about three
tons burthen, and with a crew of thirteen men. On
the 2d of June, he descended the river in company
with the last of Newport's two vessels, and, parting

CHAP. II.
1608.

with her at the capes, began his survey at cape Charles. With great fatigue and danger, he examined every river, inlet, and bay, on both sides of the Chesapeake, as far as the mouth of the Rappahannock. His provisions being exhausted, he returned, and arrived at Jamestown on the 21st of July. He found the colony in the utmost confusion and disorder. All those who came last with Newport were sick; the danger of famine was imminent; and the clamour against the president was loud, and universal. The seasonable arrival of Smith restrained their fury. The accounts he gave of his discoveries, and the hope he entertained that the waters of the Chesapeake communicated with the south sea,* extended their views and revived their spirits. They contented themselves with deposing their president, and, having in vain urged Smith to accept that office, elected his friend Mr. Scrivener as vice president.

After employing three days in making arrangements for obtaining regular supplies, and for the government of the colony, Smith again sailed with twelve men, to complete his researches into the countries on the Chesapeake.

From this voyage he returned on the seventh of September; having advanced as far as the river Susquehannah, and visited all the countries on both shores of the bay. He entered most of the large creeks, sailed up many of the great rivers to their falls, and

* This error might very possibly be produced by the Indians representing the great western lakes as seas.

made accurate observations on the extensive territories through which he passed, and on the various tribes inhabiting them, with whom he, alternately, fought, negotiated, and traded. In every situation, he displayed judgment, courage, and that presence of mind which is essential to the character of a commander; and never failed, finally, to inspire the savages he encountered, with the most exalted opinion of himself and of his nation.

When we consider that he sailed above three thousand miles in an open boat; when we contemplate the dangers and the hardships he encountered; when we reflect on the valuable additions he made to the stock of knowledge respecting America; we shall not hesitate to say that few voyages of discovery, undertaken at any time, reflect more honour on those engaged in them. "So full and exact," says Dr. Robertson, "are his accounts of that large portion of the American continent comprehended in the two provinces of Virginia and Maryland, that after the progress of information and research for a century and a half, his map exhibits no inaccurate view of both countries, and is the original, on which all subsequent delineations and descriptions have been formed.*

On his return from this expedition, Smith was chosen president of the council; and, yielding to the general wish, accepted the office. Soon after, New-

* Dr. Robertson must allude to the country below the falls of the great rivers.

CHAP. II.
1608.

port arrived with an additional supply of settlers, among whom were the two first females who adventured to the present colony; but he came without provisions.

The judicious administration of the president, however, supplied the wants of the colonists, and restrained the turbulent. Encouraged by his example, and coerced by his authority, a spirit of industry and subordination was created among them, which was the parent of plenty and of peace.*

The company in England, though disappointed in the hope of discovering a passage to the Pacific, and of finding mines of the precious metals, still indulged in golden dreams of future wealth. To increase their funds, as well as their influence and reputation, by the acquisition of additional numbers, to explain and enlarge their powers and privileges, and to ensure a colonial government conforming to their own views and wishes, the company petitioned for a new charter,

1609. which was granted on the 23d of May. Some of the first nobility and gentry of the country, and most of the companies of London, with a numerous body of merchants and tradesmen, were added to the former

New Charter. adventurers, and they were all incorporated, by the name of " The treasurer and company of adventurers of the city of London, for the first colony in Virginia." To them were granted, in absolute property, the lands extending from Cape or Point Comfort,

* Robertson. Chalmer.

along the sea coast, two hundred miles to the northward, and from the same point, along the sea coast, two hundred miles to the southward, and up into the land, throughout, from sea to sea, west and north west; and also all the islands lying within one hundred miles of the coast of both seas of the precinct aforesaid: to be holden as of the manor of East Greenwich, in free and common soccage, and paying, in lieu of all services, one-fifth of the gold and silver that should be found. The corporation was authorised to convey, under its common seal, particular portions of these lands to subjects or denizens, on such conditions as might promote the intentions of the grant. The powers of the president and council in Virginia were abrogated, and a new council in England was established, with power to the company to fill all vacancies therein by election. This council was empowered to appoint and remove all officers for the colony, and to make all ordinances for its government, not contrary to the laws of England; and to rule the colonists according to such ordinances. License was given to transport to Virginia, all persons willing to go thither, and to export merchandise free from customs for seven years. There was also granted, for twenty-one years, freedom from all subsidies in Virginia, and from all impositions on importations and exportations from or to any of the King's dominions, "except only the five pounds in the hundred due for customs." The colonists were declared to be entitled to the rights of natural subjects. The gover-

F

CHAP. II.
1609.

nor was empowered to establish martial law in case of rebellion or mutiny; and, to prevent the superstitions of the Church of Rome from taking root in the plantation, it was declared that none should pass into Virginia, but such as shall have first taken the oath of supremacy.*

The company, being thus enlarged, and enabled to take more effective measures for the settlement of the country, soon fitted out nine ships, with five hundred emigrants, Lord Delawar was constituted governor and captain-general for life; and several other offices were created. The direction of the expedition was again given to Newport; to whom, and Sir Thomas Gates, and Sir George Somers, powers were severally granted to supersede the existing administration, and to govern the colony until the arrival of Lord Delawar. With singular indiscretion, the council omitted to establish precedence among these gentlemen; who, being totally unable to settle this important point among themselves, agreed to embark on board the same vessel, and to be companions during the voyage. They were parted from the rest of the fleet in a storm, and driven on Bermudas; having on board one hundred and fifty men, a great portion of the provisions destined for the colony, and the new commission and instructions of the council. The residue of the squadron arrived safely in Virginia.

Third voyage of Newport.

"A great part of the new company," says Mr. Stith, "consisted of unruly sparks, packed off by their

* Charter.

friends to escape worse destinies at home. And the rest were chiefly made up of poor gentlemen, broken tradesmen, rakes and libertines, footmen, and such others as were much fitter to spoil and ruin a Commonwealth, than to help to raise or maintain one. This lewd company, therefore, were led by their seditious captains into many mischiefs and extravagancies. They assumed to themselves the power of disposing of the government, and conferred it sometimes on one, and sometimes on another. To day the old commission must rule, to-morrow the new, and next day neither. So that all was anarchy and distraction."

The judgment of Smith was not long suspended. With the promptness and decision which belong to vigorous minds, he determined that his own authority was not legally revoked until the arrival of the new commission, and therefore resolved to continue its exercise. Incapable of holding the reins of government with a feeble hand, he exhibited, on this emergency, that energy and good sense which never deserted him when the occasion required them. After imprisoning the chief promoters of sedition, and thereby restoring regularity and obedience, he, for the double purpose of extending the colony, and of preventing the mischiefs to be apprehended from so many turbulent spirits collected in Jamestown, detached one hundred men to the falls of James river, under the command of West, and the same number to Nansemond, under that of Martin. These per-

CHAP. II.
1609.

sons conducted their settlements with so little judgment, that they soon converted all the neighbouring Indians into enemies. After losing several parties, they found themselves in absolute need of the support and direction of Smith. These were readily afforded, until a melancholy accident deprived the colony of the aid of a man whose talents had, more than once, rescued it from that desperate condition into which folly and vice had plunged it. Returning from a visit to the detachment stationed at the falls of James river, his powder bag took fire, while he was sleeping in the boat, and, in the explosion, he was so severely wounded as to be confined to his bed. Being unable to obtain the aid of a surgeon in the colony, he embarked for England about the beginning of October.

Smith returns to England.

State of the colony.

At his departure, the colony consisted of about five hundred inhabitants. They were furnished with three ships, seven boats, commodities ready for trade, ten weeks provision in the public stores, six mares and a horse, a large stock of hogs and poultry, some sheep and goats, utensils for agriculture, nets for fishing, one hundred trained and expert soldiers well acquainted with the Indians, their language and habitations, twenty-four pieces of ordnance, and three hundred muskets, with a sufficient quantity of arms and ammunition.*

The fair prospects of the colony were soon blasted by a course of folly and crime, of riot and insubordination.

* Stith.

Numerous pretenders advanced their claims to the supreme command. The choice at length fell upon captain Percy, who derived much consideration from his virtues, as well as from his illustrious family; but his talents, at no time equal to this new and difficult station, were rendered still less competent to the task, by a long course of ill health. Being generally confined by sickness to his bed, he was incapable of maintaining his authority; and total confusion ensued, with its accustomed baneful consequences.

The Indians, no longer awed by the genius and vigour of Smith, attacked the colony on all sides. West and Martin, after losing their boats and nearly half their men, were driven into Jamestown. The stock of provisions was lavishly wasted; and famine added its desolating scourge to their other calamities. After devouring the skins of their horses, and the Indians they had killed, the survivors fed on those of their companions who had sunk under such accumulated misery. The recollection of these tremendous sufferings was long retained, and, for many years, this period was distinguished by the name of THE STARVING TIME.*

In six months, the colony was reduced, by these distresses, to sixty persons, who could not have survived ten days longer, when they were relieved from this state of despair by the arrival of Sir Thomas Gates, Sir George Somers, and captain Newport, from Bermuda.

* Robertson. Chalmer. Stith. Beverly.

CHAP. II.
610
They abandon the country.

The determination to abandon the country was immediately taken, and the wretched remnant of the colony embarked on board the vessels, and sailed for England. "None dropped a tear," says Mr. Chalmer, "because none had enjoyed one day of happiness."

Stopped by Lord Delawar.

Fortunately, they met Lord Delawar, who prevailed on them to return; and, on the 10th of June, resettled them at Jamestown.

By mildness of temper, attention to business, and judicious exercise of authority, this nobleman restored order and contentment to the colony, and again impressed the Indians with respect for the English name.

1611. Unfortunately, ill health obliged him to resign the government which he placed in the hands of Mr. Percy, and sailed for the West Indies, leaving in the colony about two hundred persons in possession of the blessings of health, plenty, and peace.

Sir Thomas Dale.

On the 10th of May, Sir Thomas Dale, who had been appointed to the government, arrived with a fresh supply of men and provisions, and found the colony relapsing into a state of anarchy, idleness, and want. It required all the authority of the new governor to maintain public order, and to compel the idle and the dissolute to labour. Some conspiracies having been detected, he proclaimed martial law, which was immediately put in execution. This severity was then deemed necessary, and is supposed to have saved the settlement.*

* Robertson. Chalmer. Stith. Beverly.

In the beginning of August, Sir Thomas Gates, CHAP II. who had been appointed to succeed Sir Thomas Dale, 1611. arrived with six ships, and a considerable supply of men and provisions. After receiving this addition to its numbers, the colony again extended itself up James river; and several new settlements were made.

Extravagant accounts of the fertility of Bermuda having reached England, the company became desirous of obtaining it as a place from which Virginia might be supplied with provisions. Application was therefore made to the crown for a new patent, to comprehend this island; and, in March, a charter was issued, granting to the treasurer and company all the islands situate in the ocean within three hundred leagues of the coast of Virginia. By this charter, the corporation was essentially new modelled. It was ordained that four general courts of the adventurers should be holden annually, for the determination of affairs of importance, and weekly meetings were directed, for the transaction of common business. To promote the effectual settlement of the plantation, license was given to open lotteries in any part of England.*

1612. New Charter.

These lotteries, which were the first ever drawn in England, brought twenty-nine thousand pounds into the treasury of the company. When they were discontinued, in 1620, on the complaint of the House of Commons, they were declared to have " supplied the real food by which Virginia had been nourished."

* Robertson. Chalmer. Stith. Beverly.

CHAP. II.
1612.

Captain Argal seizes Pocahontas.

About this time an event took place which was followed by important consequences to the colony. Provisions in Jamestown continuing to be scarce, and supplies from the neighbouring Indians, with whom the English were often at war, being necessarily uncertain, captain Argal, with two vessels, was sent round to the Potowmac for a cargo of corn. While obtaining the cargo, he understood that Pocahontas, who had remained stedfast in her attachment to the English, had absented herself from the home of her father, and lay concealed in the neighbourhood. By bribing some of those in whom she confided, Argal prevailed on her to come on board his vessel, where she was detained respectfully, and brought to Jamestown. He was induced to take this step by the hope that the possession of Pocahontas would give the English an ascendancy over her father, who was known to doat on her. In this, however, he was disappointed. Powhatan offered corn and friendship, if they would first restore his daughter, but, with a loftiness of spirit which claims respect, rejected every proposition for conciliation which should not be preceded by that act of reparation.

During her detention at Jamestown, she made an impression on the heart of Mr. Rolf, a young gentleman of estimation in the colony, who succeeded in gaining her affections. They were married with the consent of Powhatan, who was entirely reconciled to the English by that event, and continued, ever after, to be their sincere friend. This connexion led also to a treaty with the Chiccahominies, a brave and daring tribe, who submitted themselves to the English, and became their tributaries.*

About the same time, an important change took place in the internal arrangements of the colony.

Heretofore no separate property in lands had been acquired, and no individual had laboured for himself. The lands had been held, cleared, and cultivated in common, and their produce carried into a common granary, from which it was distributed to all. This system was to be ascribed, in some measure, to the unwise injunction contained in the royal instructions, directing the colonists to trade together for five years in one common stock. Its effect was such as ought to have been foreseen. Industry, deprived of its due reward, exclusive property in the produce of its toil, felt no sufficient stimulus to exertion, and the public supplies were generally inadequate to the public necessities. To remove this cause of perpetual scarcity, Sir Thomas Dale divided a considerable portion of land into lots of three acres, and granted one of them, in full property, to each individual. Although the colonists were still required to devote a large portion of labour to the public, a sudden change was made in their appearance and habits. Industry, impelled by the certainty of recompense, advanced with rapid strides; and the inhabitants were no longer in fear of wanting bread, either for themselves, or for the emigrants from England.†

Separate property in lands.

* Robertson. Chalmer. Stith. Beverly. † Idem.

CHAP. II
1614.

Early in the following year, Sir Thomas Gates returned to England, leaving the government again with Sir Thomas Dale. This gentleman detached captain Argal on an enterprise of which no immediate notice was taken, but which was afterwards recollected with indignation.

The French, who had directed their course to the more northern parts of the continent, had been among the first adventurers to North America. Their voyages of discovery are of a very early date, and their attempts to establish a colony were among the first which were made. After several abortive efforts, a permanent settlement was made in Canada, in the year 1604, and the foundation of Quebec was laid in the year 1608. In November 1603, Henry IV. appointed De Mont lieutenant-general of that part of the territory which he claimed, lying in North America, between the 40th and 46th degrees of north latitude, then called Acadié, with power to colonise and to rule it; and he soon afterwards granted to the same gentleman and his associates, an exclusive right to the commerce of peltry in Acadié and the gulph of St. Lawrence. In consequence of these grants, a settlement was formed in the subsequent year, on that coast, near the river St. Croix; and in 1605, Port Royal was built on a more northern part of the bay of Fundy.

The colony, receiving not much support from France, was feeble and unprosperous, but retained quiet possession of the country. In a time of profound peace, the expedition of Argal was directed against it. He found it totally unprepared for defence. The inhabitants, who had assiduously and successfully cultivated the friendship of the Indians, were scattered abroad in the woods, engaged in their several pursuits; and a ship and bark just arrived from France, laden with articles necessary for the use of the colony, were surprised in port, and their cargoes taken to Jamestown. After the departure of Argal, the French resumed their former station.

The pretext for this predatory expedition was, that the French, by settling in Acadié, had invaded the rights of the English, acquired by the first discovery of the continent.

Argal also paid a visit to New York, then in possession of the Dutch; which country he claimed under the pretext that captain Hudson was an Englishman, and could not transfer the benefit of his discoveries from his sovereign. He demanded possession of the place; and the Dutch governor, being unable to resist, " peaceably submitted both himself and his colony to the King of England, and the governor of Virginia under him," and consented to pay a tribute. Argal then continued his voyage to Jamestown. But another governor soon afterwards arriving from Amsterdam with better means of asserting the title of his nation, the payment of the tribute was refused, and the place put in a state of defence.*

* Robertson. Chalmer. Stith.

CHAP. II.
1614.

The advantages resulting to the colony from allowing each individual to labour, in part for himself, having soon become apparent, the system of working in common to fill the public stores, seems to have been totally relinquished; and, not long afterwards, fifty acres of land, promised by the rules of the company to each emigrant, were surveyed and delivered to those having the title.

Fifty acres of land laid off for each settler.

1615.
Tobacco.

About the same time, tobacco was first cultivated in Virginia.

This plant, although detested by the King, who even wrote a pamphlet against it, which he styled a *counter blast;* although discountenanced by the leading members of parliament, and even by the company, who issued edicts against its cultivation; although extremely unpleasant to persons not accustomed to it, and disagreeable in its effects, surmounted all opposition, and has, by an unaccountable caprice, been brought into general use, and become one of the most considerable staples of America.*

1616.

In the spring of the following year, Sir Thomas Dale sailed for England, leaving the government in the hands of Mr. George Yeardly, who, after a lax administration of one year, was succeeded by captain Argal.

Yeardly.

1617.
Argal.

Argal was a man of talents and energy, but selfish, haughty, and tyrannical. He continued martial law during a season of peace; and a Mr. Brewster, who

---

* Robertson.

was tried under this arbitrary system, for contemptuous words spoken of the governor, was sentenced to suffer death. He obtained with difficulty an appeal to the treasurer and company in England, by whom the sentence was reversed.*

While martial law was, according to Stith, the common law of the land, the governor seems to have been the sole legislator. His general edicts mark the severity of his rule. He ordered that merchandise should be sold at an advance of twenty-five *per centum*, and tobacco taken in payment at the rate of three shillings per pound, under the penalty of three years servitude to the company; that no person should traffic privately with the Indians, or teach them the use of fire arms, under pain of death; that no person should hunt deer or hogs without the governor's permission; that no man should shoot, unless in his own necessary defence, until a new supply of ammunition should arrive, on pain of a year's personal service; that none should go on board the ships at Jamestown, without the governor's leave; that every person should go to church on Sundays and holidays, under the penalty of slavery during the following week for the first offence, during a month for the second, and during a year and a day for the third. The rigour of this administration necessarily exciting much discontent, the complaints of the Virginians at length made their way to the company. Lord Delawar being dead, Mr.

* Robertson. Chalmer. Stith.

CHAP. II. Yeardly was appointed captain-general, with instruc-
1617.
Mr. Yeard- tions to examine the wrongs of the colonists, and to
ly.   redress them.*

1619.   The new governor arrived in April, and soon after, to the inexpressible joy of the inhabitants, declared his determination to convoke a colonial assembly.

This is an important era in the history of Virginia. Heretofore, all legislative authority had been exercised, either by the corporation in England, or by their officers in the colony. The people had no voice, either personally, or by their representatives, in the government of themselves; and their most important concerns were managed by persons often unacquainted with their situation, and always possessing interests different from theirs. They now felicitated themselves on having really the privileges of Englishmen.

First colo- This first assembly met at Jamestown on the 19th
nial assem-
ly.   of June. The colony being not then divided into counties, the members were elected by the different boroughs, amounting at that time to seven. From this circumstance the popular branch of the legislature received the appellation of the house of burgesses, which it retained until all connexion with England was dissolved.

The assembly, composed of the governor, the council, and burgesses, met together in one apartment, and there discussed the various matters which came before them. The laws then enacted, which,

* Robertson. Chalmer. Stith.

it is believed, are no longer extant, were transmitted to England for the approbation of the treasurer and company.*

CHAP. II.
1619.

Although the emigrations from England continued to be considerable, few females had crossed the Atlantic. Men without wives could not consider their residence in the country as permanent, and must intend after amassing some wealth, to return to their native land. To remove this impediment to the population of the colony, ninety girls, of humble fortune and spotless character, were transported by the company to Virginia; and in the subsequent year, they were followed by sixty of the same description. They were received by the young planters as a blessing which substituted domestic happiness for the cheerless gloom of solitude; and the face of the country was essentially changed.† The prospect of becoming parents was accompanied with anxieties for the welfare of their children; and the education of youth soon became an object of attention. The necessity of seminaries of learning was felt, and several steps were taken towards founding the college, afterwards established by William and Mary.

First arrival of females, 1620.

About the same time the company received orders from the King to convey to Virginia one hundred idle and dissolute persons, then in custody of the knight marshal. These were the first convicts trans-

and of convicts.

---

* Robertson. Chalmer. Stith.

† Mr. Stith says the price for a wife was at first, one hundred, and afterwards, one hundred and fifty pounds of tobacco; and a debt so contracted was made of higher dignity than any other.

CHAP. II.
1620.

ported to America. The policy which dictated this measure was soon perceived to be not less wise than it was humane. Men who, in Europe, were the pests of the body politic, made an acceptable addition to the stock of labour in the colony; and, in a new world, where the temptations to crime seldom presented themselves, many of them became useful members of society.

Heretofore the commerce of Virginia had been engrossed by the corporation. In the year 1620, this distressing and unprofitable monopoly was given up, and the trade was open to all. The free competition produced by this change of system was of essential advantage to the colony, but was the immediate cause of introducing a species of population which has had vast influence on the past, and may affect the future destinies of America, to an extent which human wisdom can neither foresee nor control. A Dutch vessel, availing itself of this commercial liberty, brought into James river twenty Africans, who were immediately purchased as slaves.*

1621.
African slaves.

In July, the company passed an ordinance establishing a frame of government for the colony. This instrument provided that there should be two supreme councils in Virginia, the one to be called the Council of State, to be appointed and displaced by the treasurer and company, and to assist the governor with advice on executive subjects; the other to be denominated the General Assembly, and to consist of the

Two councils established.

* Robertson. Chalmer. Stith.

governor, the council of state, and burgesses; to be chosen for the present, by the inhabitants of every town, hundred, or settlement, in the colony, two for each. The assembly was empowered to enact general laws for the government of the colony, reserving a negative to the governor. Its acts were not to be in force until confirmed by the general court in England, and the ratification returned under its seal. On the other hand, no order of the general court was to bind the colony until assented to by the assembly.

CHAP. II.
1621.

A controversy concerning the importation of tobacco into the European dominions of the crown, which had for some time existed between the King and the company, was, at length, adjusted.

1622.

The King had demanded high duties on that article, while he permitted its importation from the dominions of Spain, and also restrained its direct exportation from Virginia, to the warehouses of the company in Holland, to which expedient his exactions had driven them. It was at length agreed that they should enjoy the sole right of importing that commodity into the kingdom, for which they should pay a duty of nine pence per pound, in lieu of all charges, and that the whole production of the colony should be brought to England.

The industry, population, and produce of the colony, were now greatly increased. At peace with the Indians, they had extended their settlements to the Rappahannock and to the Potowmac. This change of circumstances having rendered it inconvenient to

H

58   HISTORY OF THE

CHAP. II. bring all causes to Jamestown before the governor
1622.   and council, who had heretofore exercised all judicial
power in the country, inferior courts were established, to sit in convenient places, in order to render justice more cheap and accessible to the people. Thus ori-
County   ginated the county courts of Virginia.
courts.

In this year the cup of prosperity, which the colonists had begun to taste, was dashed from their lips by an event which shook the colony to its foundation. In 1618, Powhatan died, and was succeeded, in his dominions and in his influence over all the neighbouring tribes, by Opechancanough, a bold and cunning chief, as remarkable for his jealousy and hatred of the new settlers, as for his qualifications to execute the designs suggested by his resentments. He renewed, however, the stipulations of Powhatan; and, for a considerable time, the general peace remained undisturbed. The colonists, unsuspicious of danger, observed neither the Indians nor their machinations. Engaged entirely in the pursuits of agriculture, they neglected their military exercises, and every useful precaution. Meanwhile, the Indians, being often employed as hunters, were furnished with fire arms, and taught to use them. They were admitted, at all times, freely into the habitations of the English, as harmless visitants, were fed at their tables, and lodged in their
Indian con- chambers. During this state of friendly intercourse,
spiracy to
massacre all the plan of a general massacre, which should involve
the whites. man, woman, and child, in indiscriminate slaughter, was formed with cold and unrelenting deliberation.

The tribes in the neighbourhood of the English, except those on the eastern shore of the Chesapeak, who were not trusted with the plan, were successively gained over; and, notwithstanding the perpetual intercourse between them and the white people, the most impenetrable secrecy was observed. So deep and dark was their dissimulation, that they were accustomed to borrow boats from the English to cross the river, in order to concert and mature their execrable designs.

The 22d of March was designated as the day on which all the English settlements were to be attacked. The better to disguise their intentions, and to ensure success, they brought, in the preceding evening, deer, turkies, and fish, as presents; and, even on the morning of the massacre, came freely among the whites, behaving in their usual friendly manner, until the very instant which had been appointed for the commencement of the scene of carnage. The fatal hour being arrived, they fell at once on every settlement, and murdered without distinction of age or sex. So sudden was the execution of their plan, that few perceived the weapons, or the approach of the blow, which terminated their existence. Thus, in one hour, and almost in the same instant, fell three hundred and forty-seven men, women and children; most of them by their own plantation tools.

The massacre would have been still more complete, had not information been given, the preceding night, to a Mr. Pace, by an Indian domesticated in his

CHAP. II. house, and treated as a son, who, being pressed to
1622. murder his benefactor, disclosed the plot to him. He
immediately carried the intelligence to Jamestown,
and the alarm was given to some of the nearest settlements, which were thereby saved. At some other
places, too, where the circumstances of the attack
enabled the English to seize their arms, the assailants
were repulsed.

General war.   This horrible massacre was succeeded by a vindic-
tive and exterminating war, in which the wiles of the
Indians were successfully retaliated on themselves.
During this disastrous period, many public works
were abandoned; the college institution was deserted;
the settlements were reduced from eighty to eight;
and famine superadded its afflicting scourge to the
accumulated distresses of the colony.*

As soon as intelligence of these calamitous events
reached England, a contribution was made by the adventurers for the relief of the sufferers; arms from the
tower were delivered to the treasurer and company;
and several vessels were dispatched with those articles which might best alleviate such complicated
distress.

Dissention and dissolution of the company.   But the dissolution of the company was rapidly approaching. That corporation contained many men of
the first rank and talents in the nation, who in their
assemblies, were in habits of discussing the measures
of the crown with the accustomed freedom of a popu-

* Robertson. Chalmer. Stith.

lar body. Two violent factions, which assumed the regular appearance of court and country parties, divided the company, and struggled for the ascendancy. James endeavoured to give the preponderance to the court party, but his endeavours were unsuccessful; and his failure disposed him to listen to complaints against a corporation, whose deliberations he found himself unable to control. To their mismanagement he ascribed the slow progress made by the colony, and the heavy losses that had been sustained.*

After hearing both the corporation and their accusers, the privy council determined to issue a commission, appointing persons to be named by the crown, to inquire into the affairs of Virginia from the earliest settlement of the province, and to report thereon to the government. This commission seized the charters, books, and papers of the company; and all letters and packets brought from the colony were ordered to be laid unopened before the privy council. Their report attributed the misfortunes of the colony to the corporation in England; and James, at no time a friend to popular assemblies, communicated to them his resolution to revoke the old charter and grant a new one, which should respect private property, but place power in fewer hands. The requisition that they should assent to this proposition, and surrender their charter, was accompanied with the information that the King was determined, in default of submission, to

* Robertson. Chalmer. Stith.

CHAP. II. take such proceedings for recalling their letters patent
1623.
as might be just. The company, however, resolutely determined to defend its rights; whereupon a writ of *quo warranto* was instituted in the court of King's Bench, which was decided according to the wishes of
1624. the monarch. The company was dissolved, and all
Colony taken into the its powers were revested in the crown.
hands of the
King. Above one hundred and fifty thousand pounds sterling had been expended in planting the colony; and more than nine thousand persons had been sent from England to people it. Yet, at the dissolution of the company, the annual imports from Virginia, did not exceed twenty thousand pounds in value, and the population of the country was reduced to about eighteen hundred persons.

While these things were transacting in England, the war against the Indians was prosecuted in the colony, with vigour and success. The neighbouring hostile tribes were nearly exterminated, and were driven entirely from the rivers, so that the settlements were extended in safety.

In February, the general assembly was once more convened. The several orders which had been previously made by the governor and council, were enacted into laws; and form the oldest legislative rules of action now remaining on record. Among them are various regulations respecting the church of England. But the act best representing the condition of the colonists, is a solemn declaration, " that the governor should not impose any taxes on the colony, otherwise than by the authority of the general assembly; and that he should not withdraw the inhabitants from their private labour to any service of his own." At this session, too, the privilege of exemption from arrest, while the assembly was sitting, was extended to the burgesses. Several other measures were adopted for the correction of abuses; and the laws of that session, generally, are marked with that good sense and patriotism, which are to be expected from men perfectly understanding their own situation, and legislating for themselves.

From this assembly, the royal commissioners endeavoured, in vain, to procure an address to the King, professing " their willingness to submit themselves to his princely pleasure, in revoking the ancient patents;" but a petition was agreed to and transmitted, acknowledging their satisfaction at his having taken the plantation into his more especial care, beseeching him to continue the then form of government, to confirm to Virginia and the Somers isles, the sole importation of tobacco, and soliciting that, if the promised aid of soldiers should be granted them, the governor and assembly might have a voice in directing their operations.

. Virginia having thus become a royal government, the King issued a special commission, appointing a governor and twelve councillors, to whom the entire direction of the affairs of the province was committed. No assembly was mentioned, nor was it intended to permit the continuance of that body, for, to the popu-

CHAP. II.
1624.

lar shape of the late system, James attributed the disasters of the colony. But some attention to their interests, was mingled with this subversion of political liberty. Yielding to the petitions of the English parliament and of the colonists, he issued a proclamation prohibiting the growth of tobacco in the kingdom, and the importation of it into England or Ireland, except from Virginia, or the Somers isles, and in vessels belonging to his subjects. His death prevented the completion of a legislative code for the colony, which he had commenced, and which he flattered himself, would remedy all the ills that had been experienced.

Charles I.
Arbitrary measures of the crown.
1625.

Charles I. adopted, in its full extent, the colonial system of his father. He committed to Sir George Yeardly, whom he appointed governor of Virginia, and to his council, the whole legislative and executive powers of the colony, with instructions to conform exactly to orders which should be received from him. They were empowered to make laws, and to execute them; to impose taxes, and to enforce the payment of them; to seize the property of the late company, and to apply it to the public use; and to transport the colonists to England, to be punished there for crimes committed in Virginia. To complete this hateful system, the crown exacted a monopoly of the tobacco trade, and appointed agents, to whose management that article was entirely committed.*

* Robertson. Chalmer. Stith.

The full pressure of these arbitrary regulations was not felt till Sir John Harvey, on the death of Sir George Yeardly, was appointed governor of Virginia. The mind of this gentleman is represented by the historians of the day, as having been of a structure to make even tyranny more odious. Rapacious, haughty, and unfeeling, he exercised his powers in the most offensive manner. Respect for his commission, suppressed opposition to his authority for several years. Roused, at length, almost to madness by oppression, the Virginians, in a fit of popular rage, seized their governor, and sent him a prisoner to England, accompanied by two deputies charged with the duty of representing their grievances, and his misconduct.

Charles deemed it necessary to discountenance this summary and violent proceeding, so entirely incompatible with that implicit obedience which he had ever exacted from his subjects. The deputies of the colony were sternly received; no inquiry appears to have been made into the conduct of Harvey; and, early in the succeeding year, he was sent back to Virginia, invested with all his former powers.*

The time, however, approached, when a new system of administration was to be adopted. The discontents of the nation, and his own wants, obliged Charles to determine on convening a parliament. He was probably unwilling to increase the ill temper resulting from his mal-administration at home, by bring-

* Robertson. Chalmer. Stith.

ing before the representatives of the people, complaints of the despotism which had been exercised in America.

To this change of circumstances may be ascribed, the appointment of Sir William Berkeley to succeed Harvey as governor of Virginia. In almost every respect, this gentleman was unlike his predecessor. Highly respectable for his rank and abilities, he was still more distinguished by his integrity, by the mildness of his temper, and by the gentleness of his manners. To complete the satisfaction of the colonists, he was empowered and directed to summon the burgesses of all the plantations, to meet the governor and council in the general assembly, and thereby to restore to the people their share in the government. These changes had such an effect in Virginia that, when afterward informed of a petition presented in the name of the assembly to parliament, " praying for the restoration of the ancient patents, and corporation government," the general assembly not only transmitted an explicit disavowal of it, but sent an address to the King, expressing their high sense of his favour towards them, and earnestly desiring to continue under his immediate protection. During the civil war, as well as after the establishment of the commonwealth, they continued firm in their attachment to the royal family.

1650. The House of Commons, however, having succeeded in the establishment of its power over England, was not disposed to permit its authority to be questioned in Virginia. An ordinance was passed, declaring that, as the colonies were settled at the cost and by the people of England, " they are and ought to be subordinate to, and dependent on, that nation; and subject to such laws and regulations as are or shall be made by parliament. That in Virginia and other places, the powers of government had been usurped by persons who had set themselves up in opposition to the commonwealth, who were therefore denounced as rebels and traitors; and all foreign vessels were forbidden to enter the ports of any of the English settlements in America." As the men who then governed were not in the habit of making empty declarations, the council of state was empowered to send a fleet to enforce obedience to parliament.*

Sir George Ayscue was accordingly detached with a powerful squadron, and was instructed to endeavour, by gentle means, to bring the colonists to obedience; but, if these failed, to use force, and to give freedom to such servants and slaves of those who should resist, as would serve in the troops under his command. After reducing Barbadoes, and the other islands to submission, the squadron entered the Chesapeak. Berkeley, having hired a few Dutch ships which were then trading to Virginia, made a gallant resistance; but, unable long to maintain so unequal a contest, he yielded to superior force, having first stipulated for a general amnesty. He then withdrew to

---

* Robertson. Chalmer.

a retired situation where, beloved and respected by the people, he resided as a private man, until a counter revolution called him, once more, to preside over the colony.*

After the revocation of the charter, it became more easy to obtain large grants of land. This circumstance, notwithstanding the tyranny of the provincial government, promoted emigration, and considerably increased the population of the colony. At the commencement of the civil war, Virginia was supposed to contain about twenty thousand souls.†

While the ordinance of 1650, forbidding all trade between the colonies and foreign nations, was dispensed with in favour of republican New England, it was rigorously enforced against the loyal colony of Virginia. These restrictions were the more burdensome, because England did not then furnish a sufficient market for all the produce, nor a supply for all the wants of the colonies. This severity was not calculated to detach the affections of the people from the royal family. Their discontents were cherished, too, by the great number of cavaliers who had fled to Virginia after the total defeat of their party in England. Taking advantage of an interregnum occasioned by the sudden death of governor Matthews, the people resolved to throw off their forced allegiance to the commonwealth, and called on Sir William Berkeley to resume the government. He required only their

* Robertson. Chalmer. † Idem.

solemn promise to venture their lives and fortunes with him in support of their King. This being readily given, Charles II. was proclaimed in Virginia, before intelligence had been received of the death of Cromwell. His restoration was soon afterwards effected in England; and this rash measure not only escaped chastisement, but became a meritorious service of which Virginia long boasted, and which was not entirely forgotten by the Prince.*

<small>CHAP. II
1651.

Charles II. proclaimed in Virginia.</small>

At the restoration, the colony contained about thirty thousand persons.

One of the causes which, during the government of Harvey, had disquieted Virginia, was the diminution of territory occasioned by grants of great tracts of country lying within the limits of the colony. The most remarkable of these was the grant of Maryland to Lord Baltimore.

In June 1632, Charles I. granted to that nobleman for ever, "that region bounded by a line drawn from Watkin's Point on Chesapeak bay, to the ocean on the east; thence, to that part of the estuary of Delaware ou the north, which lieth under the 40th degree, where New England is terminated; thence, in a right line, by the degree aforesaid, to the meridian of the fountain of the Potowmac; thence, following its course, by the farther bank to its confluence." The territory described in this grant was denominated Maryland, and was separated entirely from Virginia.

<small>Maryland.</small>

<small>* Robertson. Chalmer.</small>

CHAP. II.
1651.

The proprietor was empowered, with the assent of the freemen, or their delegates, whom he was required to assemble for that purpose, to make all laws for the government of the new colony, not inconsistent with the laws of England. Privileges, in other respects analogous to those given to the other colonies, were comprised in this charter; and it is remarkable that it contains no clause obliging the proprietary to submit the laws which might be enacted to the King, for his approbation or dissent; nor any reservation of the right of the crown to interfere in the government of the province.*

This is the first example of the dismemberment of a colony, and the creation of another within its original limits, by the mere act of the crown.

1632.
Arrival of a colony conducted by Calvert.

1633.

The first migration into the new colony consisted of about two hundred gentlemen with their adherents, chiefly Roman Catholics, who sailed from England under Calvert, the brother of the proprietor, in November, and, early in the following year, landed in Maryland, near the mouth of the Potowmac. Their first effort was to conciliate the good will of the natives, whose town they purchased, and called St. Mary's. This measure was as wise as it was just. By obtaining the peaceable possession of land already prepared for cultivation, the Marylanders were enabled to raise their food immediately; and this circumstance, together with their neighbourhood to Virginia,

* Chalmer. Robertson.

where the necessaries of life were then raised in abundance, secured them from famine and its concomitant diseases;—afflictions which had swept away such numbers of the first settlers of North America.

The inhabitants of Virginia presented a petition against the grant to Lord Baltimore, which was heard before the privy council in July, 1733. The decision was in favour of the continuance of the patent; leaving to the petitioners their remedy at law. To prevent farther differences, free commerce was permitted between the colonies; and they were enjoined to receive no fugitives from each other; to do no act which might bring on a war with the natives; and, on all occasions to assist each other as became fellow subjects of the same state.

In February 1635, the first assembly of Maryland was convened. It appears to have been composed of the whole body of the freemen. Their acts were, most probably, not approved by the proprietor, who transmitted, in turn, for their consideration, a code of laws prepared by himself. This code was laid before the assembly who rejected it without hesitation, and prepared a body of regulations adapted to their situation. Among these was an act of attainder against William Clayborne, who was charged with felony and sedition, with having exercised the powers of government within the province without authority, and with having excited the Indians to make war on the colony.*

* Chalmer.

CHAP. II.
1638.

As early as the year 1631, Charles had granted a license to William Clayborne, one of the council and secretary of state of Virginia, "to traffic in those parts of America for which there is already no patent granted for sole trade." To enforce this license, Harvey, then governor of Virginia, had granted his commission also, containing the same powers. Under this license and commission, Clayborne made a small settlement in the isle of Kent, near Annapolis, which he continued to claim; and refused to submit to the jurisdiction of Maryland. Not content with infusing his own turbulent spirit into the inhabitants of Kent island, he scattered jealousies among the natives, and persuaded them that "the new comers" were Spaniards, and enemies of the Virginians. Having been indicted, and found guilty of murder, piracy, and sedition, he fled from justice; whereupon his estate was seized and confiscated. Clayborne loudly denounced these proceedings as oppressive, and complained of them to his sovereign. At the same time, he prayed for a confirmation of his former license to trade, and for a grant of other lands adjoining the isle of Kent, with power to govern them. The lords commissioners of the colonies, to whom this subject was referred, determined that the lands in question belonged to Lord Baltimore; and that no plantation, or trade with the Indians, within the limits of his patent, ought to be allowed, without his permission. The other complaints made by Clayborne were not deemed proper for the interference of government.

Hitherto, the legislature had been composed of the whole body of the freemen. But the increase of population, and the extension of settlements, having rendered the exercise of the sovereign power by the people themselves intolerably burdensome, an act was passed, in 1639, " for establishing the House of Assembly." This act declared that those elected should be called burgesses, and should supply the place of the freemen who chose them, as do the representatives in the Parliament of England. These burgesses, with others called by special writ, together with the governor and secretary, were to constitute the General Assembly; but the two branches of the legislature were to sit in the same chamber. In 1650, this last regulation was changed; and an act was passed declaring that those called by special writ should form the upper house, while those chosen by the hundreds should compose the lower house; and that bills assented to by both branches of the legislature and by the governor, should be deemed the laws of the province.

CHAP II.
1639
Composed of representatives.

Perfect harmony prevailed between the proprietor and the people; and Maryland, attentive to its own affairs, remained in a state of increasing prosperity until the civil war broke out in England. This government, like that of Virginia, was attached to the royal cause; but Clayborne, who took part with the Parliament, found means to intrigue among the people, and to raise an insurrection in the province. Calvert, the governor, was obliged to fly to Virginia for pro-

1641.

CHAP. II.
1641.
tection; and the insurgents seized the reins of government. After the suppression of this revolt, and the restoration of tranquillity, an act of general pardon and oblivion was passed, from the benefits of which only a few leading individuals were excepted; but this, like most other insurrections, produced additional burdens on the people which did not so soon pass away. A duty, for seven years, of ten shillings on every hundred weight of tobacco exported in Dutch bottoms, was granted to the proprietor; the one-half of which was appropriated to satisfy claims produced by the recovery and defence of the province.*

1651. This state of repose was disturbed by the superintending care of Parliament. In September 1651, commissioners were appointed " for reducing and governing the colonies within the bay of Chesapeak." Among them was Clayborne, the evil genius of Maryland. As the proprietor had acknowledged and submitted to the authority of Parliament, he was permitted to govern the colony in the name of " the keepers of the liberties of England;" but could not long retain the possession of actual authority. The distractions of England, having found their way into Maryland, divided the colonists; and the commissioners supported with their countenance, the faction opposed to the established government. The contentions generated by this state of things, at length broke out in a civil war, which terminated in the de-

* Chalmer.

feat of the governor and the Roman Catholics. A new assembly was convened, which, being entirely under the influence of the victorious party, passed an act declaring that none who professed the popish religion could be protected in the province by the laws; that such as profess faith in God by Jesus Christ, although dissenting from the doctrine and discipline publicly held forth, should not be restrained from the exercise of their religion, provided such liberty was not extended to popery, or prelacy, or to such as, under the profession of Christ, practise licentiousness. Other laws in the same spirit were enacted; and a persecution was commenced against the Quakers, as well as against those guilty of popery, and prelacy. A scene of revolutionary turbulence ensued, in the course of which a resolution was passed declaring the upper house to be useless, which continued in force until the restoration. Philip Calvert was then appointed governor by Lord Baltimore, and the ancient order of things was restored. The colony, notwithstanding these commotions, continued to flourish; and, at the restoration, its population was estimated at twelve thousand souls.

CHAPTER III.

First ineffectual attempts of the Plymouth company to settle the country.—Settlement at New Plymouth. —Sir Henry Rosewell and company.—New charter.—Settlements prosecuted vigorously.—Government transferred to the colonists.—Boston founded. —Religious intolerance.—General court established.—Royal commission for the government of the plantations.—Contest with the French colony of Acadié.—Hugh Peters.—Henry Vane.—Mrs. Hutchison.—Maine granted to Gorges.—Quo warranto against the patent of the colony.—Religious dissentions.—Providence settled.—Rhode Island settled.—Connecticut settled.—War with the Pequods. —New Haven settled.

1606.

THE steps by which the first, or southern colony, advanced to a firm and permanent establishment, were slow and painful. The company for founding the second, or northern colony, was composed of gentlemen residing in Plymouth, and other parts of the west of England; was less wealthy, and possessed fewer resources than the first company, which resided in the capital. Their efforts were consequently more feeble, and less successful, than those which were made in the south.*

* Robertson.

The first vessel fitted out by this company was captured and confiscated by the Spaniards, who, at that time, asserted a right to exclude the ships of all other nations from navigating the American seas. Not discouraged by this misfortune, the company in the following year dispatched two other vessels, having on board about two hundred persons designed to form the proposed settlement. The colonists arrived safely on the American coast in autumn, and took possession of a piece of ground near the river Sagahadoc, where they built fort St. George. Their sufferings during the ensuing winter were extreme. Many of the company, among whom were Gilbert their admiral, and George Popham their president, sank under the diseases by which they were attacked; and the vessels which brought them supplies in the following spring, brought also the information that their principal patron, Sir John Popham, chief justice of England, was dead. Discouraged by their losses and sufferings, and by the death of a person on whom they relied chiefly for assistance, the surviving colonists determined to abandon the country, and embark on board the vessels then returning to England. The frightful pictures they drew of the country, and of the climate, deterred the company, for some time, from farther attempts to make a settlement, and their enterprizes were limited to voyages for the purposes of taking fish, and of trading with the natives for furs. One of these was made by captain Smith, so distinguished in the history of Virginia. Having explored, with great accuracy, that part of the coast which stretches from Penobscot to Cape Cod, he delineated it on a map; which he presented to the young Prince of Wales, with descriptions dictated by a sanguine mind, in which enthusiasm was combined with genius. The imagination of the Prince was so wrought upon by the glowing colours in which Smith painted the country, that he declared it should be called New England, which name it has ever since retained.*

The languishing company of Plymouth, however, could not be stimulated to engage in farther schemes of colonisation, the advantages of which were distant and uncertain, while the expense was immediate and inevitable. To a stronger motive than even interest, is New England indebted for its first settlement.

An obscure sect, which had acquired the appellation of Brownists from the name of its founder, and which had rendered itself peculiarly obnoxious by the democracy of its tenets respecting church government, had been driven by persecution to take refuge at Leyden in Holland, where its members formed a distinct society under the care of their pastor, Mr. John Robinson. There they resided several years in safe obscurity. This situation, at length, became irksome to them. Their families intermingled with the Dutch, and they saw before them, with extreme apprehension, the danger of losing their separate identity. Under the influence of these and other causes, they

* Robertson. Chalmer. Hutchison.

came to the determination of removing in a body to America.

They applied to the London company for a grant of lands; and, to promote the success of their application by the certainty of their emigrating, they said, " that they were well weaned from the delicate milk of their mother country, and inured to the difficulties of a strange land. That they were knit together in a strict and sacred bond, by virtue of which they held themselves bound to take care of the good of each other, and of the whole. That it was not with them, as with other men, whom small things could discourage, or small discontents cause to wish themselves at home again." The only privilege on which they insisted, was a license under the great seal, to practise and profess religion in that mode, which, under the impulse of conscience, they had adopted. This reasonable and moderate request was refused. James had already established the church of England in Virginia; and, although he promised to connive at their non-conformity, and not to molest them while they demeaned themselves peaceably, he positively refused to give that explicit and solemn pledge of security, which they required. This, for a short time, suspended their removal; but the causes of their discontent in Holland continuing, they, at length, determined to trust to the verbal declarations of the King, and negotiated with the Virginia company for a tract of land within the limits of their patent.*

* Robertson.

In September, they sailed from England, with only one hundred and twenty men, in a single ship. Their destination was Hudson's river; but the first land they made was Cape Cod. They soon perceived that they were not only beyond their own limits, but beyond those of the company from which they derived their title; but it was now the month of November, and consequently too late in the season again to put to sea in search of a new habitation. After exploring the coast, they chose a position for their station, to which they gave the name of New Plymouth. On the 11th of November, before landing, a solemn covenant was signed by the heads of families, and freemen, in which, after reciting that they had undertaken to plant a colony for the glory of God, and for the honour of their King and country, and professing their loyalty to their sovereign Lord King James, they combined themselves into a body politic, for the purpose of making equal laws for the general good.*

Having thus formed a compact, the obligation of which all admitted, they proceeded to the choice of a governor for one year; and to enable him the better to discharge the trust confided to him, they gave him one assistant. In 1624, three others were added; and the number was afterwards increased to seven. The supreme power resided in, and, during the infancy of the colony, was exercised by, the whole body of the male inhabitants. They assembled together, occa-

---

* Robertson. Chalmer. Hutchison.

sionally, to determine on all subjects of public concern; nor was a house of representatives established until the year 1639. They adopted the laws of England as a common rule of action, adding occasionally municipal regulations. Some of the changes in their penal code strongly mark their character and circumstances. While only a moderate fine was imposed on forgery, fornication was punished with whipping, and adultery with death.*

Misguided by their religious theories, they fell into the same error which had been committed in Virginia, and, in imitation of the primitive Christians, threw all their property into a common stock, laboured jointly for the common benefit, and were fed from the common stores. This regulation produced, even in this small and enthusiastic society, its constant effect. They were often in danger of starving; and severe whipping, administered to promote labour, only increased discontent.

The colonists landed at a season of the year which was unfavourable to the establishment of a new settlement. The winter, which was intensely cold, had already commenced; and they were not in a condition to soften its rigours. Before the return of spring, fifty of them perished with maladies increased by the hardships to which they were exposed, by the scarcity of food, and by the almost total privation of those comforts to which they had been accustomed. The

* Robertson. Chalmer. Hutchison.

survivors, as the season moderated, encountered new difficulties. Their attention to the means of providing for their future wants was interrupted by the necessity of taking up arms to defend themselves against the neighbouring savages. Fortunately for the colonists, the natives had been so wasted by pestilence, the preceding year, that they were easily subdued, and compelled to accept a peace, on equitable terms.

The colonists were supported, under these multiplied distresses, by the hope of better times, and by that high gratification which men exasperated by persecution and oppression, derived from the enjoyment of the rights of conscience, and the full exercise of the powers of self-government. From their friends in England, they received occasional but scanty supplies; and continued to struggle against surrounding difficulties, with patience and perseverance. They remained in peace, alike exempt from the notice and oppression of government. Yet, in consequence of the unproductiveness of their soil, and their adherence to the pernicious policy of a community of goods and of labour, they increased more slowly than the other colonies; and, in the year 1630, amounted to only three hundred souls.

Until the year 1630, they possessed no other title to their lands than is derived from occupancy. In that year they obtained a grant from the New Plymouth company, but were never incorporated as a body politic by royal charter. Having received no powers from the parliament or King, and being totally disregarded by the Plymouth company, they remained a mere voluntary association, yielding obedience to laws, and to magistrates, formed and chosen by themselves. In this situation they continued undisturbed, and almost unknown, more tolerant and more moderate than their neighbours, until their union with a younger, and more powerful sister, who advanced with a growth unusually rapid to a state of maturity.*

The original company of Plymouth, having done nothing effectual towards settling the territory which had been granted to them, and being unable to preserve the monopoly of their trade and fisheries, applied to James for a new and more enlarged patent. On the 3d of November, he granted that territory which lies between the 40th and 48th degrees of north latitude to the Duke of Lenox, the Marquis of Buckingham, and several others, in absolute property; and incorporated them under the name of " the council established at Plymouth, for planting and governing that country called New England;" with jurisdiction and powers similar to those which had before been conferred on the companies of south and north Virginia, and especially that of excluding all other persons whatever from trading within their boundaries and fishing in the neighbouring seas. This improvident grant, which excited the indignation of the people of England, then deeply interested in the fur

---

* Robertson. Chalmer. Hutchison.

CHAP. III.
1620.
trade and fisheries, soon engaged the attention, and received the censure of parliament. The patentees were compelled to relinquish their odious monopoly; and, being thus deprived of the funds on which they had relied to furnish the expense of supporting new settlements, they abandoned the design of attempting them. New England might have remained long unoccupied by Europeans, had not the same causes, which occasioned the emigration of the Brownists, still continued to operate. The persecution to which the puritans were exposed, increased their zeal and their numbers. In despair of obtaining at home a relaxation of those rigorous penal statutes under which they had long smarted, they looked elsewhere for that toleration which was denied them in their native land. Understanding that their brethren in New Plymouth were permitted to worship their creator according to the dictates of conscience, their attention was directed towards the same coast; and several small emigrations were made, at different times, to Massachusetts bay; so termed from the name of the Sachem who was sovereign of the country.

Mr. White, a non-conforming minister at Dorchester, formed an association of several gentlemen, who had imbibed puritanical opinions, for the purpose of conducting a colony to the bay of Massachusetts, and rendering it an asylum for the persecuted of his own persuasion. In prosecution of these views, a treaty was concluded with the council of Plymouth for the purchase of part of New England; and that

corporation, in March 1627, sold to Sir Henry Rose- CHAP. III.
well and others, all that part of New England lying 1627.
three miles to the south of Charles' river, and three Sir Henry Rosewell and others.
miles north of Merrimack river, and extending from
the Atlantic to the South sea. A small number of
planters and servants were, soon afterwards, dispatched under Endicot, who, in September, laid the foundation of Salem, the first permanent town in Massachusetts.*

The purchasers perceived their inability to accomplish the settlement of the extensive regions they had
acquired, without the aid of more opulent partners.
These were soon found in the capital; but they required that a new charter should be obtained from the
crown, comprehending their names, which should
confirm the grant to the council of Plymouth, and
confer on the grantees the powers of government. So
seldom is man instructed by the experience of others,
that, disregarding the lessons furnished by Virginia,
they likewise required that the supreme authority
should be vested in persons residing in London. The
proprietors having acceded to these requisitions, ap- New char-
plication was made to Charles for a patent conforming ter. 1628
to them, which issued on the 4th day of March, 1628.

This charter incorporated the grantees by the name
of "The governor and company of Massachusetts
bay in New England."

The whole executive power was vested in a governor,

* Robertson. Chalmer. Hutchison.

a deputy governor, and eighteen assistants; to be named, in the first instance, by the crown, and afterwards elected by the company. The governor, and seven, or more, of the assistants, were authorised to meet in monthly courts, for the dispatch of such business as concerned the company, or settlement. The legislative power was vested in the body of the proprietors, who were to assemble four times a year in person, under the denomination of the general court; and besides electing freemen, and the necessary officers of the company, were empowered to make ordinances for the good of the community, and the government of the plantation and its inhabitants; provided they should not be repugnant to the laws of England. Their lands were to be holden in free and common soccage; and the same temporary exemption from taxes, and from duties on exports and imports, which had been granted to the colony of Virginia, was accorded to them. As in the charter of Virginia, so in this, the colonists and their descendants were declared to be entitled to all the rights and privileges of natural born subjects.

The patent being obtained, the governor and council engaged with ardour in the duties assigned them. To support the expenses of a fresh embarkation, it was resolved that every person subscribing fifty pounds, should be entitled to two hundred acres of land as the first dividend. Five vessels sailed in May, carrying about two hundred persons, who reached Salem in June. At that place they found Endicot, to whom they brought a confirmation of his commission as governor. The colony consisted of three hundred persons, one hundred of whom removed to Charlestown.

CHAP. III.
1628.

Religion, which had stimulated them to remove from their native land, became the first object of their care in the country they had adopted. Being zealous puritans, they concurred in the institution of a church, establishing that form of policy, which has since been denominated independent. A confession of faith was drawn up to which the majority assented; and an association was formed in which they covenanted with the Lord, and with each other, to walk together in all his ways, as he should be pleased to reveal himself to them. Pastors, and other ecclesiastical officers, were chosen, who were installed into their sacred offices, by the imposition of the hands of the brethren.*

A church being thus formed, several were received as members who gave an account of their faith and hope as Christians; and those only were admitted into the communion, whose morals and religious tenets were approved by the elders.†.

Pleased with the work of their hands, and believing it to be perfect, they could tolerate no difference of opinion. Just escaped from persecution, they became persecutors themselves. Some few of their number, attached to the ritual of the church of England, were dissatisfied with its total abolition; and, withdrawing

* Robertson.   † Idem.

from communion with the church, met apart, to worship God in the manner they deemed most proper. At the head of this small number were two of the first patentees, who were also of the council. They were called before the governor, who, being of opinion that their non-conformity and conversation tended to sedition, sent them to England. The opposition ceased when deprived of its leaders.*

The following winter brought with it the calamities which must be uniformly sustained by the first emigrants into a wilderness, where the cold is severe, and the privations almost universal. In the course of it, nearly half their number perished, "lamenting that they did not live to see the rising glories of the faithful." The fortitude, however, of the survivors, was not shaken; nor were their brethren in England deterred from joining them. Religion supported the colonists under all their difficulties; and the intolerant spirit of the English hierarchy diminished, in the view of the puritans in England, the dangers and the sufferings to be encountered in America; and disposed them to forego every other human enjoyment, for the consoling privilege of worshipping the Supreme Being according to their own opinions. Many persons of fortune determined to seek in the new world that liberty of conscience which was denied them in the old; but, foreseeing the misrule inseparable from the residence of the legislative power in England, they

* Robertson. Chalmer. Hutchison.

demanded, as preliminary to their emigration, that the powers of government should be transferred to New England, and be exercised in the colony. The company had already incurred expenses for which they saw no prospect of a speedy reimbursement; and although they doubted the legality of the measure, were well disposed by adopting it, to obtain such important aid. A general court was therefore convened, by whom it was unanimously resolved " that the patent should be tranferred, and the government of the colony removed from London to Massachusetts bay." It was also agreed that the members of the corporation remaining in England, should retain a share in the trading stock and profits for the term of seven years.*

Such was the effect of this revolution in the system of government, that, early in the following year, fifteen hundred persons, among whom were several of family and fortune, embarked, at an expense of upwards of twenty thousand pounds, and arrived at Salem in July. Dissatisfied with this situation, they explored the country in quest of better stations; and, settling in many places around the bay, they laid the foundation of several towns, and, among others, of Boston.

The difficulty of obtaining subsistence, the difference of their food from that to which they had been accustomed, the intense cold of the winter, against which sufficient provision was not yet made, were still severely felt by the colonists, and still carried many

---

* Robertson. Chalmer. Hutchison.

of them to the grave; but that enthusiasm which had impelled them to emigrate, preserved all its force; and they met, with a firm unshaken spirit, the calamities which assailed them. Our admiration of their fortitude and of their principles, sustains, however, some diminution from observing the sternness with which they denied to others that civil and religious liberty which, through so many dangers and hardships, they sought for themselves. Their general court decreed that none should be admitted as freemen, or permitted to vote at elections, or be capable of being chosen as magistrates, or of serving as jurymen, but such as had been received into the church as members. Thus did men who had braved every hardship for freedom of conscience, deny the choicest rights of humanity, to all those who dissented from the opinion of the majority on any article of faith, or point of church discipline.

The numerous complaints of the severities exercised by the government of Massachusetts, added to the immense emigration of persons noted for their enthusiasm, seem, at length, to have made some impression on Charles; and an order was made by the King in council, to stop the ships at that time ready to sail, freighted with passengers for New England. This order, however, seems never to have been strictly executed, as the emigrations continued without any sensible diminution.

Hitherto the legislature had been composed of the whole body of the freemen. Under this system, so favourable to the views of the few who possess popular influence, the real power of the state had been chiefly engrossed by the governor and assistants, aided by the clergy. The emigration, however, having already been considerable, and the settlements having become extensive, it was found inconvenient, if not impracticable, longer to preserve a principle which their charter enjoined. In the year '1634' therefore, by common consent, the people elected delegates who met the governor and council, and constituted the general court. This important improvement in their system, rendered familiar, and probably suggested, by the practice in the mother country, although not authorised by the charter, remained unaltered, so long as that charter was permitted to exist.*

The colony of Massachusetts having been conducted, from its commencement, very much on the plan of an independent society, at length attracted the partial notice of the jealous administration in England; and a commission for " the regulation and government of the plantations" was issued to the great officers of state, and to some of the nobility, in which absolute power was granted to the archbishop of Canterbury and to others, " to make laws and constitutions concerning either their state public, or the utility of individuals." The commissioners were authorised to support the clergy by assigning them " tithes, oblations, and other profits, according to their discretion;

---

* Robertson. Chalmer. Hutchison.

CHAP. III. to inflict punishment on those who should violate their
1635. ordinances; to remove governors of plantations, and to appoint others; and to constitute tribunals and courts of justice, ecclesiastical and civil, with such authority and form as they should think proper;" but their laws were not to take effect until they had received the royal assent, and had been proclaimed in the colonies. The commissioners were also constituted a committee to hear complaints against a colony, its governor or other officers, with power to remove the offender to England for punishment. They were farther directed to cause the revocation of such letters patent, granted for the establishment of colonies, as should, upon inquiry, be found to have been unduly obtained, or to contain a grant of liberties hurtful to the royal prerogative.*

From the first settlement at Salem, the colony of Massachusetts had cultivated the friendship of their neighbours of New Plymouth. The bonds of mutual amity were now rendered more strict, not only by some appearances of a hostile disposition among the natives, but by another circumstance which excited alarm in both colonies.

The voyages for discovery and settlement, made by the English and French, to the coast of North America, having been nearly cotemporaneous, their conflicting claims soon brought them into collision with each other. The same lands were granted by

* Chalmer. Hutchison.

the sovereigns of both nations; and, under these different grants, actual settlements had been made by the French as far south and west as St. Croix, and, by the English, as far north and east as Penobscot. During the war with France, which broke out early in the reign of Charles I., that monarch granted a commission to captain Kirk for the conquest of the countries in America occupied by the French; under which, in 1629, Canada and Acadié were subdued; but, by the treaty of St. Germains, those places were restored to France without any description of their limits; and Fort Royal, Quebec, and Cape Breton, were severally surrendered by name. In 1632, a party of French from Acadié committed a robbery on a trading house established at Penobscot by the people of New Plymouth. With the intelligence of this fact, information was also brought that cardinal Richelieu had ordered some companies to Acadié, and that more were expected the next year, with priests, jesuits, and other formidable accompaniments, for a permanent settlement. The governor of Acadié established a military post at Penobscot, and, at the same time wrote to the governor of New Plymouth stating, that he had orders to displace the English as far as Pemaquid. Not being disposed to submit quietly to this invasion of territory, the government of New Plymouth undertook an expedition for the recovery of the fort at Penobscot, consisting of an English ship of war under the command of captain Girling, and a bark with twenty men belonging to the colony. The garrison received notice of this armament, and prepared for its reception by fortifying and strengthening the fort; in consequence of which Girling, after expending his ammunition and finding himself too weak to attempt the works by assault, applied to Massachusetts for aid. That colony agreed to furnish one hundred men, and to bear the expense of the expedition by private subscription; but a sufficient supply of provisions, even for this small corps, could not be immediately obtained, and the expedition was abandoned. Girling returned, and the French retained possession of Penobscot till 1654. The apprehensions entertained of these formidable neighbours contributed, in no small degree, to cement the union between Massachusetts and Plymouth.*

Two persons, afterwards distinguished in English annals, arrived this year in Boston. One was Hugh Peters, the coadjutor and chaplain of Oliver Cromwell; the other was Mr. Henry Vane, the son of sir Henry Vane, who was, at that time a privy councillor of great credit with the King. The mind of this young gentleman was so deeply imbued with the political and religious opinions of the puritans, that he appeared ready to sacrifice, for the enjoyment of them, all his bright prospects in his native land. His mortified exterior, his grave and solemn deportment, his reputation for piety and wisdom, his strong professions of attachment to liberty and to the public good,

* Hutchison.

added to his attention to some of the leading members in the church, won rapidly the affections of the people, and he was chosen their governor.

His administration commenced with more external pomp than had been usual, or would seem to be congenial either with his own professions, or with the plain and simple manners of the people whom he governed. When going to court or church, he was always preceded by two serjeants who walked with their halberts. Yet his popularity sustained no diminution, until the part he took in the religious controversies of the country detached from him many of its most judicious inhabitants.*

Independent of the meetings for public worship on every Sunday, of the stated lecture in Boston on every Thursday, and of occasional lectures in other towns, there were frequent meetings of the brethren of the churches, for religious exercises. Mrs. Hutchinson, who had been much flattered by the attentions of the governor, and of Mr. Cotton, one of the most popular of the clergy; who added eloquence to her enthusiasm, and whose husband was among the most respected men of the country; dissatisfied with the exclusion of her sex from the private meetings of the brethren, instituted a meeting of the sisters also, in which she repeated the sermons of the preceding Sunday, accompanied with remarks and expositions. These meetings were attended by a large number of

---

* Chalmer. Hutchison

CHAP. III. the most respectable of her sex; and her lectures
1636. were, for a time, generally approved. At length she
drew a distinction between the ministers through the
country. She designated a small number as being
under a covenant of grace; the others, as being under
a covenant of works. Contending for the necessity
of the former, she maintained that sanctity of life is no
evidence of justification, or of favour with God; and
that the Holy Ghost dwells personally in such as are
justified. The whole colony was divided into two
parties, equally positive, on these abstruse points,
whose resentments against each other threatened the
most serious calamities. Mr. Vane espoused, with
zeal, the wildest doctrines of Mrs. Hutchinson, and
Mr. Cotton decidedly favoured them. The lieutenant
governor Mr. Winthrop, and the majority of the
churches, were of the opposite party. Many conferences were held; days of fasting and humiliation
were appointed; a general synod was called; and,
after violent dissentions, Mrs. Hutchinson's opinions
were condemned as erroneous, and she was banished.
Many of her disciples followed her. Vane, in disgust, quitted America; unlamented even by those
who had lately admired him. He was thought too
visionary; and is said to have been too enthusiastic
even for the enthusiasts of Massachusetts.

The patentees, having no common object to prosecute, resolved to divide their lands; and, in the expectation of receiving a deed of confirmation for the
particular portion which fortune should allot to each,

cast lots, in the presence of James, for the shares each should hold in severalty. They continued, however, to act some years longer as a body politic, during which time, they granted various portions of the country to different persons; and executed under the seal of the corporation, deeds of feoffment for the lots drawn by each member of the company; patents of confirmation for which were solicited, but appear to have been granted only to Gorges, for Maine. The charter was surrendered by the company and accepted by the crown.*

Charles, in pursuance of his determination to take the government of New England into his own hands, issued a proclamation directing that none should be transported thither who had not the special license of the crown, which should be granted to those only who had taken the oaths of supremacy and allegiance, and had conformed to the discipline of the church of England. This order, however, could not be completely executed; and the emigrations, which were entirely of non-comformists, still continued. Those who were disgusted with the ceremonials rigidly exacted in England, estimated so highly the simple frame of church policy established in Massachusetts, that numbers surmounted every difficulty, to seek an asylum in this new Jerusalem. Among them were men of the first political influence and mental attainments. Pymm, Hampden, Hazlerig, and Cromwell,

* Chalmer. Hutchison.

CHAP. III.
1637.
with many others who afterwards performed a conspicuous part in that revolution which brought the head of Charles to the block, are said to have been actually on board a vessel prepared to sail for New England, and to have been stopped by the special orders of the privy council.*

1638.
The commissioners for the regulation and government of the plantations having reported that Massachusetts had violated its charter, a writ of *quo warranto* was issued, on which judgment was given in favour of the crown. The process was never served on any member of the corporation; and it is therefore probable that the judgment was not final. The privy council however ordered the governor and company to send their patent to England to be surrendered. The general court answered this order by a petition to the commissioners in which they said, " we dare not question your Lordship's proceedings in requiring our patent to be sent unto you; we only desire to open our griefs; and if in any thing we have offended his Majesty or your Lordships, we humbly prostrate ourselves at the foot stool of supreme authority; we are sincerely ready to yield all due obedience to both; we are not conscious that we have offended in any thing, as our government is according to law; we pray that we may be heard before condemnation, and that we may be suffered to live in the wilderness." Fortunately for the colonists, Charles and his com-

* Hume.

missioners found too much employment at home, to have leisure for carrying into complete execution, a system aimed at the subversion of what was most dear to the hearts of Americans.

To the religious dissentions which distracted Massachusetts, and to the rigour with which conformity was exacted, is to be attributed the first settlement of the other colonies of New England. As early as the year 1634, Roger Williams, a popular preacher at Salem, who had refused to hold communion with the church at Boston, because its members refused to make a public declaration of their repentance for having held communion with the church of England during their residence in that country, was charged with many exceptionable tenets. Among several which mark his wild enthusiasm, one is found in total opposition, to the spirit of the times and to the severity of his other doctrines. He maintained, that to punish a man for any matter of conscience is persecution, and that even papists and Armenians are entitled to freedom of conscience in worship, provided the peace of civil society be secured. The divines of Massachusetts, in opposition to this doctrine, contended that they did not persecute men for conscience, but corrected them for sinning against conscience; and so they did not persecute, but punish heretics. This unintelligible sophism not convincing Williams, he was, for this, and for his other heresies, banished by the magistrates, as a disturber of the peace of the church, and of the commonwealth.

CHAP. III.
1638.

Providence settled.

Many of his disciples followed him into exile, and, travelling south until they passed the line of Massachusetts, purchased a tract of land of the Narraghansetts, then a powerful tribe of Indians, where, in 1635, they made a settlement to which they gave the name of Providence. After fixing the place of their future residence, they entered into a voluntary association, and framed a government composed of the whole body of freemen. After the manner of Massachusetts, they created a church by collecting a religious society; but, as one of the causes of their migration had been the tenet that all were entitled to freedom of conscience in worship, entire toleration was established. The new settlers cultivated with assiduity the good will of the natives, with whom a long peace was preserved.*

The banishment of Williams was soon followed by that of Mrs. Hutchinson. She was accompanied by many of her disciples, who, pursuing the steps of Williams, and, arriving in his neighbourhood, purchased a tract of land from the same tribe,

Rhode Island settled.

and founded Rhode Island. Imitating the conduct of their neighbours, they formed a similar association for the establishment of civil government, and adopted the same principles of toleration. In consequence of this conduct the island soon became so populous as to furnish settlers for the adjacent shores.†

1634.

Connecticut too is a colony of Massachusetts. As early as the year 1634, several persons, among whom

* Chalmer. Hutchison. † Chalmer.

was Mr. Hooker, a favourite minister of the church, applied to the general court of Massachusetts for permission to pursue their fortunes in some new and better land. This permission was not granted at that time; and, it being then the received opinion that the oath of a freeman, as well as the original compact, bound every member of the society so as not to leave him the right to separate himself from it without the consent of the whole, this emigration was suspended. The general court, however, did not long withhold its assent. The country having been explored, and a place selected on the west side of the river Connecticut, a commission was granted to the petitioners to remove, on the condition of their still continuing under the jurisdiction of Massachusetts, some few huts had been erected the preceding year in which a small number of emigrants had wintered; and, the fall succeeding, about sixty persons traversed the wilderness in families. In 1636, about one hundred persons, led by Pynchon, Hooker, and Haynes, followed the first emigrants, and founded the towns of Hartford, Springfield, and Weathersfield. There are some peculiarities attending this commission and this settlement, which deserve to be noticed.

The country to be settled was, confessedly, without the limits of Massachusetts; yet Roger Ludlow was authorised to promulgate the orders which might be necessary for the plantations; to inflict corporal punishment, imprisonment, and fines; to determine all differences in a judicial way; and to convene the

CHAP. III.
1636.

inhabitants in a general court, if it should be necessary. This signal exercise of authority grew out of the principle, solemnly asserted by the general court of Massachusetts, that the oath of fidelity to the commonwealth was binding, although the person should no longer reside within its limits.

There were other difficulties attending the title of the settlers. The Dutch at Manhadoes, or New York, claimed a right to the river, as its first discoverers. In addition to this hostile title, Lord Say and Seal, and Lord Brooke, with some others, contemplating a retreat in the new world from the despotism with which England was threatened, had made choice of Connecticut river for that purpose, and had built a fort at its mouth, called Saybrooke. The emigrants from Massachusetts, however, kept possession; and proceeded to clear and cultivate the country. They purchased the rights of Lord Say and Seal, and Lord Brooke, and their partners; and the Dutch, being too feeble to maintain their title by the sword, gradually receded from the river. The emigrants, disclaiming the authority of Massachusetts, entered into a voluntary association for the establishment of a government, which, in its form, was like those established in the other colonies of New England. The principal difference between their constitution and that of Massachusetts was, that they imparted the right of freemen to those who were not members of the Church.*

* All the powers of government for nearly three years, seem to have been in the magistrates. Two were appointed in each town, who directed all the affairs of the plantation. The freemen appear to have had no voice in making the

These new establishments gave great and just alarm to the Piquods, a powerful tribe of Indians on the south of Massachusetts. They foresaw their own ruin in this extension of the English settlements; and the disposition excited by this apprehension soon displayed itself in private murders, and other acts of hostility. With a policy suggested by a strong sense of danger, they sought a reconciliation with the Narraghansetts, their ancient enemies and rivals; and requested them to forget their long cherished animosities, and to co-operate cordially against a common enemy whose continuing encroachments threatened to overwhelm both in one common destruction. Noticing the rapid progress of the English settlements, they urged, with reason, that, although a present friendship subsisted between the Narraghansetts and the new comers, yet all, in turn, must be dispossessed of their country, and this dangerous friendship could promise no other good than the wretched privilege of being last devoured.

These representations could not efface from the bosoms of the Narraghansetts, that deep rooted enmity which neighbours, not bound together by ligaments of sufficient strength to prevent reciprocal acts of hostility, too often feel for each other. Dreading still less the power of a foreign nation, than that of

laws, or in any part of the government except in some instances of general and uncommon concern. In these instances committees were sent from the several towns to a general meeting. During this term, juries seem not to have been employed in any case.

CHAP III.
1636.

men with whom they had been in the habit of contending, they not only refused to join the Piquods, but communicated their proposition to the government of Massachusetts, with whom they formed an alliance against that tribe. Open war being resolved on by both parties, Captain Underhill was sent to the relief of fort Saybrooke which had been besieged by the Indians; and the three colonies, Massachusetts, Plymouth, and Connecticut, agreed to march their united forces into the country of the Piquods, to effect their entire destruction. The troops of Connecticut were first in motion. Those of Massachusetts were detained by the controversy concerning the covenant of works, and of grace, which had insinuated itself into all the transactions of that colony. Their little army, when collected, found itself divided by this metaphysical point; and the stronger party, believing that the blessing of God could not be expected to crown with success the arms of such unhallowed men as their opponents in faith on this question, refused to march until their small band was purified by expelling the unclean, and introducing others whose tenets were unexceptionable.

War with the Piquods.

While this operation was performing, the troops of Connecticut, reinforced by a body of friendly Indians and by a small detachment from Saybrooke, determined to march against the enemy. The Piquods had taken two positions which they had surrounded with palisadoes, and had resolved to defend. The nearest was on a small eminence surrounded by a swamp near the head of Mystic river. Against this fort the first attack was made. The Indians, deceived by a movement of the vessels from Saybrooke to Narraghansett, believed the expedition to have been abandoned; and celebrated, in perfect security, the supposed evacuation of their country. About day-break, while they were asleep, the English approached, and the surprise would have been complete, had they not been alarmed by the barking of a dog. They immediately gave the war whoop, and flew undismayed to arms. The English rushed to the attack, forced their way through the works, and set fire to the Indian wigwams. The confusion soon became general, and almost every man was killed or taken.

Soon after this action, the troops of Massachusetts arrived, and it was resolved to pursue the victory. Several skirmishes terminated unfavourably to the Piquods; and, in a short time, they received another total defeat, which put an end to the war. A few only of this once powerful nation survived, who, abandoning their country, dispersed themselves among the neighbouring tribes, and were incorporated with them.*

This vigorous essay in arms of the New England colonists impressed on the Indians a high opinion of their courage and military superiority; but their victory was sullied with cruelties which cannot be recollected without mingled regret and censure.

Immediately after the termination of this war New Haven was settled.

A small emigration from England conducted by Eaton and Davenport, arrived at Boston in June. Unwilling to remain where power and influence were already in the hands of others, they refused to continue within the jurisdiction of Massachusetts; and, disregarding the threats at Manhadoes, settled themselves west of Connecticut river, on a place which they named New Haven. Their institutions, civil and ecclesiastical, were in the same spirit with those of their elder sister, Massachusetts.

The colony was now in a very flourishing condition. Twenty-one thousand two hundred emigrants had arrived from England; and, although they devoted great part of their attention to the abstruse points of theology which employed the casuists of that day, they were not unmindful of those solid acquisitions which permanently improve the condition of man. Sober, industrious, and economical, they laboured indefatigably in opening and improving the country, and were unremitting in their efforts to furnish themselves with those supplies which are to be drawn from the bosom of the earth. Of these, they soon raised a surplus for which fresh emigrants offered a profitable market; and their foreign trade in lumber, added to their fish and furs, furnished them with the means of making remittances to England for those manufactures which they found it advantageous to import. Their fisheries had become so important as to attract the attention of government. For their encouragement, a law was passed exempting property employed in catching, curing, or transporting fish, from all duties and taxes, and the fishermen, and ship builders, from militia duty. By the same law, all persons were restrained from using cod or bass fish for manure.

CHAPTER IV.

Massachusetts claims New Hampshire and part of Maine.—Dissentions among the inhabitants.—Confederation of the New England colonies.—Rhode Island excluded from it.—Separate chambers provided for the two branches of the Legislature.—New England takes part with Parliament.—Treaty with Acadié.—Petition of the non-conformists.—Disputes between Massachusetts and Connecticut.—War between England and Holland.—Machinations of the Dutch at Manhadoes among the Indians.—Massachusetts refuses to join the united colonies in the war.—Application of New Haven to Cromwell for assistance.—Peace with the Dutch.—Expedition of Sedgewic against Acadié.—Religious intolerance.

1639. The government of Massachusetts, induced by the rapidity with which the colony had attained its present strength to form sanguine hopes of future importance, instituted an inquiry into the extent of their patent, with a view to the enlargement of territory. To facilitate this object, commissioners were appointed to explore the Merrimack, and to ascertain its northernmost point. The charter conveyed to the grantees all the lands within lines to be drawn three miles south of Charles river, and the same distance north of the Merrimack. The government construed this description as authorising a line to be drawn due east from a point three miles north of the head of Merrimack, which soon leaves that river, and includes all New Hampshire, and a considerable part of Maine. In pursuance of this exposition of the charter, the general court asserted its jurisdiction over New Hampshire, in which there were a few scattered habitations, and proceeded to authorise settlements in that country.*

CHAP. IV.
1639.

Massachusetts claims New Hampshire and part of Maine.

The attempts which had been made to colonise the northern and eastern parts of New England had proved almost entirely unsuccessful. Sir Ferdinando Gorges and John Mason had built a small house at the mouth of Piscataqua, about the year 1623; and, nearly at the same time, others erected a few huts along the coast from Merrimack eastward to Sagadahock for the purpose of fishing. In 1631, Gorges and Mason sent over a small party of planters and fishermen under the conduct of a Mr. Williams, who laid the foundation of Portsmouth.

When the Plymouth company divided New England among its members, that territory lying along the coast from Merrimack river, and for sixty miles into the country to the river Piscataqua, was granted to Mason, and was called New Hampshire; that territory north-eastward of New Hampshire, to the river Kennebec, and sixty miles into the country, was

---

* Chalmer. Hutchison.

CHAP IV.
1639. granted to sir Ferdinando Gorges. In 1639, Gorges obtained a patent for this district under the name of Maine, comprehending the lands for one hundred, instead of sixty miles, into the country, together with the powers of sovereignty. He framed a system of government which, being purely executive, could not even preserve itself. After struggling with a long course of confusion, and drawing out, for several years, a miserable political existence, Maine submitted itself to the jurisdiction of Massachusetts, and consented to become a part of that colony. In the course of the years 1651 and 1652, this junction was affected, and Maine was erected into a county, the towns of which sent deputies to the general court at Boston. To this county was conceded the peculiar privilege that its inhabitants, although not members of the church, should be entitled to the rights of freemen on taking the oath.*

The settlements in New Hampshire, too, were maintaining only a doubtful and feeble existence, when they drew a recruit of inhabitants from the same causes which had peopled Rhode Island and Connecticut.

1637. In 1637, when Mrs. Hutchinson and other Antinomians were exiled, Mr. Wheelright, her brother in law, a popular preacher, was likewise banished. He carried with him a considerable number of his followers; and, just passing the north-eastern boundary of

* Chalmer. Hutchison.

Massachusetts, planted the town of Exeter. These emigrants immediately formed themselves, according to the manner of New England, into a body politic for their own government.

A few persons arrived soon afterwards from England, and laid the foundation of the town of Dover. They also established a distinct government. Their first act proved to be the source of future discord. The majority chose one Underhill as governor; but a respectable minority was opposed to his election. To this cause of discontent was added another of irresistable influence. They were divided on the subject of the covenant of works, and of grace. These dissentions soon grew into a civil war, which was happily terminated by Williams, who was, according to the practice of small societies torn by civil broils, invited by the weaker party to its aid. He marched from Portsmouth at the head of a small military force; and, banishing the governor, and the leaders of the Antinomian faction, restored peace to this distracted village.

Massachusetts had asserted a right over this territory. Her claim derived aid, not only from the factions which agitated these feeble settlements, but also from the uncertainty of the tenure by which the inhabitants held their lands. Only the settlers at Portsmouth had acquired a title from Mason; and the others were, consequently, unfriendly to his pretensions. These causes produced a voluntary offer of submission to the government of Massachusetts,

CHAP. IV.
1639.

1640.

CHAP. IV.
1640.

which was accepted; and the general court passed an order, declaring the inhabitants of Piscataqua to be within their jurisdiction, with the privileges of participating in all their rights, and of being exempted from all " public charges, other than those which shall arise for, or among themselves, or from any action, or course that may be taken for their own good or benefit." Under the protecting wing of this more powerful neighbour, New Hampshire attained the growth which afterwards enabled her to stand alone; and long remembered with affection the benefits she had received.*

Charles, environed with difficulties arising from his own misrule, was at length compelled to meet his Parliament; and, in November, the great council of the nation was again assembled. The circumstances which had caused such considerable emigrations to New England, existed no longer. The puritans were not only exempt from persecution, but became the strongest party in the nation; and, from this time, New England is supposed to have derived no increase of population from the parent state.†

Confederation of the New England colonies.

About the same period many evidences were given of a general combination of the neighbouring Indians against the settlements of New England; and apprehensions were also entertained of hostility from the Dutch at Manhadoes. A sense of impending danger suggested the policy of forming a confederacy of

* Chalmer. Hutchison.   † Hutchison.

the sister colonies for their mutual defence; and so confirmed had the habit of self-government become since the attention of England was absorbed in her domestic dissentions, that it was not thought necessary to consult the parent state on this important measure. After mature deliberation, articles of confederation were digested; and in May 1643, they were conclusively adopted.*

By them the united colonies of New England, viz. Massachusetts, Plymouth, Connecticut, and New Haven, entered into a firm and perpetual league, offensive and defensive.

Each colony retained a distinct and separate jurisdiction; no two colonies could join in one jurisdiction without the consent of the whole; and no other colony could be received into the confederacy without the like consent.

The charge of all wars was to be borne by the colonies respectively, in proportion to the male inhabitants of each, between sixteen and sixty years of age.

On notice of an invasion given by three magistrates of any colony, the confederates were immediately to furnish their respective quotas. These were fixed at

* This was an union, says Mr. Trumbull, of the highest consequence to the New England colonies. It made them formidable to the Dutch and Indians, and respectable among their French neighbours. It was happily adapted to maintain harmony among themselves, and to secure the rights and peace of the country. It was one of the principal means of the preservation of the colonies, during the civil wars, and unsettled state of affairs in England. It was the great source of mutual defence in Philip's war; and of the most eminent service in civilising the Indians, and propagating the Gospel among them. The union subsisted more than forty years, until the abrogation of the charters of the New England colonies by king James II.

P

one hundred from Massachusetts, and forty-five from each of the other parties to the agreement. If a larger armament should be found necessary, commissioners were to meet, and ascertain the number of men to be required.

Two commissioners from each government, being church members, were to meet annually on the first Monday in September. Six possessed the power of binding the whole. Any measure approved by a majority of less than six was to be referred to the general court of each colony, and the consent of all was necessary to its adoption.

They were to choose annually a president from their own body, and had power to frame laws or rules of a civil nature, and of general concern. Of this description were rules which respected their conduct towards the Indians, and measures to be taken with fugitives from one colony to another.

No colony was permitted, without the general consent, to engage in war, but in sudden and inevitable cases.

If, on any extraordinary meeting of the commissioners, their whole number should not assemble, any four who should meet were empowered to determine on a war, and to call for the respective quotas of the several colonies; but not less than six could determine on the justice of the war, or settle the expenses, or levy the money for its support.

If any colony should be charged with breaking an article of the agreement, or with doing an injury to another colony, the complaint was to be submitted to the consideration and determination of the commissioners of such colonies as should be disinterested.*

This union, the result of good sense, and of a judicious consideration of the real interests of the colonies, remained in force until their charters were dissolved. Rhode Island, at the instance of Massachusetts, was excluded; and her commissioners were not admitted into the congress of deputies which formed the confederation.

<small>CHAP IV.
1643.

Rhode Island excluded from it.</small>

On her petitioning at a subsequent period to be received as a member, her request was refused, unless she would consent to be incorporated with Plymouth. This condition being deemed inadmissible, she never was taken into the confederacy. From the formation of this league, its members were considered by their neighbours as one body with regard to external affairs, and such as were of general concern; though the internal and particular objects of each continued to be managed by its own magistrates and legislature.

The vigorous and prudent measures pursued by the united colonies, disconcerted the plans of the Indians, and preserved peace.

Rhode Island and Providence plantations, excluded from the general confederacy, were under the necessity of courting the friendship of the neighbouring Indians. So successful were their endeavours that, in the year 1644, they obtained from the chiefs of the Narraghansetts a formal surrender of their country.†

<small>* Chalmer. Hutchison. Trumbull.   † Chalmer.</small>

CHAP. IV.
1643.

1644.

The first general assembly, consisting of the collective freemen of the plantations, was convened in May, 1647. In this body the supreme authority of the nation resided. The executive duties were performed by a governor and four assistants, chosen from among the freemen by their several towns; and the same persons constituted also the supreme court for the administration of justice. Every township, forming within itself a corporation, elected a council of six, for the management of its peculiar affairs, and for the settlement of its disputes.*

Hitherto the governor, assistants, and representatives, of Massachusetts had assembled in the same chamber, and deliberated together. At first their relative powers do not seem to have been accurately understood; nor the mode of deciding controverted questions to have been well defined. The representatives being the most numerous body, contended that every question should be decided by a majority of the whole, while the assistants asserted their right to a negative. More than once, this contest suspended the proceedings of the general court. But the assistants having, with the aid of the clergy, succeeded on each occasion, the representatives yielded the point, and moved that separate chambers should be provided for the two branches of the legislature. This motion being carried in the affirmative, their deliberations were afterwards conducted apart from each other.

This regulation was subsequently modified with

* Chalmer.

respect to judicial proceedings; for the legislature was the court of the last resort. If, in these, the two houses differed, the vote was to be taken conjointly.

CHAP. IV.
1644.

In England, the contests between the King and Parliament, at length ripened into open war. The colonies of New England took an early and sincere part on the side of Parliament. Their interests were committed to such agents as might best conciliate the favour of the House of Commons, who, in return, manifested the impression received from them, and from the general conduct of their northern colonies, by passing a resolution exempting from the payment of "duties or other customs," until the house should order otherwise, all merchandises exported to or from New England.* And, in 1644, the general court passed an ordinance declaring " that what person soever shall by word, writing, or action, endeavour to disturb our peace directly or indirectly by drawing a party under pretence that he is for the King of England, and such as join with him against the Parliament, shall be accounted as an offender of a high nature against this commonwealth, and to be proceeded with either capitally or otherwise, according to the quality and degree of his offence; provided always that this shall not be extended against any merchant, strangers and shipmen that come hither merely for

New England takes part with Parliament

---

* In the subsequent year Parliament exempted New England from all taxes "until both houses should otherwise direct;" and, in 1646, all the colonies were exempted from all talliages except the excise, " provided their productions should be exported only in English bottoms."

CHAP IV. trade or merchandise, albeit they should come from
1644. any of those parts that are in the hands of the King,
and such as adhere to him against the Parliament;
carrying themselves here quietly, and free from rail-
ing, or nourishing any faction, mutiny, or sedition
among us as aforesaid."*

These manifestations of mutual kindness were not
interrupted by an ordinance of Parliament, passed in
in 1643, appointing the earl of Warwick governor in
chief and lord high admiral of the colonies, with a
council of five peers, and twelve commoners, to assist
him; and empowering him, in conjunction with his
associates, to examine the state of their affairs; to
send for papers and persons; to remove governors
and officers, appointing others in their places; and to
assign over to them such part of the powers then
granted as he should think proper. Jealous as were
the people of New England of measures endangering
their liberty, they do not appear to have been alarmed
at this extraordinary exercise of power. So true is it
that men close their eyes on encroachments committed by that party to which they are attached, in the
delusive hope that power, in such hands, will always
be wielded against their adversaries, never against
themselves.

This prosperous state of things was still farther improved by a transaction which is the more worthy of
notice as being an additional evidence of the extent
to which the colonies of New England then exercised

* Hutchison.

the powers of self-government. A treaty of peace and commerce was entered into between the governor of Massachusetts, styling himself governor of New England, and Monsieur D'Aulney, lieutenant general of the King of France in Acadié. This treaty was laid before the commissioners for the colonies and received their sanction.

<small>CHAP IV.
1644.

Treaty with Acadié.</small>

The rigid adherence of Massachusetts to the principle of withholding the privilege of a freeman from all who dissented from the majority in any religious opinion, could not fail to generate perpetual discontents. A petition was presented to the general court, signed by several persons highly respectable for their situation and character, but, not being church members, excluded from the common rights of society, complaining that the fundamental laws of England were not acknowledged by the colony ; and that they were denied those civil and religious privileges to which they were entitled, as freeborn Englishmen, of good moral conduct. Their prayer to be admitted to the rights, or to be relieved from the burdens, of society, was accompanied with observations conveying a very intelligible censure on the proceedings of the colony, and a threat of applying to Parliament, should the prayer of their petition be rejected.

<small>1646.

Petition of the nonconformists.</small>

The most popular governments not being always the most inclined to tolerate opinions differing from those of the majority, this petition gave great offence, and its signers were req ired to attend the court. Their plea, that the right to petition government was

CHAP. IV.
1646.

sacred, was answered by saying that they were not accused for petitioning, but for using contemptuous and seditious expressions. They were required to find sureties for their good behaviour; and, on refusing to acknowledge their offence, were fined at the discretion of the court. An appeal from this decision having been refused, they sent deputies to lay their case before Parliament; but the clergy exerted themselves on the occasion; and the celebrated Cotton, in one of his sermons, asserted " that if any should carry writings or complaints against the people of God in that country to England, it would be as Jonas in the ship." A storm having risen during the passage, the mariners, impressed with the prophecy of Cotton, insisted that the obnoxious papers should be thrown overboard; and the deputies were constrained to consign their credentials to the waves. On their arrival in England, they found Parliament but little disposed to listen to their complaints. The agents of Massachusetts had received instructions to counteract their efforts; and the governments of New England were too high in favour, to admit of a rigid scrutiny into their conduct.*

In some of the internal dissentions which agitated Massachusetts, Winthrop, a man of great influence, always among their first magistrates, and often their governor, was charged while deputy governor with some arbitrary conduct. He defended himself at the bar, in the presence of a vast concourse of people;

* Chalmer. Hutchison.

and, having been honourably acquitted, addressed them from the bench, in a speech which was highly approved.

As this speech tends to illustrate the political opinions of the day, an extract from it may not be unworthy of regard. "The questions," he said, "which have troubled the country of late, and from which these disturbances in the state have arisen, have been about the authority of the magistrate and the liberty of the people. Magistracy is certainly an appointment from God. We take an oath to govern you according to God's law, and our own; and if we commit errors, not willingly, but for want of skill, you ought to bear with us, because, being chosen from among yourselves, we are but men, and subject to the like passions as yourselves. Nor would I have you mistake your own liberty. There is a freedom of doing what we list, without regard to law or justice; this liberty is indeed inconsistent with authority; but civil, moral, and federal liberty, consists in every man's enjoying his property, and having the benefit of the laws of his country; which is very consistent with a due subjection to the civil magistrate. And for this you ought to contend, with the hazard of your lives."*

During the remnant of his life, he was annually chosen governor.

About this time, a controversy which had long subsisted between Massachusetts, and Connecticut,

* Hutchison.

was terminated. The latter, for the purpose of maintaining Saybrooke, had laid a duty on all goods exported from Connecticut river. The inhabitants of Springfield, a town of Massachusetts lying on the river, having refused to pay this duty, the cause was laid before the commissioners of the united colonies; and, after hearing the parties, those of Plymouth and New Haven adjourned the final decision of the case until the next meeting, in order to hear farther objections from Massachusetts, but directed that, in the meantime, the duty should be paid.

At the meeting in 1648, Massachusetts insisted on the production of the patent of Connecticut. It was perfectly well known that the original patent could not be procured; and the agents for Connecticut, after stating this fact, offered an authentic copy. The commissioners recommended that the boundary line should be run, to ascertain whether Springfield was really in Massachusetts, but still directed that the duty should continue to be paid. On this order being made, the commissioners of Massachusetts produced a law of their general court, reciting the controversy, with the orders which had been made in it, and imposing a duty on all goods belonging to the inhabitants of Plymouth, Connecticut, or New Haven, which should be imported within the castle, or exported from any part of the bay, and subjecting them to forfeiture for non-payment. The commissioners remonstrated strongly against this measure, and recommended it to the general court of Massachusetts, seriously to consider whether such proceedings were reconcilable with " the law of love," and the tenor of the articles of confederation. In the mean time, they begged to be excused from " all farther agitations concerning Springfield."

In this state of the controversy fort Saybrooke was consumed by fire, and Connecticut forbore to re-build it, or to demand the duty. In the following year, Massachusetts repealed the ordinance which had so successfully decided the contest.*

Thus does a member of a confederacy, feeling its own strength, and the weakness of those with whom it is associated, deride the legitimate decisions of the federal body, when opposed to its own interest or passions, and obey the general will, only when that will is dictated by itself.

Although, while civil war raged in the mother country, New England had been permitted to govern itself as an independent nation, Parliament seems to have entertained very decisive opinions respecting the subordination of the provinces, and its own controlling power. The measures taken for giving effect to these opinions, involved all the colonies equally. The council of state was authorised to displace governors and magistrates, and to appoint others. Massachusetts was required to take a new patent, and to hold its courts, not in the name of the colony, but in the name of the Parliament. The general court, unwilling to comply with these requisitions, transmitted a

* Chalmer. Hutchison.

CHAP. IV.
1651.
petition to Parliament, styling that body " the supreme authority," and expressing for it the highest respect. They stated their uniform attachment to Parliament during the civil war, the aid they had given, and the losses they had sustained. After speaking of the favours they had received, they expressed the hope " that it will not go worse with them than it did under the late King; and that the frame of this government will not be changed, and governors and magistrates imposed on them against their will." They declared, however, their entire submission to the will of Parliament; and, avowing for that body the most zealous attachment, prayed a favourable answer to their humble petition.

But the united colonies had lately given great umbrage by supplying Virginia, and Barbadoes, then enemies of the commonwealth, with warlike stores and other commodities. It was also matter of real complaint that their exemption from the payment of duties enabled them to enrich themselves at the expense of others; and a revocation of their privileges in this respect was seriously contemplated. Yet the requisitions concerning their charter were never complied with, and do not appear to have been repeated.*

In this year, war was declared by England against Holland. The united colonies, accustomed to conduct their affairs in their own way, did not think themselves involved in this contest, unless engaged in it by some act of their own. The Dutch at Man-

* Chalmer. Hutchison.

hadoes, too weak to encounter their English neighbours, solicited the continuance of peace; and, as the trade carried on between them was mutually advantageous, this request was readily granted. Intelligence however was soon brought by the Indians, that the Dutch were privately inciting them to a general confederacy for the purpose of extirpating the English. This intelligence gave the more alarm, because the massacre at Amboyna was then fresh in the recollection of the colonists. An extraordinary meeting of the commissioners was called at Boston, who were divided in opinion with regard to the propriety of declaring war. In consequence of this division, a conference was held before the general court and several elders of Massachusetts. The elders, being requested to give their opinion in writing, stated " that the proofs and presumptions of the execrable plot, tending to the destruction of so many of the dear saints of God, imputed to the Dutch governor, and the fiscal, were of such weight as to induce them to believe the reality of it; yet they were not so fully conclusive as to clear up a present proceeding to war before the world, and to bear up their hearts with that fullness of persuasion which was mete, in commending the case to God in prayer, and to the people in exhortations; and that it would be safest for the colonies to forbear the use of the sword; but advised to be in a posture of defence until the mind of God should be more fully known either for a settled peace, or more

CHAP. IV.
1651.

1653.
Machinations of the Dutch with the Indians.

manifest grounds of war."* With this opinion of the elders, the vote of the general court concurred.

The intelligence of the practices of the Dutch governor with the Indians becoming more certain, all the commissioners except Mr. Bradstreet of Massachusetts, declared in favour of war. Their proceedings were immediately interrupted by a declaration of the general court of Massachusetts, that no determination of the commissioners, although they should be unanimous, should bind the general court to join in an offensive war which should appear to be unjust. A serious altercation ensued, in the course of which the other colonies pressed the war as a measure essential to their safety; but Massachusetts adhered inflexibly to its first resolution. This additional evidence of the incompetency of their union to bind one member, stronger than all the rest, threatened a dissolution of the confederacy; and that event seems to have been prevented only by the inability of the others to stand alone. Alarmed at their situation, and irritated by the conduct of their elder sister, Connecticut and New Haven represented to Cromwell, then lord protector of England, the danger to which the colonies were exposed from the Dutch and the Indians; and the hazard the smaller provinces must continue to incur, unless the league between them could be maintained and executed according to its true intent, and the interpretation which its articles had uniformly received.

With his usual promptness and decision, Crom-

* Chalmer. Hutchison.

well detached a small armament for the reduction of the Dutch colony, and recommended to Massachusetts to furnish aid to the expedition. Although the legitimate requisitions of the government of the union had been ineffectual, the recommendation of the lord protector was not to be disregarded; and the general court passed a resolution conforming to it. A treaty of peace, which was signed in April, saved the Dutch colony.*

The progress of the French in their neighbourhood had been viewed with regret and apprehension by all New England. Sedgewic, the commander of the forces which had been destined against Manhadoes, animated with the vigour of his master, was easily prevailed on to turn his arms against a people, whose religious tenets he detested, and whose country he hated. He soon dislodged the French from Penobscot, and subdued all Acadié. The ministers of his most christian majesty, pending the negotiations for the treaty of Westminster, demanded restitution of the forts Pentagoet, St. Johns, and Port Royal; but, each nation having claims on the country, their pretensions were referred to the arbitrators appointed to adjust the damages committed on either side since the year 1640; and the restitution of Acadié was postponed for future discussion.

Cromwell seems not to have intended to restore the countries he had conquered. He granted to St. Etienne, Crown and Temple, for ever, the territory de-

* Chalmer. Hutchison.

nominated Acadie, and part of the country commonly called Nova Scotia, extending along the coast to Pentagoet, and to the river St. George.

Until the restoration, the colonies of New England continued in a state of unexampled prosperity. Those regulations respecting navigation, which were rigorously enforced against others less in favour, were dispensed with for their benefit. They maintained external peace by the vigour and sagacity with which their government was administered; and, improved the advantages which the times afforded them by industry and attention to their interests. In this period of prosperity, they acquired a degree of strength and consistence which enabled them to struggle through the difficulties that afterwards assailed them.

These sober industrious people were peculiarly attentive to the instruction of youth. Education was among the first objects of their care. In addition to private institutions, they had brought the college at Cambridge to a state of forwardness which reflects much credit on their character. As early as the year 1636, the general court had bestowed four hundred pounds on a public school at Newtown, the name by which Cambridge was then known. Two years afterwards, an additional donation was made by the reverend Mr. John Harvard, in consequence of which the institution received the name of Harvard college. In 1642, this college was placed under the government of the governor, and deputy governor, and of the magistrates, and ministers of the six next adjacent towns, who, with the president were incorporated for that purpose; and, in 1650, its first charter was granted.*

It is to be lamented that the same people possessed a degree of bigotry in religion, and a spirit of intolerance, which their enlightened posterity will view with regret. During this period of prosperity, the government maintained the severity of its institutions against all those who dissented from the church; and exerted itself assiduously in what was thought the holy work of punishing heretics, and introducing conformity in matters of faith. In this time, the sect denominated Quakers appeared. They were fined, imprisoned, whipped, and, at length put to death; but could not be totally suppressed. As enthusiastic as their persecutors, they gloried in their sufferings, and deemed themselves the martyrs of truth.

* Chalmer. Hutchison.

R

CHAPTER V.

Transactions succeeding the restoration of Charles II. —Contests between Connecticut and New Haven. —Discontents in Virginia.—Grant to the Duke of York.—Commissioners appointed by the crown.— Conquest of the Dutch settlements.—Conduct of Massachusetts to the royal commissioners.—Their recall.—Massachusetts evades a summons to appear before the King and council.—Settlement of Carolina.—Form of government.—Constitution of Mr. Locke.—Discontents in the county of Albemarle.— Invasion from Florida.—Abolition of the constitution of Mr. Locke.—Bacon's rebellion.—His death. —Assembly deprived of judicial power.—Discontents in Virginia.—Population of the colony.

1660. THE restoration of Charles II. was soon known in America, and excited, in the different colonies very different emotions. In Virginia, and in Maryland, the intelligence was received with transport, and the King was proclaimed amidst acclamations of unfeigned joy. In Massachusetts, the unwelcome information was heard with doubt, and in silence. Republicans in religion and in politics, all their affections were engaged in favour of the revolutionary party in England, and they saw, in the restoration of monarchy, much more to fear than to hope for themselves. Nor were they mistaken in their forebodings.

No sooner was Charles seated on the throne, than Parliament voted a duty of five *per centum* on all merchandises exported from, or imported into, any of the dominions belonging to the English crown ; and, in the course of the same session, the celebrated navigation act was re-enacted. The difficulty of carrying this system into execution among a distant people, accustomed to the advantages of a free trade, was foreseen ; and the law directed that the governors of the several plantations should, before entering into office, take an oath faithfully to observe it.*

As some compensation to the colonists for these commercial restraints, it was also enacted that no tobacco should be planted or made in England or Ireland, Guernsey, or Jersey. These regulations confined the trade of the colonies to England ; and conferred on them, exclusively, the production of tobacco.

Charles, on ascending the throne, transmitted to Sir William Berkeley a commission as governor of Virginia, with instructions to summon an assembly, and to assure it of his intention to grant a general pardon to all persons, other than those who were attainted by act of Parliament ; provided all acts passed during the rebellion, derogating from the obedience due to the King and his government, should be repealed.

The assembly, which had been summoned in

* Chalmer. Hutchison.

CHAP V. March 1660, in the name of the King, though he was
1660.
not then acknowledged in England, and which had
been prorogued by the governor to the following
1661. March, then convened, and engaged in the arduous
task of revising the laws of the colony. One of the
motives assigned for this revision strongly marks the
temper of the day. It is that they may " repeal and
expunge all unnecessary acts, and chiefly such as
might keep in memory their forced deviation from his
majesty's obedience."*

This laborious work was accomplished; and, in its
execution, the first object of attention was religion.
The church of England was established by law, and
provision was made for its ministers. To preserve
the purity and unity of its doctrines and discipline,
those only who had been ordained by some bishop in
England, and who should subscribe an engagement
to conform to the constitution of the church of England and the laws there established, could be inducted
by the governor: and no others were permitted to
preach. The day of the execution of Charles I. was
ordered to be kept as a fast; and the anniversaries of
the birth, and of the restoration of Charles II. to be
celebrated as holy days. The duties on exports and
tonnage were rendered perpetual; the privilege of the
burgesses from arrest was established, and their number fixed; the courts of justice were organised; and
many useful laws were passed, regulating the interior
affairs of the colony.†

* Virginia Laws. Chalmer.   † Idem.

AMERICAN COLONIES. 133

An effort was made to encourage manufactures, especially that of silk. For each pound of that article which should be raised, a premium of fifty pounds of tobacco was given; and every person was enjoined to plant a number of mulberry trees proportioned to his quantity of land, in order to furnish food for the silk worm. But the labour of the colony had been long directed to the culture of tobacco, and Indian corn; and new systems of culture can seldom be introduced until their necessity becomes apparent. This attempt to multiply the objects of labour did not succeed, and the acts on the subject were soon repealed.

CHAP. V.
1661.

In Maryland, the legislature was also convened, and, as in Virginia, their first employment was to manifest their satisfaction with the restoration; after which they entered upon subjects of general utility.

Rhode Island, excluded from the confederacy of the other New England colonies, and dreading danger to her independence from Massachusetts, was well pleased at the establishment of an authority which could overawe the strong, and protect the weak. Charles II. was immediately proclaimed; and an agent was deputed to the court of that monarch, for the purpose of soliciting a patent, confirming the right of the inhabitants to the soil, and jurisdiction of the country. The object of the mission was obtained, and the patentees were incorporated by the name of "The governor and company of the English colony of Rhode Island and Providence." The legislative power was vested in an assembly to consist of the

1662.

Rhode Island incorporated.

CHAP. V.
1662.

governor, deputy governor, the assistants, and such of the freemen as should be chosen by the towns. The presence of the governor or his deputy, and of six assistants, was required to constitute an assembly. They were empowered to pass laws adapted to the situation of the colony, and not repugnant to those of England. "That part of the dominions of the crown in New England containing the islands in Narraghansetts bay, and the countries and parts adjacent," was granted to the governor and company and their successors, with the privilege to pass through, and trade with, any other English colonies.*

Patent to Connecticut.

In Connecticut, the intelligence of the restoration was not attended by any manifestation of joy or sorrow. Winthrop was deputed to attend to the interests of the colony; and, in April, 1662, he obtained a charter incorporating them by the name of "The governor and company of the English colony of Connecticut in New England." The executive as in the other colonies of New England, consisted of a governor, deputy governor, and assistants. The legislature was composed of the members of the executive, and of two deputies from every town. It was authorised to appoint annually the governor, assistants, and other officers; to erect courts of justice, and to make such laws as might be necessary for the colony, with the usual proviso, that they should not be contrary to those of England. To this corporation, the King granted that part of his dominions in New England,

* Chalmer.

AMERICAN COLONIES. 135

bounded, on the east, by Narraghansetts bay, on the north, by the southern line of Massachusetts, on the south, by the sea, and extending in longitude from east to west, with the line of Massachusetts, to the south sea.

CHAP V.
1662.

By this charter, New Haven was, without being consulted included in Connecticut. The freemen of that province, dissatisfied with this measure, determined in general meeting, " that it was not lawful to join;" and unanimously resolved to adhere to their former association. A committee was appointed to address the assembly of Connecticut on this interesting subject. They insisted, not that the charter was void, but that it did not include them.

1663.

Contest between Connecticut and New Haven.

A negotiation between the two provinces was commenced, in which the people of New Haven maintained their right to a separate government with inflexible perseverance, and with a considerable degree of exasperation. They appealed to the crown from the explanation given by Connecticut to the charter; and governor Winthrop, the agent who had obtained that instrument, and who flattered himself with being able, on his return, to conciliate the contending parties, deemed it advisable to arrest all proceeding on their petition, by pledging himself that no injury should be done to New Haven by Connecticut; and that the incorporation of the two colonies should be effected only by the voluntary consent of both.

The government of Connecticut, however, still persisting to assert its jurisdiction, attempted to exercise it by claiming obedience from the people, appointing constables in their towns, disavowing the authority of the general court of New Haven, and protecting those who denied it. Complaints of these proceedings were laid before the commissioners of the united colonies, who declared that New Haven was still an integral member of the union, and that its jurisdiction could not be infringed without a breach of the articles of confederation.

Disregarding this decision, Connecticut pursued unremittingly, the object of incorporation. The inhabitants of New Haven were encouraged to refuse the payment of taxes imposed by their legislature; and, when distress was made on the disobedient, assistance was obtained from Hartford. These proceedings seemed only to increase the irritation on the part of New Haven, where a deep sense of injury was entertained, and a solemn resolution taken to break off all farther treaty on the subject.

This state of things was entirely changed by a piece of intelligence which gave the most serious alarm to all New England. Information was received that the King had granted to his brother, the duke of York, all the lands claimed by the Dutch, to which he had annexed a considerable part of the territory over which the northern colonies had exercised jurisdiction; and that an armament for the purpose of taking possession of the grant might soon be expected. To this it was added, that commissioners were to come at the same time, empowered to settle the disputes, and to new model the governments, of the colonies.

The commissioners of the united colonies, perceiving the necessity of accommodating internal differences, now took a decided part in favour of the proposed incorporation. The most intelligent inhabitants of New Haven became converts to the same opinion; but the prejudices imbibed by the mass of the people being still insurmountable, a vote in favour of the union could not be obtained.

At length, after the arrival of the commissioners appointed by the crown, and a manifestation of their opinion in favour of the incorporation; after a long course of negotiation which terminated in a compact establishing certain principles of equality required by the jealousy of New Haven; the union was completed, and the representatives of the two colonies met in the same assembly.

During the frequent changes which took place in England after the death of Cromwell, Massachusetts preserved a cautious neutrality; and seemed disposed to avail herself of any favourable occurrences, without exposing herself to the resentments of that party which might ultimately obtain the ascendancy. Although expressly ordered, she did not proclaim Richard as lord-protector; nor did she take any step to recognise the authority of Parliament. The first intelligence of the restoration of Charles was received with the hesitation of men who are unwilling to believe a fact too well supported by evidence to be dis-

CHAP V. credited; and when they were informed of it in a
1663. manner not to be questioned, they neither proclaimed
the King, nor manifested, by any public act, their admission of his authority. This was not the only testimony of their dissatisfaction. Whaley and Goff, two of the judges of Charles I. came passengers in the vessel which brought this intelligence, and were received with distinction by the government, and with affection by the people.*

In a session of the general court, held in October, 1660, an address to the King was moved; but reports of the yet unsettled state of the kingdom being received, the motion did not prevail. They had seen so many changes in the course of a few months, as to think it not improbable that an address to the King might find the executive power in the hands of a committee of safety, or council of state. This uncertain state of things was not of long continuance. In November, a ship arrived from Bristol, bringing positive advices of the joyful and universal submission of the nation to the King, with letters from their agent, and from others, informing them that petitions had been presented against the colony, by those who thought themselves aggrieved by its proceedings. The time for deliberation was passed. A general court was convened, and a loyal address to the King was voted, in which, with considerable ability, though in the peculiar language of the day, they justified their whole conduct; and, without abandoning any

* Chalmer. Trumbull.

opinion concerning their own rights, professed unlimited attachment to their sovereign. A similar address was made to Parliament; and letters were written to those noblemen who were the known friends of the colony, soliciting their interposition in its behalf. A gracious answer being returned by the King, a day of thanksgiving was appointed to acknowledge their gratitude to Heaven for inclining the heart of his majesty favourably to receive and answer their address.

Their apprehensions however of danger from the revolution in England still continued. Reports prevailed that their commercial intercourse with Virginia and the islands was to be interdicted; and that a governor-general might be expected whose authority should extend over all the colonies. On this occasion, the general court came to several resolutions, respecting the rights of the people, and the obedience due from them, which are strongly expressive of their deliberate opinions on these interesting subjects.

It was resolved,

That the patent (under God) is the first and main foundation of the civil polity of the colony.

That the governor and company are, by the patent, a body politic, invested with the power to make freemen.

That the freemen have authority to choose annually a governor, deputy governor, assistants, representatives, and all other officers.

That the government thus constituted hath full

power, both legislative and executive, for the government of all the people, whether inhabitants or strangers, without appeals; save only in the case of laws repugnant to those of England.

That the government is privileged by all means, even by force of arms, to defend itself both by land and sea, against all who should attempt injury to the plantation or its inhabitants, and that in their opinion, any imposition prejudicial to the country, contrary to any just law of theirs, (not repugnant to the laws of England) would be an infringement of their rights.*

These strong and characteristic resolutions were accompanied by a recognition of the duties to which they were bound by their allegiance. These were declared to consist, in upholding that colony as belonging of right to his majesty, and not to subject it to any foreign prince; in preserving his person and dominions; and in settling the peace and prosperity of the King and nation, by punishing crimes, and by propagating the Gospel.†

It was, at the same time, determined that the royal warrant, which had been received sometime before, for apprehending Whaley and Goff, ought to be faithfully executed. These persons however were permitted to escape to Connecticut, where they were received with every demonstration of regard, and to remain during life in New England, only taking care not to appear in public.

At length, in August 1661, it was determined to

---

* Hutchison. Chalmer.   † Idem.

proclaim the King; but, as if unable to conceal the reluctance with which this step was taken, an order was made, on the same day, prohibiting all disorderly behaviour on the occasion, and, in particular, directing that no man should presume to drink his majesty's health, " which," adds the order, " he hath in a special manner forbid."

Farther intelligence being received from England of the increasing complaints against the government of Massachusetts, agents were deputed with instructions to represent the colonists as loyal and obedient subjects, to remove any ill impressions that had been made against them, and to learn the disposition of his majesty toward them ; but to do nothing which might prejudice their charter.

The agents, who engaged reluctantly in a service from which they rightly augured to themselves censure rather than approbation, were received more favourably than had been expected. They soon returned with a letter from the King, confirming their charter, and containing a pardon for all treasons committed during the late troubles, with the exception of those only who were attainted by act of Parliament. But the royal missive also required that the general court should review its ordinances, and repeal such of them as were repugnant to the authority of the crown; that the oath of allegiance should be taken by every person; that justice should be administered in the King's name; that all who desired it, should be permitted to use the book of common prayer, and to perform their devotions according to the ceremonials of the church of England; and that freeholders of competent estates, not vicious, should be allowed to vote in the election of officers, though they were of different persuasions in church government.*

These requisitions gave much disquiet; and that alone seems ever to have been complied with which directed judicial proceedings to be carried on in the name of the King. The agents, on their return were ill received by the people; and were considered as having sacrificed the interests of their country, because, with the agreeable, were mingled some bitter though unavoidable ingredients.

During these transactions, the Parliament of England proceeded to complete its system of confining the trade of the colonies to the mother country. It was enacted that no commodity of the growth or manufacture of Europe, shall be imported into the settlements of England, in Asia, Africa, or America, but such as shall be shipped in England, and proceed directly in English bottoms, navigated by Englishmen. Salt for the fisheries, wine from Madeira and the Azores; and servants, horses, and victuals, from Scotland and Ireland, were excepted from this general rule.

To counterbalance these restrictions, duties were imposed on salted and dried fish caught or imported by other vessels than those belonging to subjects of the crown; and additional regulations were made for

* Hutchison. Chalmer.

enforcing the prohibition of the culture of tobacco in England.

CHAP. V.
1663.

These commercial restrictions were the never failing source of discontent and controversy between the mother country and her colonies. Even in those of the south, where similar restraints had been enforced by Cromwell, they were executed imperfectly; but, in New England, where the governors were elected by the people, they appear to have been, for some time, entirely disregarded.*

The good humour which prevailed in Virginia on the restoration of Charles to the throne, was not of long duration. The restraints on commerce, and the continually decreasing price of tobacco, soon excited considerable discontents. The legislature endeavoured, by prohibiting its culture for a limited time, to raise its value; but, Maryland refusing to concur in the measure, the attempt was unsuccessful. Other legislative remedies were applied with as little advantage. Acts were passed suspending all proceedings in the courts of law, except for goods imported; giving to country creditors priority in payment of debts; and to contracts made within the colony, precedence in all courts of justice. Such expedients as these have never removed the discontents which produced them.

Discontents in Virginia.

The English government seems, at all times, to have questioned the right of the Dutch to their settlements in America; and never to have formally relin-

* Hutchison. Chalmer.

CHAP. V.
1664

Grant to the duke of York.

quished its claim to that territory. Charles now determined to assert it; and granted to his brother the duke of York " all that part of the main land of New England, beginning at a certain place called and known by the name of St. Croix, next adjoining to New England in America, and from thence extending along the sea coast unto a certain place called Pemaquie, or Pemaquid, and so up the river thereof to the farthest head of the same, as it tendeth northward; and extending from thence to the river Kernbequin, and so upwards by the shortest course to the river Canada northward; and also all that island or islands commonly called by the general name or names of Meitowax, or Long Island, situate and being towards the west of Cape Cod, and the narrow Highgansetts, abutting upon the main land between the two rivers there called and known by the several names of Connecticut and Hudson's river, and all the land from the west side of Connecticut river to the east side of Delaware bay, and also all those several islands called or known by the names of Martha's Vineyard or Nantucks, otherwise Nantucket."

Comissioners appointed by the crown.

To reduce this country, part of which was then in the peaceable possession of the Dutch, colonel Nichols was dispatched with four frigates, carrying three hundred soldiers. In the same ships, came four commissioners, of whom colonel Nichols was one, " empowered to hear and determine complaints and appeals in causes, as well military as civil and criminal, within New England; and to proceed in all things for settling the peace and security of the country." Intelligence of this deputation preceded its arrival, and the preparation made for its reception, evidences the disposition then prevailing in Massachusetts. A committee was appointed to repair on board the ships as soon as they should appear, and to communicate to their commanders the desire of the local government that the inferior officers and soldiers should be ordered, when they came on shore to refresh themselves, " at no time to exceed a convenient number, to come unarmed, to observe an orderly conduct, and to give no offence to the people and laws of the country." As if to manifest in a still more solemn manner their hostility, to the objects of the commissioners, a day of fasting and prayer was appointed to implore the mercy of God under their many distractions and troubles.*

The commissioners arrived in July, and their commission was immediately laid before the council, with a letter from the King requiring prompt assistance for the expedition against New Netherlands.

The general court, which was immediately convened, after having first resolved " that they would bear faith and true allegiance to his majesty, and adhere to their patent, so dearly obtained, and so long enjoyed, by undoubted right in the sight of God and man," determined to raise two hundred men for the expedition. In the mean time colonel Nichols proceeded to Manhadoes. The auxiliary force raised by Massachusetts was rendered unnecessary by the capitula-

Conquest of the Dutch colony.

* Chalmer. Hutchison.

T

tion of New Amsterdam, which was soon followed by the surrender of the whole province.

The year after captain Argal had subdued Manhadoes, the garrison, having obtained a reinforcement from Holland, returned to their ancient allegiance. In 1621, the states general made a grant of the country to the West India company, who erected a fort called Good Hope on Connecticut (which they denominated Fresh) river, and another called Nassau on the east side of Delaware bay. The fort on Connecticut river, however, did not protect that frontier against the people of New England, who continued to extend their settlements towards the south. The Dutch remonstrated in vain against these encroachments, and were under the necessity of receding as their more powerful neighbours advanced, until the eastern part of Long Island, and the country within a few miles of the Hudson were relinquished. Farther south, the Dutch had built fort Casimir (now New Castle) on the Delaware. This fort was taken from them by the Swedes, who claimed the western shore of that river, but was retaken by the Dutch, who, at the same time, conquered Christina, and received the submission of the few Swedes who were scattered on the margin of the river. They also made a settlement at cape Henlopen, which attracted the attention of lord Baltimore, who sent a commission to New Castle ordering the Dutch governor to remove beyond the 40th degree of north latitude, to which his lordship's claim extended. This mandate however was not obeyed.

On the appearance of colonel Nichols before New Amsterdam, Stuyvesant, the governor, was disposed to defend the place; but the inhabitants, feeling no inclination for the contest, took part with their invaders; and Stuyvesant was compelled to sign a capitulation, by which he surrendered the town to the English, stipulating for the inhabitants their property, and the rights of free denizens. New Amsterdam took the name of New York, and the island of Manhattans that of York Island.*

Hudson's, and the south, or Delaware river, were still to be reduced. Carteret commanded the expedition against fort Orange, up Hudson's river, which surrendered on the twenty-fourth of September, and received the name of Albany. While at that place, he formed a league with the five nations, which proved eminently useful to the views of the English in America.

The command of the expedition against the settlement on the Delaware was given to sir Robert Carr, who completed the conquest of that country.

Thus did England acquire all that fine country lying between her southern and northern colonies; an acquisition deriving not less importance from its situation, than from its extent and fertility.

Nichols took possession of the conquered territo-

---

* Chalmer. Smith.

CHAP V.
1664.

ry, but was compelled to surrender a part of it to Carteret.

Soon after the patent to the duke of York, and before the conquest of New Netherlands, that prince had granted to lord Berkeley, and sir George Carteret, all that tract of land adjacent to New England, to the westward of Long Island, bounded on the east, south, and west, by the river Hudson, the sea, and the Delaware; and, on the north, by forty-one degrees and forty minutes north latitude. This country was denominated New Jersey.*

The conquest of New Netherlands being achieved, the commissioners entered on the other duties assigned them. A great part of Connecticut had been included in the patent to the duke of York; and a controversy concerning limits arose between that colony and New York. In December, their boundaries were adjusted by the commissioners in a manner which appears to have been satisfactory to all parties.

In Plymouth, and in Rhode Island, the commissioners found no difficulty in the full exercise of the powers committed to them. In Massachusetts, they were considered as men clothed with an authority subversive of the liberties of the colony, which the sovereign could not rightfully confer. The people of that province had been long in habits of self-government, and seem to have entertained opinions which justified their practice. They did not acknow-

* Chalmer. Smith.

ledge that allegiance to the crown which is due from English subjects residing within the realm; but considered themselves as purchasers from independent sovereigns of the territory which they occupied, and as owing to England, only that voluntary subjection which was created and defined by their charter. They considered this instrument as a compact between the mother country and themselves, and as enumerating all the cases in which obedience was due from them. In this spirit, they agreed, soon after the arrival of the commissioners, on an address to the crown. This address, in which they express great apprehension of danger to their rights from the extraordinary powers granted to men not appointed in conformity with their charter, is drawn up in a style of much earnestness and sincerity, and concludes with these remarkable words, "let our government live, our patent live, our magistrates live, our religious enjoyments live; so shall we all yet have farther cause to say from our hearts, let the King live for ever." This address was accompanied with letters to many of the nobility supposed to possess influence at court, praying their intercession in behalf of the colony; but neither the address, nor the letters were favourably received.*

In April the commissioners arrived at Boston, and their communications with the general court commenced. The suspicions which these two bodies entertained of each other, opposed great obstacles to any cordial co-operation between them. The papers,

* Hutchison.

CHAP. V.
1665.

on the part of the commissioners, display high ideas of their own authority, as the representatives of the crown, and a pre conceived opinion that there was a disposition in the government to resist that authority. Those on the part of the general court manifest a wish to avoid a contest with the crown, and a desire to gratify his majesty, so far as professions of loyalty and submission could gratify him; but they manifest also a conviction of having done nothing improper, and a stedfast determination to make no concession incompatible with their rights. With these impressions, the correspondence soon became an altercation. The commissioners, finding their object was to be obtained neither by reasoning, nor by threats, attempted a practical assertion of their powers by summoning the parties before them, in order to hear and decide a complaint against the governor and company. The general court, with a decision which marked alike their vigour, and the high value they placed on their privileges, announced by sound of trumpet, their disapprobation of this proceeding, which they termed inconsistent with the laws and established authority; and declared that, in observance of their duty to God and to his majesty, and of the trust reposed in them by his majesty's good subjects in the colony, they could not consent to such proceedings, nor countenance those who would so act, or such as would abet them.

As a ground of compromise, the court stated their willingness to hear the case themselves in the presence of the commissioners, who would thereby be enabled to understand its merits; but this proposition was at once rejected, and every effort towards reconciliation proved unavailing.*

From Massachusetts, the commissioners proceeded to New Hampshire and Maine. They decided in favour of the claims of Mason and Gorges, and erected a royal government in each province, appointed justices of the peace, and exercised other acts of sovereignty; after which they returned to Boston. The general court, declaring that their proceedings to the eastward tended to the disturbance of the public peace, asked a conference on the subject, which was refused with a bitterness of expression that put an end to all farther communication between the parties. Massachusetts, soon afterwards, re-established her authority both in New Hampshire and Maine.

Charles, on being informed of these transactions, recalled his commissioners, and ordered the general court to send agents to England, to answer the complaints made against its proceedings. The court, having more than once experienced the benefits of procrastination, affected at first to disbelieve the authenticity of the letter; and afterwards excused themselves from sending agents by saying that the ablest among them could not support their cause better than had already been done.

During these transactions in the north, new colonies were forming in the south.

* Chalmer. Hutchison

CHAP. V.
1666.

In the year 1663, that tract of country extending from the 36th degree of north latitude to the river St. Matheo, was made a province by the name of Carolina, and granted to lord Clarendon, the duke of Albemarle, lord Craven, lord Berkeley, lord Ashley, sir George Carteret, sir John Colleton, and sir William Berkeley, in absolute property for ever. This charter bears a strong resemblance to that of Maryland, and was probably copied from it.

Settlement of Carolina.

The proprietors took immediate measures for the settlement of their colony. Its constitution consisted of a governor, to be chosen by themselves from thirteen persons nominated by the colonists; and an assembly to be composed of the governor, council, and representatives of the people, who should have power to make laws not contrary to those of England, which were to remain in force until the dissent of the proprietors should be published. Perfect freedom in religion was promised; and, as an inducement to emigration, one hundred acres of land, at the price of a half penny for each acre, were allowed for every freeman, and fifty for every servant, who should, within the space of five years, be settled in the province.

A small settlement had been made on Albemarle sound by some emigrants from Virginia, the superintendance of which had been conferred, by the proprietors, on sir William Berkeley, then governor of that colony; with instructions to visit it, to appoint a governor and council of six persons for the management of its affairs, and to grant lands to the inhabitants on the same terms that those in Virginia might be obtained.

The attention of the proprietors was next turned to the country south of cape Fear, which, as far as the river St. Matheo, was erected into a county by the name of Clarendon. Considerable numbers from Barbadoes emigrated into it, one of whom, Mr. John Yeamans, was appointed commander in chief; and, in 1665, a separate government was erected in it, similar to that in Albemarle.

The proprietors having discovered some valuable lands not comprehended in their original patent, obtained a new charter which bestowed on them a more extensive territory. This charter grants that province within the King's dominions in America, extending north eastward to Carahtuke inlet, thence in a straight line to Wyonok, which lies under 36 degrees 30 minutes north latitude; south westward to the 29th degree of north latitude; and from the Atlantic ocean to the South sea. Powers of government and privileges analogous to those comprised in other colonial charters, were also contained in this.

The people of Albemarle, employed like those of Virginia, in the cultivation of corn and tobacco, received their scanty supplies principally from New England; and carried on their small commerce in the vessels of those colonies. Their progress was slow, but they were contented. A new constitution was given them, by which the executive power was placed in a governor, to act by the advice of a council of twelve, six of whom were to be chosen by himself, and the others by the assembly, which was composed of the governor, the council, and twelve delegates, to be elected annually by the freeholders. Perfect freedom in religion was established, and all were entitled to equal privileges, on taking the oaths of allegiance to the King, and of fidelity to the proprietors.

The first acts of this legislature indicate the condition and opinions of the people. It was declared that none should be sued, during five years, for any cause of action arising out of the country; and that no person should accept a power of attorney to receive debts contracted abroad.

The proprietors, dissatisfied with their own systems, applied to Mr. Locke for the plan of a constitution. They supposed that this profound and acute reasoner must be deeply skilled in the science of government. In compliance with their request, he framed a body of fundamental laws which were approved and adopted. A palatine for life was to be chosen from among the proprietors, who was to act as president of the palatine court, which was to be composed of all those who were entrusted with the execution of the powers granted by the charter. A body of hereditary nobility was created, to be denominated Landgraves, and Caciques, the former to be invested with four baronies, consisting each of four thousand acres, and the latter to have two, containing each two thousand acres of land. These estates were to descend with the dignities for ever.

The provincial legislature, denominated a Parliament was to consist of the proprietors, in the absence of any one of whom, his place was to be supplied by a deputy appointed by himself; of the nobility; and of the representatives of the freeholders, who were elected by districts. These discordant materials were to compose a single body which could initiate nothing. The bills to be laid before it were to be prepared in a grand council composed of the governor, the nobility, and the deputies of the proprietors, who were invested also with the executive power. At the end of every century, the laws were to become void without the formality of a repeal. Various judicatories were erected, and numerous minute perplexing regulations were made. This constitution, which was declared to be perpetual, soon furnished additional evidence, to the many afforded by history, of the great but neglected truth, that experience is the only safe school in which the science of government is to be acquired; and that the theories of the closet must have the stamp of practice, before they can be received with implicit confidence.

The duke of Albemarle was chosen the first palatine, but did not long survive his election; and lord Berkeley was appointed his successor. The other proprietors were also named to high offices; and Mr. Locke was created a landgrave.

After this change of constitution, the attention of the proprietors was first directed to the south. A settlement was made at Port Royal, under the conduct of William Sayle, who had been appointed governor of that part of the coast which lies south west of cape Carteret. He was accompanied by Joseph West, who was intrusted with the commercial affairs of the proprietors, and who, with the governor, conducted the whole mercantile business of the colony.

William Sayle, after leading the first colony to Port Royal, and convening a parliament in which there were neither landgraves nor caciques, became the victim of the climate; after which, the authority of sir John Yeamans, who had hitherto governed the settlement at cape Fear, was extended over the territory south-west of cape Carteret. In the same year, the foundation of *old Charlestown* was laid, which continued, for some time, to be the capital of the southern settlements.

While these exertions were making in the south, great dissatisfaction was excited in Albemarle. In 1670, Stevens, the governor, had been ordered to introduce into that settlement, the constitution prepared by Mr. Locke. This innovation was strenuously opposed; and the discontent it produced was increased by a rumour, which was not the less mischievous for being untrue, that the proprietors designed to dismember the province. There was also another cause which increased the ill humour pervading that small society. The proprietors attempted to stop the trade carried on in the vessels of New England; and the attempt produced the constant effect of such measures—much ill temper both on the part of those who carried on the traffic, and of those for whom it was conducted.

At length, these discontents broke out into open insurrection. The insurgents, led by Culpeper, who had been appointed surveyor-general of Carolina, obtained possession of the country, seized the revenues, and imprisoned the president, with seven deputies who had been named by the proprietors. Having taken possession of the government, they established courts of justice, appointed officers, called a parliament, and, for several years, exercised the powers of an independent state; yet they never, formally, disclaimed the power of the proprietors.

At this time, the titheables of Albemarle, a term designating all the men, with the negroes and Indian women, between sixteen and sixty years of age, amounted only to fourteen hundred; and the exports consisted of a few cattle, a small quantity of Indian corn, and about eight hundred thousand weight of tobacco.

About this time, an event occurred in the southern settlements, showing as well the poverty of the people, as the manner in which the affairs of the proprietors were conducted. Joseph West, their agent, was appointed to succeed Yeamans in the government; and, the colony being unable to pay his salary, the plantation, and mercantile stock of the proprietors, were assigned to him in satisfaction of his claims.

In England, the opinion had been long entertained that the southern colonies were adapted to the production of those articles which succeed in the warmer climates of Europe. In pursuance of this opinion,

CHAP. V.
1688.

Charles, in 1679, employed two vessels to transport foreign protestants into the southern colony for the purpose of raising wine, oil, silk, and other productions of the south; and, to encourage the growth of these articles, exempted them, for a limited time, from taxation. The effort, however, did not succeed.

Old Charlestown being found an inconvenient place for the seat of government, the present Charleston became the metropolis of South Carolina. This situation was deemed so unhealthy, that directions were given to search out some other position for a town. The seat of government, however, remained unaltered until the connexion with Great Britain was dissolved.

Carolina continued to increase slowly in wealth and population without any remarkable incident, except the invasion of its most southern settlement by the Spaniards from St. Augustine. This was occasioned, in part, by the jealousy with which the English colony inspired its neighbours, but was principally, and immediately attributable to the countenance given, in Charleston, to the buccaneers who then infested those seas, and who were particularly hostile to the Spaniards. It was with difficulty the colonists were prevented by the proprietors from taking ample vengeance for this injury. Their resentments, though restrained, were not extinguished; and, until the annexation of the Floridas to the British crown, these colonies continued to view each other with distrust and enmity.

The dissatisfaction of the colony with its constitution grew with its population. After some time a settled purpose was disclosed, to thwart and oppose the wishes of the proprietors in every thing. Wearied with a continued struggle to support a system not adapted to the condition of the people, the proprietors at length, abandoned the constitution of Mr. Locke, and restored the ancient form of government.*

<small>CHAP V.
1688.

Constitution of Mr. Locke abandoned.</small>

The discontents which arose in Virginia soon after the restoration, continued to augment. To the regularly decreasing price of tobacco, and the restraints imposed on commerce by the acts of navigation, other causes of dissatisfaction were soon added. Large grants of land were made to the favourites of the crown: and considerable burdens were produced, and injuries inflicted by the hostility of the Indians. Agents were deputed to remonstrate against these improvident grants, as well as to promote the views of the colony with regard to other objects of great moment; and a considerable tax was imposed to support the expense of the deputation. They are said to have been on the point of obtaining the objects of their mission, when all farther proceedings were suspended in consequence of a rebellion, which, for a time, wore a very serious aspect.

<small>Discontents of Virginia.</small>

At the head of the insurgents was colonel Nathaniel Bacon, a gentleman who had received his education, in England, at the inns of court; and had been appointed a member of the council soon after his arri-

<small>Bacon's rebellion.</small>

---

* Chalmer. History of South Carolina and Georgia.

CHAP. V.
1663.
val in Virginia. Young, bold, and ambitious; possessing an engaging person, and commanding elocution; he was well calculated to rouse and direct the passions of the people. Treading the path by which ambition marches to power, he harangued the people on their grievances, increased their irritation against the causes of their disgust, and ascribed the evils with which they thought themselves oppressed to those who governed them, while he professed no other object than their good. He declaimed particularly against the languor with which the Indian war had been prosecuted; and, striking the note to which their feelings were most responsive, declared that, by proper exertions, it might have been already terminated.

The people, viewing him as their only friend, and believing the zeal he manifested to be produced solely by his devotion to their cause gave him their whole confidence and elected him their general. In return,

1676. he assured them that he would never lay down his arms until he had avenged their sufferings on the savages, and redressed their other grievances.

He applied to the governor for a commission appointing him general to prosecute the war against the Indians. A temporising policy being pursued, he entered Jamestown at the head of six hundred armed men, and obtained all he demanded, from an intimidated government. No sooner had he withdrawn from the capital than the governor, at the request of the assembly which was then in session, issued a proclamation declaring him a rebel, and commanding his followers to deliver him up, and to retire to their respective homes. Bacon and his army, equally incensed at this piece of impotent indiscretion, returned to Jamestown, and the governor fled to Accomack.

The general of the insurgents called a convention of his friends, who inveighed against the governor, for having, without cause, endeavoured to foment a civil war in the country, and after failing in this attempt, for having abdicated the government, to the great astonishment of the people. They stated farther that, the governor having informed the King " that their commander and his followers were rebellious, and having advised his majesty to send forces to reduce them, it consisted with the welfare of the colony, and with their allegiance to his sacred majesty, to oppose and suppress all forces whatsoever until the King be fully informed of the state of the case by such persons as shall be sent by Nathaniel Bacon in behalf of the people." This extraordinary manifesto was concluded with the recommendation of an oath, first taken by the members of the convention, to join the general and his army against the common enemy in all points whatever; and to endeavour to discover and apprehend such evil disposed persons as design to create a civil war by raising forces against him, and the army under his command.

In the mean time, the governor collected a considerable force which crossed the bay under the command of major Robert Beverly, and several sharp

CHAP. V.
1676.

skirmishes were fought. A civil war was commenced; agriculture declined; Jamestown was burnt by the insurgents; those parts of the country which remained in peace were pillaged; and the wives of those who supported the government were carried to camp, where they were very harshly treated. Virginia was relieved from this threatening state of things, and from the encreasing calamities it portended, by the sudden death of Bacon.

His death.
1677.

Having lost their leader, the malcontents were incapable of farther agreement among themselves. They began, separately, to make terms with the government, and all opposition soon ended. Sir William Berkeley was re-instated in his authority, and an assembly was convened, which seems to have been actuated by the spirit of revenge common to those who suffer in civil contests.*

The real motives and objects of this rebellion are not perfectly understood. Many were disposed to think that Bacon's original design extended no farther than to gratify the common resentments against the Indians, and to acquire that reputation and influence which result from conducting a popular war successfully. Others believed that he intended to seize the government. Whatever may have been his object, the insurrection produced much misery, and no good, to Virginia.†

Soon after the restoration of domestic quiet, sir William Berkeley returned to England, and was suc-

* Chalmer. Beverly. † Idem.

ceeded by Herbert Jeffreys, who relieved the colony from one of its complaints by making peace with the Indians.

CHAP V.
1667.

About the year 1680, an essential change was made in the jurisprudence of Virginia. In early times, the assembly was the supreme appellate court of the province. During the administration of lord Culpeper, a controversy arose between the burgesses, and counsellors, who composed also the general court, concerning the right of the latter to sit as a part of the assembly, on appeals from their own decisions. The burgesses claimed, exclusively, the privilege of judging in the last resort. This controversy was determined by taking all judicial power from the assembly, and allowing an appeal from judgments of the general court to the King in council, where the matter in contest exceeded the value of three hundred pounds sterling.*

1680.

Assembly deprived of judicial power.

From the rebellion of Bacon to the revolution in 1688, the history of Virginia affords no remarkable occurrence. The low price of tobacco, that perpetual source of dissatisfaction, still continued to disquiet the country. Combinations were formed among the people to raise its value by preventing, for a time, the growth of the article; and disorderly parties assembled to destroy the tobacco plants in the beds when it was too late to sow the seed again. Violent measures were adopted to prevent these practices, and several individuals were executed.

* Chalmer. Beverly.

CHAP V.
1680
Population.

These discontents did not arrest the growth of the colony. A letter from sir William Berkeley, dated in June, 1671, states its population at forty thousand, and its militia at eight thousand. A letter from lord Culpeper in December, 1681, supposes that there might then be in the colony fifteen thousand fighting men. This calculation however is probably exaggerated, as the report of general Smith, prepared in 1680 from actual returns, represents the militia as then consisting of eight thousand five hundred and sixty-eight men, of whom thirteen hundred were cavalry.*

* Chalmer.

CHAPTER VI.

*Prosperity of New England.—War with Philip.—
—Edward Randolph arrives in Boston.—Maine
adjudged to Gorges.—Purchased by Massachusetts.
—Royal government erected in New Hampshire.—
—Complaints against Massachusetts.—Their letters patent cancelled.—Death of Charles II.—
—James II. proclaimed.—New commission for the
government of New England.—Sir Edmond Andros.—The charter of Rhode Island abrogated.—
Odious measures of the new government.—Andros
deposed.—William and Mary proclaimed.—Review
of proceedings in New York and the Jerseys.—
Pennsylvania granted to William Penn.—Frame
of government.—Foundation of Philadelphia laid.—
Assembly convened.—First acts of the legislature.
Boundary line with lord Baltimore settled.*

AFTER the departure of the commissioners, New England was for some time quiet and prosperous. The plague, the fire of London, and the discontents of the people of England, engrossed the attention of the King, and suspended the execution of his plans respecting Massachusetts. In the mean time, that colony disregarded the acts of navigation, traded as

1680.
Prosperity of New England.

CHAP. VI.
1680.

War with Philip.

1675.

an independent state, and governed New Hampshire and Maine without opposition.*

This state of prosperous repose was interrupted by a combination of Indians so formidable, and a war so bloody, as to threaten the very existence of all New England. This combination was formed by Philip, the second son of Massassoet. The father and eldest son had cultivated the friendship of the colonists; but Philip, equally brave and intelligent, saw the continuing growth of the English with apprehension, and by his conduct soon excited their suspicion. He gave explicit assurances of his pacific disposition; but, from the year 1670 till 1675, when hostilities commenced, he was secretly preparing for them. The war was carried on with great vigour and various success: the savages, led by an intrepid chief, who believed that the fate of his country depended on the entire destruction of the English, made exertions of which they had not been thought capable. Several battles were fought; and all that barbarous fury which distinguishes Indian warfare, was displayed in its full extent. Wherever the Indians marched, their route was marked with murder, fire, and desolation. Massachusetts, New Hampshire, and Plymouth, were the greatest sufferers. In those provinces especially, the

* From a paper in possession of the British administration, it appears that in 1673, New England was supposed to contain one hundred and twenty thousand souls, of whom sixteen thousand were able to bear arms. Three-fourths of the wealth and population of the country, were in Massachusetts and its dependencies. The town of Boston alone contained fifteen hundred families.

Indians were so intermingled with the whites, that there was scarcely a part of the country in perfect security, or a family which had not to bewail the loss of a relation or friend. For a considerable time no decisive advantage was gained. At length, the steady efforts of the English prevailed; and in August 1676, when the tide of success was running strong in favour of the colonists, Philip, after losing his family and chief counsellors, was himself killed by one of his own nation, whom he had offended. After his death, the war was soon terminated by the submission of the Indians. Never had the people of New England been engaged in so fierce, so bloody, and so desolating a conflict. Though the warriors of the nation of which Philip was prince, were estimated at only five hundred men, he had, by alliances, increased his force to three thousand. In this estimate the eastern Indians are not included. Many houses, and flourishing villages were reduced to ashes, and six hundred persons were either killed in battle, or murdered privately.*

While this war was raging with its utmost violence, the government of Massachusetts was under the necessity of directing a part of its attention to the claims of Mason and Gorges. The efforts of Charles to procure an appearance of the colony before the council having proved ineffectual, he determined to give judgment in its absence, unless an appearance should be entered within six months. Edward Ran-

* Chalmer. Hutchison.

dolph, who was dispatched to give notice of this determination, arrived in Boston in the summer of 1676; and, as other letters brought by the same vessel gave assurance that this resolution would be adhered to, the general court hastened the departure of deputies to represent the colony, and support its interests.

It was the opinion of the King in council that the line of Massachusetts did not run more than three miles north of the Merrimack; and Maine was adjudged to Gorges. The claim of Mason to New Hampshire being confined to the soil, all title to which, though so long exercised, was now waved by Massachusetts; and the terre-tenants not being before the court, that part of the case was decided so far only as respected the boundary of Massachusetts, which, being against the pretensions of that colony, its jurisdiction over New Hampshire ceased. Charles had been for some time treating for the purchase both of New Hampshire and Maine which he intended to bestow on his favourite son, the duke of Monmouth, but his poverty had prevented the contract. Massachusetts, though not ignorant of this fact, finding that the decision respecting Maine would be in favour of Gorges, purchased his title for twelve hundred pounds sterling. The offended monarch insisted on a relinquishment of the contract; but Massachusetts, apologising for what had been done, retained the purchase, and governed the country as a subordinate province.*

* Chalmer. Hatchison.

New Hampshire having become a distinct colony, a royal government was erected in that province; the legislature of which voted an affectionate address to Massachusetts, avowing a willingness to have retained their ancient connexion, had such been the pleasure of their common sovereign.

CHAP. VI.
1679.
Royal government in New Hampshire.

The temper and conduct of Massachusetts remaining unchanged, the charges against its government were renewed. The complaints of the Quakers were perseveringly urged; and the neglect of the acts of navigation, constituted a serious accusation against the colony. The general court, in a letter to their agents, declared these acts " to be an invasion of the rights, liberty, and property, of the subjects of his majesty in the colony, they not being represented in Parliament." But as his majesty had signified his pleasure that they should be conformed to, " they had made provision by a law of the colony that they should be strictly attended to from time to time, although it greatly discouraged trade, and was a great damage to his majesty's plantation." Their agents gave correct information of the state of things in England, and assured them that only a fair compliance with the regulations respecting trade could secure them from an open breach with the crown. These honest representations produced the usual effect of unwelcome truths. They diminished the popularity of the agents, and excited a suspicion in Boston that they had not supported the interests of the colony with sufficient zeal. On their return, they brought

Y

with them a letter containing the requisitions of the King; and were soon followed by Randolph, who had been appointed collector at Boston. The general court began to manifest some disposition to appease their sovereign, and passed several laws for this purpose; but still declined complying with his directions to send agents with full powers to attend to the new ordering of the province; and the collector encountered insuperable obstacles in his attempts to execute the laws of trade. Almost every suit he instituted for the recovery of penalties or forfeitures was decided against him, at the costs of the prosecutor. These difficulties induced him to return to England, to solicit additional powers, which were equally disregarded.

The complaints of the King on these subjects were answered by professions of loyalty, and by partial compliances with the demands of the crown; but the main subject of contest remained unaltered.

At length, being convinced that the King was determined to annul the charter, Massachusetts so far yielded to his will, as to appoint agents to represent the colony. But persons empowered to submit to such regulations as might be made by government, were, in other words, persons appointed to surrender the charter. They were therefore instructed not to do, or consent to, any thing that might infringe the liberties granted by charter, or the government established thereby. These powers were declared to be insufficient; and the agents were informed that, unless others, in every respect satisfactory, should be immediately obtained, it was his majesty's pleasure that a *quo warranto* should be issued without delay. This unpleasant intelligence was immediately communicated to the general court, accompanied with information of the proceedings which had lately taken place in England. In that country, many corporations had surrendered their charters; and, on the refusal of London, a *quo warranto* had issued against the city, which had been decided in favour of the crown. The question whether it was advisable to submit to his majesty's pleasure, or to permit the *quo warranto* to issue, was seriously referred to the general court, and was as seriously taken into consideration throughout the colony. In concurrence with the common sentiment, the general court determined that "it was better to die by other hands than their own." On receiving this final resolution, the fatal writ was issued, and was committed to the care of Randolph, who brought also a declaration of the King, that if the colony, before the writ should be prosecuted, would submit to his pleasure, he would regulate their charter for his service, and their good; and would make no farther alterations in it than should be necessary for the support of his government in the province. The governor and assistants passed a vote of submission; but, the deputies refusing their assent thereto, the high court of chancery, in Trinity term 1684, decreed against the governor.

CHAP. VI. and company, " that their letters patent, and the en-
1684. rolment thereof be cancelled."

1685. Charles did not survive this decree long enough to complete his system respecting the New England colonies, or to establish a new government for Massa-
Death of chusetts. He died early in the following year; and
Charles II. his successor, from whose stern temper, and high toned opinions, the most gloomy presages had been
James II. drawn, was proclaimed, in Boston, with melancholy
proclaimed. pomp.

Their presages were soon verified. Immediately after James had ascended the throne, a commission was issued for a president and council, as a temporary government for Massachusetts, New Hampshire, Maine, and Narraghansetts; whose powers were entirely executive and judicial. This commission reach-
1686. ed Boston in May, and was laid before the general court, not as a body invested with political authority, but as one composed of individuals of the first respectability and influence in the province. The general court agreed unanimously to an address, in answer to this communication, declaring " that the liberty of the subject is abridged, by the new system, both in matters of legislation and in laying taxes; and that it highly concerns them to whom it is directed to consider whether it be safe;" and added " that, if the newly appointed officers, mean to take upon themselves the government of the people, though they could not give their assent thereto, they should demean themselves as loyal subjects, and humbly make their addresses to

God, and, in due time, to their gracious prince, for relief."

CHAP VI
1686.

Mr. Dudley, the president named in the commission, was a native of Massachusetts, and seems to have mingled with his respect for the constitutional prerogative of the crown, a due regard for the rights of the people. Any immediate alterations, therefore, in the interior arrangements of the country were avoided; and the commissioners transmitted a memorial to the lords of the council for the colonies, stating the necessity of a well regulated assembly to represent the people, and soliciting an abatement of the taxes. This moderate conduct did not accord with the wishes of that class of men who court power wherever it may be placed. These sought the favour of their sovereign by prostrating every obstacle to the execution of his will; and soon transmitted complaints to administration, charging the commissioners with conniving at violations of the laws respecting trade, and countenancing ancient principles in religion and government.

James was dissatisfied with the conduct of his commissioners; and was also of opinion that a wise policy required a consolidation of the colonies, and a permanent administration for New England. With a view to this object, he appointed Sir Edmond Andros, who had governed New York, captain-general and vice-admiral of Massachusetts, New Hampshire, Maine, New Plymouth, Pemaquid, and Narraghansetts; and empowered him, with the consent of a council to be

Sir Edmond Andros.

appointed by the crown, to make ordinances not inconsistent with the laws of the realm, which should be submitted to the King for his approbation or dissent; and to impose taxes for the support of government.

In December 1685, Andros arrived at Boston, where he was received with the respect which was due to the representative of the crown. In pursuance of his orders, he dissolved the government of Rhode Island, broke its seal, and assumed the administration of the colony. In the preceding year, articles of high misdemeanour had been exhibited against that colony and referred to Sayer, the attorney general, with orders to issue a writ of *quo warranto* to annul their patent. The assembly stopped farther proceedings, by passing an act formally surrendering their charter. Their submission, however, availed them nothing. Their fate was involved in that of Massachusetts.*

Odious measures of government. In pursuance of the determination to break the charters and unite the colonies, articles of misdemeanour had been also exhibited against the governor and company of Connecticut, on which a writ of *quo warranto* had been issued. The government of that colony addressed a letter to the secretary of state, desiring, with many professions of loyalty, to remain in its present situation; but, if it should be the purpose of his majesty to dispose otherwise of them, submitting to his royal commands, and requesting to be annexed to

* Chalmer. Hutchison.

Massachusetts. No farther proceedings were had on the *quo warranto*, and Andros was ordered to accept the submission of the colony, and annex it to Massachusetts. This order was executed in October, when Andros appeared in Hartford at the head of a small corps of regular troops, demanded the charter, and declared the government to be dissolved. The colony submitted, but the charter was concealed in a tree, which was venerated long afterwards and is still in existence.*

The grand legislative council, composed of individuals selected by the crown throughout the united colonies, readily assembled, and proceeded to execute the duties assigned to it.

The measures of the new government were not calculated to diminish the odium excited by its objectionable from. The fees of office were enormous; and the regulations respecting divine worship, marriages, the acts of navigation, and taxes, were deemed highly oppressive. In addition to these causes of discontent, the governor general took occasion to cast a doubt on the validity of the titles by which lands were holden.

To obtain relief from these oppressive grievances, Mather, an eminent politician and divine, was deputed by the colonies of New England to lay their complaints before the King. He was graciously received, but could effect no substantial change in the colonial administration. James had determined to reduce all

---

* Trumbull. Hutchison. Chalmer.

CHAP. VI.
1688.

the governments, proprietory as well as royal, to an immediate dependence on the crown; and, to effect this purpose, had directed writs of *quo warranto* to issue against those charters which still remained in force. This plan was adopted, not only for the purpose of establishing his favourite system of government, but also of forming a barrier to the encroachments of France, by combining the force of the colonies as far as the Delaware. During this reign, Canada was pushed south of Lake Champlain; and fortresses were erected within the immense forests which then separated that province from New York and New England. With a view to this union of force, a new commission was made out for Andros, annexing New York and the Jerseys to his government, and appointing Francis Nicholson his lieutenant.

The dissatisfaction of the people continued to increase; and every act of the government, even those which were in themselves laudable, was viewed through the medium of prejudice.

1689. At length these latent ill humours burst forth into action. Some vague intelligence was received concerning the proceedings of the Prince of Orange in England. The old magistrates and leading men silently wished, and secretly prayed, that success might attend him, but determined to commit nothing unnecessarily to hazard, and quietly to await an event, which no movement of theirs could accelerate or retard.

The people were less prudent. Stung with the recollection of past injuries, their impatience, on the first prospect of relief, could not be restrained. On the 18th of April, without any apparent preconcerted plan, a sudden insurrection broke out in Boston, and about fifty of the most unpopular individuals, including the governors, were seized and imprisoned; and the government was once more placed in the hands of the ancient magistrates. All apprehensions of danger from this precipitate measure were soon quieted by the information that William and Mary had been crowned King and Queen of England. They were immediately proclaimed in Boston with unusual pomp, and with demonstrations of unaffected joy.*

Andros deposed.

William and Mary proclaimed.

The example of Massachusetts was quickly followed by Connecticut and Rhode Island. Andros was no sooner known to be in prison than he was deposed also in Connecticut; and, in both colonies the ancient form of government was restored.

In New Hampshire a convention was called, which determined to re-annex that colony to Massachusetts, and deputies were elected to represent them in the general court. This re-union continued to be their wish, but was opposed by the King, who, in 1692, appointed for it a distinct governor.

In order to bring the affairs of the middle colonies to this period, it will be necessary briefly to review the transactions of several years.

The treaty of Breda, which restored Acadié to France, confirmed New Netherlands to England. Quiet possession of that valuable territory was re-

Review of proceedings in New York and New Jersey.

* Chalmer. Hutchison.

CHAP. VI.
1689.

tained until 1673, when, England being engaged again in war with Holland, a small Dutch squadron appeared before the fort at New York, which surrendered without firing a shot. The example was followed by the city and country; and, in a few days, the submission of New Netherlands was complete. After this acquisition the old claim to Long Island was renewed, and some attempts were made to wrest it from Connecticut. That province however, after consulting its confederates, and finding that offensive operations would be agreeable to the union, declared war against the Dutch; and not content with defending its own possessions, prepared an expedition against New York. The termination of the war between England and Holland prevented its prosecution, and restored to the English the possessions they had lost.*

To remove all controversy concerning his title, which had been acquired while the granted lands were in possession of the Dutch, the duke of York, after the peace of 1674, obtained a renewal of his patent, and appointed sir Edmond Andros governor of his territories in America. This commission included New Jersey, his former grant of which he supposed to be annulled by the conquest thereof in 1673. Andros, disregarding the decision of the commissioners, claimed for the duke that part of Connecticut which lies west of the river of that name; and, during the war with Philip, endeavoured to support

* Trumbull. Hutchison.

his claim by force. The determined resistance of Connecticut compelled him to relinquish an attempt on Saybrooke; after which he returned to New York. The taxes which had been laid by the Dutch were collected, and duties, for a limited time, were imposed, by authority of the duke. This proceeding excited great discontent. The public resentment was directed, first against the governor, whose conduct was inquired into and approved by his master, and afterwards against the collector, who was seized and sent to England; but never prosecuted. The representatives of the duke in New York, feeling the difficulty of governing a high spirited people on principles repugnant to all their settled opinions, repeatedly, but ineffectually, urged him to place the colony on the same footing with its neighbours, by creating a local legislature, one branch of which should be elected by the people. It was not until the year 1683, when the revenue laws were about to expire, when the right of the duke to re-enact them was denied in America, and doubted in England, that he could be prevailed on to appoint a new governor with instructions to convene an assembly.*

In 1674, lord Berkeley assigned his interest in the Jerseys to William Penn and his associates. They afterwards acquired the title of sir George Carteret also, and immediately conveyed one-half of their interest to the earl of Perth and others, who, in 1683,

* Smith.

obtained a conveyance from the duke of York directly to themselves.

During these transactions, continual efforts were made to re-annex the Jerseys to New York. Carteret had endeavoured to participate in the advantages of commerce by establishing a port at Amboy; but Andros seized and condemned the vessels trading thither, and was supported by the duke in this exercise of power. The assembly of New York claimed the right of taxing the people of Jersey; and the collector, continued to exercise his former authority within their territory. On his complaining, after the accession of the duke of York to the throne, that every vessel he prosecuted was discharged by the verdict of the jury, a writ of *quo warranto* was directed. The English judges did not then hold their offices during good behaviour; and the proprietors of East Jersey, confident that the cause would be decided against them, surrendered their patent to the crown, praying only a grant of the soil. The Jerseys were, soon afterwards, annexed to New England.*

Dongan, who, in 1683, had succeeded Andros in the government of New York, took a deep interest in the affairs of the five nations, who had been engaged in bloody wars with Canada. The French, by establishing a settlement at Detroit, and a fort at Michilimackinack, had been enabled to extend their commerce among the numerous tribes of Indians who hunted on the banks of the great lakes, and the up-

* Chalmer. Smith.

per branches of the Mississippi. They excluded the people of New York from any share in this gainful commerce; in consequence of which Dongan solicited and obtained permission to aid the five nations. This order, however, was soon countermanded; and a treaty was concluded, stipulating that no assistance should be given to the savages by the English colonists; soon after which Dongan was recalled, and New York was annexed to New England.

From the accession of James to the throne, he had discontinued the assemblies of New York, and empowered the governor, with the consent of his council, to make laws "as near as might be" to those of England. The reinstatement of this arbitrary system gave general disgust, and, together with the apprehension that the Roman Catholic religion would be established, prepared the people of New York, as well as those of the other colonies, for that revolution which wrested power from hands accustomed to abuse it. On receiving intelligence of the revolution at Boston, the militia were raised by a captain Jacob Leisler, who took possession of the fort in the name of King William, and drove Nicholson, the lieutenant governor, out of the country. This event gave rise to two parties, who long divided New York, and whose mutual animosities were the source of much uneasiness and mischief to the province.*

William Penn having gained some knowledge of the country west of the Delaware, formed the design

* Chalmer. Smith.

CHAP. VI.
1689
Pennsylvania granted to William Penn.

of acquiring that territory as a separate estate. On his petition, a charter was issued in 1681, granting to him, in absolute property, by the name of Pennsylvania, that tract of country bounded on the east by the river Delaware, extending westward five degrees of longitude, stretching to the north from twelve miles north of New Castle to the forty-third degree of latitude, and limited on the south by a circle of twelve miles, drawn round New Castle to the beginning of the fortieth degree of latitude.

In this charter, the acts of navigation were recognised, a local legislature was created, and provision made that a duplicate of its laws should be transmitted, within five years, to the King in council; any of which that were repugnant to those of England, or inconsistent with the authority of the crown, might be declared void in six months. This charter conveyed nearly the same powers and privileges with that of Maryland, but recognised the right of Parliament to tax the colony.

Penn soon commenced the settlement of the province, and immediately asserted a claim to a part of the territory which had been supposed by lord Baltimore to be within the bounds of Maryland. In this claim originated a controversy between the two proprietors, productive of considerable inconvenience and irritation to both.

He published a frame of government for Pennsylvania, the chief intention of which was declared to be " for the support of power in reverence with the people, and to secure the people from the abuse of power; that they may be free by their just obedience, and the magistrates honourable for their just administration; for liberty without obedience is confusion, and obedience without liberty is slavery."

CHAP. VI.
1689.

This scheme of fundamental law contains many provisions indicating good sense and just notions of government, but was too complex for an infant settlement; and, after many fruitless attempts to amend it, was laid aside, and a more simple form was adopted, resembling in its principal features, those established in the other colonies, which remained until the proprietary government itself was dissolved.

In August 1682, Penn obtained from the duke of York a conveyance of the town of New Castle, with the territory twelve miles around it, and that tract of land extending thence southward, on the Delaware, to cape Henlopen. Soon after this grant was issued, he embarked for America, accompanied by about two thousand emigrants; and, in the October following, landed on the banks of the Delaware. In addition to the colonists sent out by himself, he found, on his arrival several small settlements of Swedes, Dutch, Finlanders, and English, amounting to about three thousand persons. Penn cultivated the good will of the natives, from whom he purchased such lands as were necessary for the present use of the colonists. At this time the foundation of Philadelphia was laid, which, we are assured contained near one hundred houses within twelve months from its commencement.

Foundation of Philadelphia.

CHAP VI.
1689.

An assembly was convened which, instead of being composed of all the freemen, according to the frame of government, was, at the request of the people themselves, constituted of their representatives. Among the laws which were enacted was one annexing the territories lately purchased from the duke of York to the province, and extending to them all its privileges. Universal freedom in religion was established; and every foreigner who promised allegiance to the King, and obedience to the proprietor was declared a freeman.*

In the hope of extending his limits to the Chesapeake, Penn, soon after his arrival, met lord Baltimore for the purpose of adjusting their boundaries. The patent of that nobleman calls for the fortieth degree of north latitude, and he proposed to determine the intersection of that degree with the Delaware by actual observation. Penn, on the contrary, insisted on finding the fortieth degree by mensuration from the capes of Virginia, the true situation of which had been already ascertained. Each adhering firmly to his own proposition, the controversy was referred to the committee of plantations, who, after the crown had descended on James, decided that the peninsula between the bays of Chesapeake and Delaware, should be divided into two equal parts by a line drawn from the latitude of cape Henlopen to the fortieth degree, and adjudged that the land lying from that line towards the Delaware should belong to his majesty, and the

* History of Pennsylvania. Chalmer.

other moiety to lord Baltimore. This adjudication was ordered to be immediately executed.

CHAP. VI.
1689.

Pennsylvania was slow in acknowledging the Prince and Princess of Orange. The government continued to be administered in the name of James for some time after his abdication was known. At length, however, William and Mary were proclaimed; and Penn had the address to efface the unfavourable impressions which this delay was calculated to make on them.

CHAPTER VII.

New charter of Massachusetts.—Affairs of New York. —War with France.—Schenectady destroyed.— Expedition against Port Royal.—Against Quebec. —Acadié recovered by France.—Pemaquid taken. —Attempt on St. Johns.—Peace.—Affairs of New York.—Of Virginia.—Disputes between England and France respecting boundary in America.—Recommencement of hostilities.—Quotas of the respective colonies.—Treaty of neutrality between France and the five nations.—Expedition against Port Royal.—Incursion into Massachusetts.—Plan for the invasion of Canada.—Port Royal taken.—Expedition against Quebec.—Treaty of Utrecht.—Affairs of New York.—Of Carolina.—Expedition against St. Augustine.—Attempt to establish the Episcopal church.—Invasion of the colony.—Bills of credit issued.—Legislature continues itself.—Massacre in North Carolina by the Indians.—Tuscaroras defeated.—Scheme of a Bank.

1689.

THE revolution which placed the Prince and Princess of Orange on the throne, revived in Massachusetts, the hope of recovering the ancient charter. Elections were held by authority of the temporary government, and the representatives requested the council to exercise, until orders should be received from England, the powers and authorities vested in that body by the charter. The council acceded to this proposition; and the ancient system was re-established.

It was soon perceived by the agents of Massachusetts that the old charter would not be restored, and that the King was determined to retain the appointment of the governor in his own hands. The colony, however, was authorised to exercise the powers of government according to the ancient system, until a new arrangement should be made. The vessel by which these directions were transmitted, carried also orders that sir Edmond Andros, and those imprisoned with him, should be sent to England.

The general court deputed additional agents, with instructions to solicit the confirmation of their beloved charter; but these solicitations were ineffectual. The King was inflexible; and, at length, a new charter was framed, more eligible than the first in many respects, but introducing some changes which affected radically the independence that had been long practically possessed by the colony. The governor was to be appointed by the crown, was enabled to call, adjourn, prorogue, and dissolve the assembly at pleasure; he had the appointment solely, of all military officers; and, with the consent of his council, of all officers belonging to the courts of justice.

Sir William Phipps, the first governor, arrived in May, and immediately issued writs for a general as-

CHAP. VII.
1692.

sembly, which met in June, and accepted the charter; though a considerable party had been formed to oppose it. This instrument annexed Plymouth and Nova Scotia to Massachusetts; but, contrary to the wishes of both colonies, omitted New Hampshire, which became permanently a separate government.*

Affairs of New York.

In New York, Leisler, who had obtained the entire control of the lower country, associated with himself in the government, a few trusty partisans, denominated a committee of safety, over whom he presided. Some of the principal inhabitants of the city, dissatisfied at seeing a man of low birth, without education, in possession of supreme power, retired to Albany, where a convention of the people was assembled, who determined to hold the fort and country for the King and Queen, but not to submit to the authority of Leisler. On receiving intelligence of these transactions, Jacob Milbourne was detached with a small force to reduce the place; but, finding that the people adhered to the convention, and that his harangues against James and popery made no impression on them, he returned to New York. The next spring he appeared again before the fort; and, being favoured by an irruption of the Indians, obtained possession of it. The principal members of the convention absconded, upon which their effects were seized and confiscated. This harsh measure produced resentments which were transmitted from father to son.

Leisler retained the supreme power, without farther

* Hutchison.

opposition, until the arrival of sir Henry Slaughter, who had been appointed governor of the province. Though informed of the commission which Slaughter bore, this infatuated man refused to yield the government to him; and showed a disposition, without the ability, to resist. This ill judged obstinacy threw the governor, who soon obtained possession of the fort, into the arms of the opposite party. Leisler and Milbourne were arrested, tried for high treason, condemned, and executed. Their estates were confiscated, but were afterwards restored to their families.*

While these things were passing in the interior, the colonies of New England and New York were engaged in a bloody and desolating war with the French of Canada, and with the Indians. The English people had long viewed with apprehension, the advances of France towards universal dominion; and with infinite disgust, the influence of Louis XIV. in their cabinet. On the elevation of the Prince of Orange to the throne, they entered with alacrity into all his views for opposing barriers to the power, and restraints on the ambition, of that haughty monarch. The war which was proclaimed between the two nations, extended itself to their possessions in America. De Calliers, who sailed from Canada to France in 1688, had formed a plan for the conquest of New York, which was adopted by his government. Caffiniere commanded the ships which sailed from Rochefort on this expedition, subject however to the count

* Smith.

CHAP. VII. de Frontignac, who was general of the land forces
1692. destined to march from Canada by the route of the
river Sorel and of lake Champlain. The fleet and
troops arrived at Chebucta, whence the count proceeded to Quebec leaving orders with Caffiniere to
sail to New York.

On reaching Quebec, the count found all Canada
in the utmost distress. In the preceding summer,
twelve hundred warriors of the Five nations had suddenly landed on the island of Montreal, and put to
death about one thousand of the inhabitants whom
they found in perfect security. The place was again
attacked in October, and the lower part of the island
entirely destroyed. In consequence of these calamitous events, fort Frontignac, on lake Ontario, was
evacuated, and two vessels which had been constructed there were burnt.

Count Frontignac, who, in his sixty-eighth year,
possessed the activity of youth, after remaining a few
days on shore, re-embarked in a canoe for Montreal.
In the hope of conciliating the Five nations, he held a
great council with them at Onondago, where the Indians showed some disposition towards a peace without concluding one. To influence their deliberations,
and raise the depressed spirits of the Canadians, he
sent out several parties against the English colonies.
That against New York, consisting of about two
hundred French, and some Indians; after marching
twenty-two days with their provisions on their backs,
through a wilderness covered deep with snow, arri-

ved, on 8th of February 1690, about eleven at night, at Schenectady, a village a few miles north-west of Albany. Finding the gates open and unguarded, they immediately entered the town, the inhabitants of which were asleep; and, dividing themselves into small parties, invested every house at the same time. No alarm was given until the doors were broken open; and then was commenced the perpetration of those barbarities which add so much to the ordinary horrors of war. The whole village was instantly in flames; pregnant women were ripped open and their infants cast into the flames, or dashed against the posts of the doors. Sixty persons were massacred, twenty-seven carried into captivity, and those who escaped fled naked, through a deep snow and storm to Albany. In the flight, twenty-five lost their limbs from the intensity of the cold. The town was pillaged until about noon the next day, when the enemy marched off with their plunder. Being pursued by a party of young men from Albany, about twenty-five of them were killed and captured.*

In the spring and summer of 1689, several settlements and forts in New Hampshire and Maine, were successfully attacked by the Indians; who, wherever they were victorious, perpetrated their usual cruelties. Knowing that these depredations originated in Canada and Acadié, the general court of Massachusetts planned an expedition against both Port Royal and Quebec. Early in the spring, eight small vessels,

Expedition against Port Royal.

* Smith.

CHAP. VII. carrying seven or eight hundred men, sailed under
1692. the command of sir William Phipps; and, almost without opposition, took possession of Port Royal, and of the whole coast between that place and New England. The fleet returned in May, having taken nearly plunder enough to discharge the expense of the equipment. But two detachments made about the same time by count Frontignac, attacked the Salmon falls, and fort Casco, where they killed and took about one hundred and eighty persons.

A vessel had been dispatched to England in April with letters urging the importance of conquering Canada, and soliciting the aid of the King to that enterprise. He was however too much occupied in Europe to attend to America; and it was determined to prosecute the expedition without his assistance.

Against Quebec

New York and Connecticut, engaged to furnish a body of men, to march, by the way of lake Champlain, against Montreal, while the troops of Massachusetts should proceed by sea to Quebec. The fleet, consisting of between thirty and forty vessels, the largest of which carried forty-four guns, sailed from Nantucket the ninth of August, having on board two thousand men. This expedition also was commanded by sir William Phipps, a brave man, but not qualified for so difficult an enterprise. He did not arrive before Quebec until October, when it was too late for a regular seige. Instead of availing himself of the first impression, sir William is charged with having wasted two or three days in sight of the place, after which he summoned it to surrender. Having performed this ceremony, he landed between twelve and thirteen hundred men, and marched until night, under a scattering fire from an enemy concealed in the woods. At night, a deserter gave such an account of the French force as entirely discouraged him.

Connecticut and New York were disappointed in receiving the assistance expected from the Five nations; who furnished neither the warriors they had promised, nor canoes to transport their troops over the lakes. The commissary too had neglected to lay up the necessary supplies of provisions. These disappointments, obliged the party destined against Montreal to retreat without making an attempt on that place; which enabled the French general to oppose the whole force of Canada to Phipps.

The evening after the troops were landed, the ships were drawn up before the place, but received more damage from the batteries than they could do to the town. After wasting a few days in unavailing parade, the army re-embarked with precipitation, and returned to Boston.

The general court, so far from suspecting that the expedition might possibly miscarry, seem to have counted, not only on success, but on acquiring sufficient treasure from the enemy to pay their soldiers. The army, finding the government totally unprepared to satisfy its claims, was on the point of mutinying. In this state of difficulty, bills of credit were issued, and were received in lieu of money. A tax was im-

CHAP. VII.
1692.

posed at the same time, payable in the paper notes of the colony at five per centum above par. Notwithstanding the exertions to keep up its credit, the paper depreciated to fourteen shillings in the pound, which depreciation was, almost entirely, sustained by the army. As the time for collecting the tax approached, the paper rose above par, but this appreciation was gained by the holders.*

Colonel Phipps, soon after his return from Canada, embarked for England, to renew the solicitations of the colony for aid in another attempt on Quebec. Though unsuccessful in this application, the government of the province was bestowed on him; and, this character, he returned to Boston. A desultory war continued to be carried on, which, without furnishing any events that would now be interesting, produced heavy expense, and much individual misery.

Canada being considered as the source of all the evils, its conquest continued to be the favourite object of Massachusetts. At length, King William yielded to the solicitations of that colony and determined to

1693. employ a force for the reduction of Quebec. Unfortunately the first part of the plan was to be executed in the West Indies, where the capture of Martinique was contemplated. While on that service a contagious fever attacked both the land and sea forces; and, before they reached Boston, thirteen hundred sailors, and eighteen hundred soldiers, were buried.

* See note No. 1, of the Appendix.

The survivors not being in a condition to prosecute the enterprise, it was abandoned.*

CHAP. VII.
1693.

On the conquest of Acadié by sir William Phipps, the government of Massachusetts had been extended over that province; but, as the prejudices and affections of the inhabitants were entirely on the side of France, it was soon perceived that a military force alone could preserve the acquisition; and Massachusetts was unable, at her own expense, to support a sufficient body of troops for the defence of the country. Port Royal was recovered by Villebonne, after which all Acadié shook off the government of Massachusetts, and resumed its allegiance to France. About the same time a fort at Pemaquid was attacked and carried by Iberville.

1696.

In December, the treaty of peace which had been concluded at Riswick was proclaimed at Boston; and hostilities with the French in Canada immediately ceased. The depredations of the Indians continued but a short time after this event; and, in the course of the following year, general tranquillity was restored.

Peace.

The frontiers of New Hampshire had been not less harassed during the war, than those of Massachusetts. Perpetual and distressing incursions had been made into the country, which were marked by the burning of undefended habitations, and the massacre of men, women, and children.†

1697.

The frontiers of New York were covered by the

Affairs of New York.

* Hutchison. Belknap. † Belknap.

CHAP. VII.
1697.

Five nations. Hostilities were carried on between them and the French, but they were not attended by any material circumstance.

During the war the English government meditated a union of the colonies for the purpose of forming an army to defend New York; and the governors were instructed to propose to the several provinces to raise the quota of troops assigned to each* by the crown. Though this plan never took effect, the fact is of some interest.

Of Virginia.
The influence of the French not yet extending far enough south to involve the colonies beyond New York in the calamities of Indian warfare, few occurrences took place among them which deserve attention. In Virginia, the college of William and Mary, to which a charter had been granted in 1692, was liberally endowed, and was established at Williamsburg by an act of assembly which passed in the year 1693. In 1698, the state-house at Jamestown, with many valuable papers, was consumed by fire; and, in the following year, the legislature passed an act for removing the seat of government to Williamsburg,

---

* The quotas assigned by the crown are as follows:

To Massachusetts Bay	350
Rhode Island and Providence plantations	48
Connecticut	120
New York	200
Pennsylvania	80
Maryland	160
Virginia	240
Total	1,198.

then called the middle plantation, and for building a CHAP. VII. 1697. capitol at that place.

By the treaty of Riswick, it was agreed that France and England should mutually restore to each other all conquests made during the war; and it was farther stipulated that commissioners should be appointed to examine and determine the rights and pretentions of each monarch to the places situated in Hudson's bay.

The consequences of not ascertaining boundaries were soon perceived. The English claimed as far west as the St. Croix, while France asserted her right to the whole country east of the Kennebeck.

These claims remained unsettled; and were mingled with other differences of more importance, which soon occasioned the re-commencement of hostilities. War renewed.

The whole weight of the war in America fell on New England. Previous to its commencement, the earl of Bellamont, who was, at that time governor of New York as well as of Massachusetts and of New Hampshire, had required that the quotas of men, assigned by the crown to the different colonies for the defence of New York, should be furnished. This requisition however was not complied with; and, before hostilities began, a treaty of neutrality was negotiated between the Five nations and the governor of Canada, which was assented to by lord Cornbury, then governor of New York. This treaty preserved the peace of that province, but left Massachusetts 1702.

CHAP VII
1702.

and New Hampshire to struggle with the combined force of the French and their Indian allies :—a struggle which seems to have been viewed by New York with the utmost composure.

Hostilities between Great Britain and France were immediately followed by incursions of French and Indians into the exposed parts of New England. A predatory and desolating war, attended with no striking circumstance, but with considerable expense and great individual distress, was carried on for some years. During its continuance, propositions were made for a cessation of hostilities; and the negotiations on this subject were protracted to a considerable length; but Dudley, who had succeeded the earl of Bellamont as governor of Massachusetts and New Hampshire, declined engaging for the neutrality of those provinces, in the hope that Nova Scotia and Canada might be subdued in the course of the war.

1707.

The battle of Almanza, in Spain, having induced the British cabinet to direct an armament intended for New England to European objects, Dudley determined to make an attempt on Acadié, though no aid should arrive from England. With this view, he applied, early in the spring, to the assemblies of both his provinces, and to the colonies of Connecticut and Rhode Island; requesting them to raise one thousand men for the expedition. Connecticut declined furnishing her quota; but the other three colonies raised the whole number, who were disposed into two regiments, one commanded by colonel Wainright, and the other by colonel Hilton. On the 13th of May, they embarked at Nantucket on board a fleet of transports furnished with whale boats, under convoy of a man of war and a galley. The chief command was given to colonel March, who had behaved gallantly in several encounters with the Indians, but had never been engaged in such service as this. They arrived before Port Royal in a few days, and landed without opposition. After making some ineffectual attempts to bombard the fort, a disagreement among the officers, and a misapprehension of the state of the fort and garrison, induced the troops to re-embark in a disorderly manner.* Dudley, who was unwilling to relinquish the enterprise, directed the army to remain in its position till farther orders. March was beloved by the soldiers, and was known to be brave, but his capacity was doubted. It was therefore thought unsafe either to recal him, to place an officer over him, or to continue him in the chief command. The expedient devised in this perplexity was, to send a commission to the army, composed of three members of the council, invested with all the powers which the governor himself, if present, would possess. These commissioners arrived at Casco about the middle of July, where they found the army insubordinate, and indisposed to the service. The troops, however, were again embarked, and arrived at Passamaquodi, on the seventh of August. The spirits of the general were broken, and his health was impaired.

* Belknap.

CHAP. VII
1707.

While dispositions for landing the army were making, he declared his inability to act, and the command devolved on colonel Wainright. The landing was effected on the 10th of August; but the troops could not be inspired with that union and firmness which are essential to success. After devoting ten days to inefficient, unmeaning operations, they re-embarked, and returned, sickly, fatigued and dispirited.

1708.

During this unfortunate expedition, the frontiers were kept in perpetual alarm by small parties of Indians; and, in the succeeding year, a formidable armament was destined by Vaudreuil, the governor of Canada, against New England. This enterprise was not fully prosecuted, in consequence of the failure of several Indian tribes to furnish the number of warriors expected from them. A considerable force, however penetrated into Massachusetts, and burnt a part of the town of Haverhill; where about one hundred persons were killed and many others carried off as prisoners. These invaders were pursued and overtaken by a body of troops collected in the neighbourhood, who killed a few of them, and recovered several of their own countrymen.

Incursion into Massachusetts.

The new England colonies, still attributing all these calamities to the French were earnest in their solicitations to the crown, for aids which might enable them to conquer Canada. Their application was supported by the representations of Francis Nicholson, who had been lieutenant governor, first of New York, and afterward of Virginia; of Samuel Veitch, a trader to Nova Scotia, and of colonel Schuyler, a gentleman of great influence in New York, who undertook a voyage to England for the purpose of communicating his sentiments more fully to administration, and carried with him resolutions of the assembly, expressing the high opinion that body entertained of his merit. Influenced by these representations, the British cabinet determined to undertake an expedition against the French settlements on the continent of North America, and on New Foundland, to consist of a squadron, having on board five regiments of regular troops, which were to be at Boston by the middle of May, 1709, where they were to be joined by twelve hundred men to be raised in Massachusetts and Rhode Island. Fifteen hundred men also were to be raised in the governments south of Rhode Island, who should proceed, by the way of lake Champlain, against Montreal. All the colonies, except Pennsylvania, executed with punctuality the part assigned to them. Nicholson, who was appointed to command the troops destined against Montreal, marched to Wood creek, where he was ordered to continue, until the arrival of the forces from Europe; that the two armies might co-operate with each other. The New England troops, who had been assembled at Boston remained at that place till September, expecting the arrival of the fleet and army from England. About that time, Nicholson returned from Wood creek, and it was obviously too late to proceed against Quebec. A meeting of the commanding officers, and governors of provinces was requested, in order to deliberate on future operations. A few days before this meeting was to take place, a ship arrived from England, with the intelligence that the armament intended for America had been ordered to Portugal, and with directions to hold a council of war, in order to determine on the propriety of employing the troops raised in America, against Port Royal; in which event the ships of war then at Boston were to aid the expedition. The commanders of the ships, except captain, afterwards admiral, Matthews, refused to engage in this service; and, it being unsafe to proceed without convoy, the men were disbanded.*

A congress, composed of governors, and of delegates from several of the assemblies, met at Rhode Island, and recommended the appointment of agents to assist colonel Nicholson in representing the state of the country to the Queen, and soliciting troops for an expedition against Canada, the next spring. Government seems at first to have thought favourably of this proposal, but finally determined to proceed only against Port Royal. Five frigates and a bomb ketch, which were assigned for this service, arrived with Nicholson, in July. Although the troops were then to be raised, the whole armament, consisting of one regiment of marines, and four regiments of infantry, sailed from Boston the 18th of September; and, on the 24th arrived before Port Royal. The place was immediately invested, and, after the exchange of a few

* Belknap. Hutchinson.

shot and shells, was surrendered. Vietch was appointed governor, and its name, in compliment to the Queen, was changed to Annapolis.

After the reduction of Port Royal, Nicholson returned to England to renew the often repeated solicitations for an expedition against Canada. The ministry was now changed; and the colonists despaired of obtaining from those in power, any aids against the French. Contrary to the general expectation, his application succeeded; and he arrived at Boston, in June, with orders to the governors as far south as Pennsylvania, to get their quotas of men and provisions in readiness to act with the fleet and army expected from Europe. Within sixteen days, while the several governors were yet deliberating on the subject of these orders, the fleet arrived. The service according perfectly with the wishes of the people as well as of the governors, every practicable exertion was made; and difficulties were overcome which, on other occasions, might have been deemed insurmountable. To supply the money which the English treasury could not then advance, the general court of Massachusetts issued bills of credit to the amount of forty thousand pounds; and the example was followed by Connecticut, New York, and New Jersey. Provisions were obtained by impressment.

The army consisted of seven veteran regiments, who had served under the duke of Marlborough; one regiment of marines; and two regiments of provincials; amounting, in the whole, to six thousand five

CHAP VII.
1711.

hundred men; a force equal to that which afterwards reduced Quebec, when in a much better state of defence. This armament sailed from Boston on the 30th of July. Their sanguine hopes were all blasted in one fatal night. On the 23d of August, in the river St. Lawrence, the weather being thick and dark, eight transports were wrecked on Egg Island, near the north shore, and one thousand persons perished. The next day the fleet put back, and was eight days beating down the river against an easterly wind, which, in two, would have carried it to Quebec. After holding a fruitless consultation respecting an attempt on Placentia, the expedition was abandoned; and the squadron sailed for England. Loud complaints were made, and heavy charges reciprocated, on this occasion. The ignorance of the pilots, the obstinacy of the admiral, the detention of the fleet at Boston, its late arrival there, the want of seasonable orders, and the secret intentions of the ministry, were all subjects of bitter altercation; but no regular inquiry was ever made into the causes of the miscarriage.

The plan of this campaign embraced also an attack on Montreal. Four thousand men raised in Connecticut, New York, and New Jersey, and commanded by colonel Nicholson, marched against that place by the way of Albany and lake Champlain. The failure of the expedition against Quebec enabling the governor of Canada to turn his whole force towards the lakes, Nicholson was under the necessity of making a precipitate retreat.

No other event of importance took place during this war, which was terminated by the treaty of Utrecht. By the 12th article of this treaty, France ceded to England " all Nova Scotia or Acadié, with its ancient boundaries, as also the city of Port Royal, now called Annapolis Royal, and all other things in those parts which depend on the said lands." This territory, which had been comprehended in the grant made to the Plymouth company, was, with the consent of that company, afterwards granted by James as King of Scotland, under the name of Nova Scotia, to sir William Alexander.

In New York, the Leislerian and anti-Leislerian parties continued to persecute each other. To this calamity was added, in the year 1702, the still heavier affliction of a malignant fever, imported in a vessel from the West Indies, which, in almost every instance, proved mortal. A similar disease raged, about the same time, in several other sea port towns; and was probably the same which has since produced such fatal effects under the name of the yellow fever.

In the same year, lord Cornbury, a needy and profligate nobleman, was appointed governor of the province. He embraced the anti-Leislerian party, that being then the strongest. On meeting the assembly, he urged the necessity of providing money for the public exigencies; and, as he had arranged himself with the ruling party, the vote of supply was liberal.

It was soon perceived that the confidence in the governor was misplaced. Considerable sums levied for objects of great interest, were applied to his private use. The system adopted in New York, for collecting and keeping public money, was calculated to favour this peculation. The colony having no treasurer, its revenue came into the hands of the receiver general for the crown, whence it was drawn by a warrant from the governor. Contests soon arose, between his lordship and the legislature, on the subject of money; the house requiring a statement of disbursements, and the appointment of a treasurer, to be controled by them. At length, in 1706, an act was passed raising three thousand pounds for fortifications, and directing the money to be placed in the hands of a person named by the legislature. The assent of the governor to this act was not given till the succeeding year, and was then accompanied with a message stating, that he had it in command from the Queen " to permit the general assembly to name their own treasurer when they raised extraordinary supplies for particular uses and which are no part of the standing and constant revenue."

The continual demands of the governor for money, his misapplication of it, his extortion in the form of fees, and his haughty tyrannical conduct increased the irritation subsisting between him and the legislature. At length, the Queen yielded to the complaints of both New York and New Jersey, and consented to recal him.

During these altercations, some spirited resolutions were entered into by the assembly; one of which claims particular notice. It is in these words. "Resolved, that the imposing and levying of any monies upon her majesty's subjects in this colony, under any pretence or colour whatsoever, without their consent in general assembly, is a grievance, and violation of the people's property."

This strong assertion of a principle, which afterwards dismembered the British empire, then passed away without notice. It was probably understood to be directed only against the assumption of that power by the governor.*

In Carolina, the vexatious contests with the proprietors still continued. The public attention was, for a time diverted from these, by hostilities with their neighbours of Florida. Before the declaration of war made against France and Spain, had been officially communicated, it was reported in the colonies that this event had taken place, and Mr. Moore, the governor of the southern settlements, proposed to the assembly an expedition against St. Augustine. Temperate men were opposed to this enterprise; but the

---

* So early as the year 1692, the difference of opinion between the mother country and the colonies on the great point, which afterwards separated them, made its appearance. The legislature of Massachusetts, employed in establishing a code of laws under their new charter, passed an act containing the general principles respecting the liberty of the subject, that are asserted in *magna charta*, in which was the memorable clause, "no aid, tax, tallage, assessment, custom, benevolence, or imposition whatsoever, shall be laid, assessed, imposed, or levied, on any of his majesty's subjects or their estates, on any pretence whatsoever, but by the act and consent of the governor, council, and representatives of the people, assembled in general court."

It is scarcely necessary to add that the royal assent to this act was refused.

CHAP. VII.
1702.

assurances of the governor, that Florida would be an easy conquest, and that immense treasure would be the reward of their valour, were too seductive to be resisted. A great majority of the assembly declared in favour of the expedition, and voted the sum of two thousand pounds sterling for its prosecution. Six hundred militia were embodied for the service, and an equal number of Indians engaged as auxiliaries.

Expedition against St. Augustine.

In the plan of operations which had been concerted, colonel Daniel was to move by the inland passage, with a party of militia and Indians, and attack the town by land; while the governor, with the main body should proceed by sea, and block up the harbour. Colonel Daniel executed his part of the plan with promptitude and vigour. He advanced against the town, which he entered and plundered before the governor reached the harbour. The Spaniards, however, had been apprised of the preparations making at Charleston, and had laid up provisions for four months, in the castle, into which they retired, as Daniel entered the town. On the arrival of the governor, the place was completely invested; but, it being impossible to carry the castle without battering artillery, colonel Daniel was dispatched to Jamaica for cannon, bombs, and mortars. During his absence, two small Spanish vessels of war were seen off the mouth of the harbour; upon which the governor raised the siege, abandoned his transports, and made a precipitate retreat to Carolina. Colonel Daniel returned soon afterwards, and, having no suspicion that the siege was raised, stood in for the harbour. He fortunately discovered his situation in time to escape, though with much difficulty."

CHAP. VII.
1702.

This rash and ill conducted expedition entailed on the colony a debt of six thousand pounds sterling. The ignominy attached to it was soon wiped off by one that was attended with better success. The Appalachian Indians, who were attached to the Spaniards, had become extremely troublesome to the inhabitants of the frontiers. The governor, at the head of a body of militia and friendly Indians, marched into the heart of their settlements, laid their towns in ashes, made several prisoners, and compelled them to sue for peace, and submit to the British government.*

Soon after this transaction, sir Nathaniel Johnson, who had been appointed to succeed Mr. Moor arrived in Charleston. He endeavoured, but ineffectually to turn the attention of the colonists to the culture of silk. This article, as well as cotton was neglected, and rice became the great staple of the country.

Governor Johnson.

During his administration, the contests between the proprietors and the people increased. An attempt to establish the Episcopal church was added to other pre-existing causes of discord. The colony having been settled by emigrants from different nations, of different religious persuasions, the indiscreet endeavour to produce uniformity, could not fail to increase their irritation. The influence of the governor in the legislature obtained the passage of such acts as were

Attempt to establish the Episcopal church.

* History of South Carolina.

D d

CHAP. VII.
1702.

assurances of the governor, that Florida would be an easy conquest, and that immense treasure would be the reward of their valour, were too seductive to be resisted. A great majority of the assembly declared in favour of the expedition, and voted the sum of two thousand pounds sterling for its prosecution. Six hundred militia were embodied for the service, and an equal number of Indians engaged as auxiliaries.

Expedition against St. Augustine.

In the plan of operations which had been concerted, colonel Daniel was to move by the inland passage, with a party of militia and Indians, and attack the town by land; while the governor, with the main body should proceed by sea, and block up the harbour. Colonel Daniel executed his part of the plan with promptitude and vigour. He advanced against the town, which he entered and plundered before the governor reached the harbour. The Spaniards, however, had been apprised of the preparations making at Charleston, and had laid up provisions for four months, in the castle, into which they retired, as Daniel entered the town. On the arrival of the governor, the place was completely invested; but, it being impossible to carry the castle without battering artillery, colonel Daniel was dispatched to Jamaica for cannon, bombs, and mortars. During his absence, two small Spanish vessels of war were seen off the mouth of the harbour; upon which the governor raised the siege, abandoned his transports, and made a precipitate retreat to Carolina. Colonel Daniel returned soon afterwards, and, having no suspicion that the siege was raised, stood in for the harbour. He fortunately discovered his situation in time to escape, though with much difficulty."

<small>CHAP. VII.
1702.</small>

This rash and ill conducted expedition entailed on the colony a debt of six thousand pounds sterling. The ignominy attached to it was soon wiped off by one that was attended with better success. The Appalachian Indians, who were attached to the Spaniards, had become extremely troublesome to the inhabitants of the frontiers. The governor, at the head of a body of militia and friendly Indians, marched into the heart of their settlements, laid their towns in ashes, made several prisoners, and compelled them to sue for peace, and submit to the British government.*

Soon after this transaction, sir Nathaniel Johnson, who had been appointed to succeed Mr. Moor arrived in Charleston. He endeavoured, but ineffectually to turn the attention of the colonists to the culture of silk. This article, as well as cotton was neglected, and rice became the great staple of the country. <small>Governor Johnson.</small>

During his administration, the contests between the proprietors and the people increased. An attempt to establish the Episcopal church was added to other pre-existing causes of discord. The colony having been settled by emigrants from different nations, of different religious persuasions, the indiscreet endeavour to produce uniformity, could not fail to increase their irritation. The influence of the governor in the legislature obtained the passage of such acts as were <small>Attempt to establish the Episcopal church.</small>

* History of South Carolina.

CHAP. VII.
1702.

necessary for his purpose; but many petitions against them were laid before parliament; and the house of lords presented so decisive an address to her majesty on the subject, that a writ of *quo warranto* against the charter was directed. This measure, however, was not put in execution; and the attention of the colonists was diverted, for a time, from these intestine broils, by the appearance of danger from abroad.

1704.

Spain claimed the whole country, as part of Florida; and was preparing an expedition to enforce this claim. Governor Johnson, who had acquired some military skill in European service, having received intelligence of these preparations, made great exertions to fortify the entrance into the harbour of Charleston, and to put the province in a state of defence.

There was reason to rejoice that these precautions were used; for, although no armament arrived from Europe, yet an expedition planned in the Havanna, was carried into execution.

Colony invaded.

A French frigate and four armed Spanish sloops, commanded by Monsieur Le Febour, sailed for Charleston, with orders to touch at St. Augustine for men. His force is said to have amounted to about eight hundred. A government cruizer descried this squadron off the bar of St. Augustine, and brought the intelligence to Charleston. Scarcely had the captain delivered his information, when signals from Sullivan's island announced its appearance off the coast. The alarm was immediately given, and the militia of the town were under arms. In the evening the fleet reached Charleston bar, but deferred attempting to pass it until the morning.

After consuming a day in sounding the south bar, the Spanish flotilla crossed it, and anchored above Sullivan's island. The governor then directed some pieces of heavy artillery to be placed in the vessels in the harbour; and gave the command of them to William Rhet. A summons to surrender being rejected, a party of the enemy landed on James' island, and burnt a few houses. Another party, consisting of one hundred and sixty men, landed, about the same time, on the opposite side of the river. Both these were attacked and defeated.

Encouraged by this success, Johnson determined to attack the invaders by sea. In execution of this determination, Rhet, with six small vessels, proceeded down the river to the place where the hostile flotilla rode at anchor which, at his approach, precipitately re-crossed the bar. For some days it was believed that the enterprise was abandoned; but while the inhabitants were rejoicing at their deliverance, advice was received that a ship of force had been seen in Sewee bay, and had landed a number of men. On examining his prisoners, the governor was informed that the enemy had expected a ship of war with a reinforcement of two hundred men, under the command of Monsieur Arbuset. Taking his measures with the promptness of an experienced officer, he ordered captain Fenwick to pass the river, and march against the detachment which had landed; while Rhet, with

CHAP VII.
1704

two small armed vessels, sailed round by sea, with orders to meet the ship in Sewee bay. Fenwick came up with the party on shore, charged them briskly, and drove them to their ship, which, on the appearance of Rhet, surrendered without firing a shot. The prize, with about ninety prisoners was brought up to Charleston.

Thus was terminated with the loss of near three hundred men killed and prisoners, among the latter of whom were the general and some naval officers, the invasion of Carolina by Monsieur Le Febour. It seems to have been undertaken in the confidence that the colony was too weak for resistance; and was conducted without skill or courage.

Bills of credit.

To defray the expenses incurred in repelling this invasion, bills of credit to the amount of eight thousand pounds were issued. The effect of this emission was such a depreciation of the currency under the form of a rise in the price of commodities and of exchange, that one hundred and fifty pounds in paper, were given for one hundred pounds sterling.

1707.

Lord Granville, the palatine, a bigoted churchman, under whose influence violent measures had been taken for the establishment of religious conformity in Carolina, died in the year 1707. He was succeeded by lord Craven, who, though of the same religious tenets, supported them with moderation. His disposition to indulge, and thereby mollify, the dissenters, was considered by the zealots of the established church, as endangering religion; and the legislature, which was elected under the influence of the late palatine, and of his governor, dreading a change in the administration, adopted the extraordinary measure of continuing itself " for two years, and for the time and term of eighteen months after the change of government, whether by the death of the present governor, or the succession of another in his time."* Thus adding one other humiliating proof to those which perpetually occur, that principles are deplorably weak, when opposed by the passions.

CHAP. VII.
1707.

1708.
Legislature continues itself.

In the year 1712, the Indians in North Carolina, alarmed, as their countrymen had been in the other colonies, by the encreasing population and regular encroachments of the whites, formed with their accustomed secrecy, the plan of exterminating in one night these formidable neighbours. No indication of their design was given until they broke into the houses of the planters. The slaughter on Roanoke was immense. In that settlement alone, one hundred and thirty-seven persons were murdered. A few escaped by concealing themselves in the woods, who, the next day, gave the alarm. The remaining whites were collected together in a place of safety, and guarded by the militia until assistance could be received from South Carolina.

1712.

Massacre in North Carolina by the Indians.

This was prompt and effectual. The assembly at Charleston voted four thousand pounds for the service; and colonel Barnwell was detached with six hundred militia, and three hundred and sixty Indians,

* Chalmer.

CHAP. VII
1712.

to the relief of the afflicted North Carolinians. With the utmost celerity he passed through the difficult and dangerous wilderness which then separated the northern from the southern settlements; and, attack-

Indians defeated.

ing the savages with unexpected fury, killed three hundred of them, and made one hundred prisoners. The survivors retreated to the Tuscorora town, and took refuge within a wooden breast-work, in which they were surrounded by the whites. After sustaining considerable loss, they sued for peace and obtained it; but soon afterwards abandoned their country, and united themselves with the Iroquois, or Five nations.

The expense of this expedition greatly transcended the scanty means of South Carolina. To supply the exigencies of government, and to promote the convenience of commerce, the legislature determined to issue forty-eight thousand pounds in bills of credit, to be denominated bank bills. This money was to be lent out, at interest, on security, and to be redeemed gradually by the annual payment of one-twelfth part of the sum loaned. The bills were made a legal tender; and the creditor who should refuse them, lost his debt.

After the emission of these bills, exchange rose, the first year, to one hundred and fifty, and in the second to two hundred per centum, above par. The effect of this depreciation, and of the tender laws which accompanied it, on creditors, and on morals, was obvious and certain.

CHAPTER VIII.

Proceedings of the legislature of Massachusetts.—Intrigues of the French among the Indians.—War with the savages.—Peace.—Controversy with the governor.—Decided in England.—Contests concerning the governor's salary.—The assembly adjourned to Salem.—Contest concerning the salary terminated.—Great depreciation of the paper currency.—Scheme of a land bank.—Company dissolved by act of Parliament.—Governor Shirley arrives.—Review of transactions in New York.

THE heavy expenses of Massachusetts during the late war had produced such large emissions of paper money, that a considerable depreciation took place, and specie disappeared. The consequent rise of exchange, instead of being attributed to its true cause, was ascribed to the decay of trade.

The colony, having now leisure for its domestic concerns, turned its attention to this interesting subject.

Three parties were formed. The first, a small one, actuated by the principle that "honesty is the best policy," was in favour of calling in the paper money, and relying on the industry of the people, to replace it with a circulating medium of greater stability.

1714.

Affairs of Massachusetts.

The second proposed a private bank, which was to issue bills of credit, to be received by all the members of the company, but at no certain value compared with gold and silver. It was not intended to deposit specie in the bank for the redemption of its notes as they might be offered; but to pledge real estates as security that the company would perform its engagements.

The third party was in favour of a loan of bills from the government, to any of the inhabitants who would mortgage real estate to secure their re-payment in a specified term of years; the interest to be paid annually, and applied to the support of government.

The first party, perceiving its numerical weakness, joined the third; and the whole province was divided between a public and private bank.

At length, the party for the public bank prevailed in the general court, and fifty thousand pounds were issued and placed in the hands of trustees; to be lent for five years, at an interest of five *per centum per annum*, one-fifth part of the principal to be paid annually.

This scheme failing to improve the commerce of the colony, governor Shute, who had succeeded Dudley, reminded the assembly of the bad state of trade, which he ascribed to the scarcity of money; and recommended the consideration of some effectual measures to supply this want. The result of this recommendation was a second loan of one hundred thousand pounds for ten years, to be placed in the hands of commissioners in each county, in proportion to its taxes. The whole currency soon depreciated to such a degree, that the entire sum in circulation did not represent more real value, than was represented by that which was circulating before the emission. The governor had now sufficient leisure, and the general court furnished him with sufficient motives, to reflect on the policy he had recommended. An attempt to raise his salary as money depreciated, did not succeed, and only the usual nominal sum was voted for his support.

In Massachusetts, peace abroad was the signal for dissention at home. Independent in her opinions and habits, she had been accustomed to consider herself rather as a sister kingdom, acknowledging one common sovereign with England, than as a colony. The election of all the branches of the legislature, a principle common to New England, contributed, especially while the mother country was occupied with her own internal divisions, to nourish these opinions and habits. Although the new charter of Massachusetts modified the independence of that colony, by vesting the appointment of the governor in the crown, yet the course of thinking which had prevailed from the settlement of the country, had gained too much strength to be immediately changed; and Massachusetts sought, by private influence over her chief magistrate, to compensate herself for the loss of his appointment. With this view, it had become usual for the general court to testify its satisfaction with his conduct by

CHAP. VIII
1719.

presents; and this measure was also adopted in other colonies.

Apprehending that this practice might dispose the governors to conciliate the legislatures at the expense of their duty to the crown, the Queen had given peremptory orders to receive no more gifts; and to obtain acts fixing their salaries permanently at a sum named by herself. The mandate respecting presents was, of course, obeyed; and some of the colonies complied with the requisition respecting the salary; but in Massachusetts and New York, it was steadily resisted.

A controling power over salaries was a source of influence which was pertinaciously maintained; and its efficay was tried in all the conflicts between Massachusetts and her Governor. Almost every important measure brought before the legislature, was productive of contests between these departments. They disagreed, not only on the policy of particular acts, but on the limits of their power. The Governor claimed the right of negativing the speaker chosen by the representatives, which was denied by them; and, each party persisting in its pretensions, the assembly was dissolved, and new elections took place. The same members being generally re-chosen, the house of representatives assembled with increased irritation, and passed some angry resolutions respecting its dissolution. The governor, in turn, charged the house with encroachments on the power of the executive; among other instances of which, he men-

1720.

tioned certain resolutions passed on the commencement of hostilities by the Indians, which were deemed equivalent to a declaration of war, and had therefore been rejected.

Disagreements were multiplied between them. Paper money and trade were inexhaustible sources of discontent. New elections produced no change of temper. After war was formally declared against the Indians, the house endeavoured to exercise executive powers in its prosecution; and, the council not concurring with them, the representatives attempted, in one instance, to act alone.

The measures recommended by the governor to successive assemblies, were disregarded; irritating resolves were adopted and reiterated; and a course of angry crimination and recrimination took place between them in the progress of which the governor's salary was reduced in its nominal as well as real amount; and the sum granted, instead of being voted, as had been usual, at the commencement of the session, was reserved to its close.

In the midst of these contests, governor Shute, who had privately solicited and obtained leave to return to England, suddenly embarked on board the Sea Horse man of war, leaving the controversy concerning the extent of the executive power, to devolve on the lieutenant governor.*

The house of representatives persisted in asserting its control over objects which had been deemed with-

* Hutchison.

in the province of the executive; but its resolutions were generally negatived by the council. This produced some altercation between the two branches of the legislature; but they at length united in the passage of a resolution desiring their agent in England to take the best measures for protecting the interests of the colony, which were believed to be in danger from the representations of governor Shute.

Intrigues of the French with the Indians.

During these contests in the interior, the frontiers had suffered severely from the depredations of the Indians. The French had acquired great influence over all the eastern tribes. Jesuit missionaries generally resided among them, who obtained a great ascendancy in their councils. After the cession of Nova Scotia to Great Britain, father Rahlé, a missionary residing among the savages of that province exerted successfully, all his address to excite their jealousies and resentments against the English. By his acts, and those of other missionaries, all the eastern Indians, as well as those of Canada, were combined against New England. They made incursions into Massachusetts, in consequence of which, some troops were detached to the village in which Rahlé resided, for the purpose of seizing his person. He received intimation of their approach in time to make his escape; but they secured his papers, among which were some showing that in exciting the savages to war against the English colonists, he had acted under the authority of the governor of Canada, who had secretly promised to supply them with arms and ammunition.

Envoys were deputed with a remonstrance against conduct so incompatible with the state of peace then subsisting between France and England. The governor received this embassy politely, and, at first, denied any interference in the quarrel, alleging that the Indians were independent nations who made war and peace without being controled by him. On being shown his letters to Rahlé, he changed his language, and gave assurances of his future good offices in effecting a peace. On the faith of these assurances, conferences were held with some Indian chiefs then in Canada; several captives were ransomed; and, soon after the return of the commissioners to New England, the war was terminated by a treaty of peace signed at Boston.*

Meanwhile the complaints of governor Shute against the house of representatives were heard in England. Every question was decided against the house. In most of them, the existing charter was deemed sufficiently explicit; but, on two points, it was thought advisable to have explanatory articles. These were, the right of the governor to negative the appointment of the speaker, and the right of the house on the subject of adjournment. An explanatory charter therefore passed the seals, affirming the power claimed by the governor to negative a speaker, and denying to the house of representatives the right of ad-

* Hutchison. Belknap.

CHAP VIII journing itself for a longer time than two days. This
1726. charter was submitted to the general court, to be accepted or refused; but it was accompanied with the intimation that, in the event of its being refused, the whole controversy between the governor and house of representatives would be laid before Parliament. The conduct of the representatives had been so generally condemned in England, as to excite fears that an act to vacate the charter, would be the consequence of a parliamentary inquiry. The temper of the house too had undergone a change. The violence and irritation which marked its proceedings in the contest with governor Shute had subsided; and a majority determined to accept the New charter.

The trade of the province still languished, and complaints of the scarcity of money were as loud as
1727. when only specie was in circulation. To remedy these evils, a bill for emitting a farther sum in paper passed both houses, but was rejected by the lieutenant governor, as being inconsistent with his instructions. The house of representatives, thereupon, postponed the consideration of salaries till the next session. The assembly was then adjourned at its own request, and, after a recess of a fortnight, was again convened. As an expedient to elude the instructions to the governor which interdicted his assent to any act for issuing bills of credit, except for charges of government, a bill passed with the title of " an act for raising and settling a public revenue for and towards defraying the necessary charges of government, by

an emission of sixty thousand pounds in bills of credit." This bill providing for the payment of the salaries to which several members of the council were entitled, passed that house also; and the lieutenant governor gave a reluctant assent to it. Its passage into a law furnishes strong evidence of the influence which the control over salaries gave to the house of representatives.

Mr. Burnet who had been appointed governor of Massachusetts and New Hampshire, was received with great pomp in Boston. At the first meeting of the assembly, he stated the King's instructions to insist on an established salary, and his intention firmly to adhere to them. The assembly was not less firm in its determination to resist this demand; and, that no additional and unnecessary obloquy might be encountered, resolved, not to mingle any difference concerning the amount of the salary, with the great question of its depending on the will of the legislature. As soon therefore as the compliments usual on the arrival of a governor had passed, the house voted one thousand seven hundred pounds towards his support, and to defray the charges of his journey. This vote was understood to give him, as a present salary, a sum equal to one thousand pounds sterling per annum. The governor declared his inability to assent to this bill, it being inconsistent with his instructions. After a week's deliberation, the assembly granted three hundred pounds for the expenses of his journey, which he accepted; and, in a distinct vote, the farther,

CHAP VIII 1728. sum of one thousand four hundred pounds was granted toward his support. The latter vote was accompanied with a joint message from both houses, wherein they asserted their undoubted right as Englishmen, and their privilege by the charter, to raise and apply money for the support of government; and their willingness to give the governor an ample and honourable support; but they apprehended it would be most for his majesty's service to do so without establishing a fixed salary. The governor returned an answer on the same day, in which he said, that, if they really intended to give him an ample and honourable support, they could have no just objection to making their purpose effectual by fixing his salary; for he would never accept a grant of the kind then offered.

The council was disposed to avoid the contest, and to grant a salary to the present governor for a certain time; but the house of representatives, remaining firm to its purpose, sent a message to the governor requesting that the court might rise. He answered, that a compliance with this request would put it out of the power of the legislature to pay immediate regard to the King's instructions; and he would not grant a recess, until the business of the session should be finished. The representatives then declared that, " in faithfulness to the people, they could not come into an act for establishing a salary on the governor or commander in chief for the time being," and, therefore, renewed their request that the court might rise.

Both the governor and the house of representatives

seem, thus far, to have made their declarations with some reserve. A salary during his own administration might, perhaps, have satisfied him, though he demanded that one should be settled, generally, on the commander in chief for the time being; and the house had not yet declared against settling a salary on him for a limited time. Each desired that the other should make some concession. Both declined; both were irritated by long altercation; and, at length, instead of mutually advancing, fixed at the opposite extremes. After several ineffectual efforts on each side, the representatives sent a message to the governor, stating at large the motives which induced the resolution they had formed. The governor returned a prompt answer, in which he also detailed the reasons in support of the demand he had made. These two papers, manifesting the principles and objects of both parties, deserve attention even at this period.

The house, not long after receiving this message, far from making any advances towards a compliance with his request, came to two resolutions strongly expressive of its determination not to recede from the ground which had been taken.

These resolutions gave the first indication, on the part of the representatives, of a fixed purpose to make no advance towards a compromise. They induced the governor to remind the court of the danger to which the proceedings of that body might expose the charter. This caution did not deter the house from preparing, and transmitting to the several towns of the province a statement of the controversy, which concludes with saying " we dare neither come into a fixed salary on the governor for ever, nor for a limited time, for the following reasons :

First, Because it is an untrodden path which neither we, nor out predecessors have gone in, and we cannot certainly foresee the many dangers that may be in it, nor can we depart from that way which has been found safe and comfortable.

Secondly, Because it is the undoubted right of all Englishmen, by *magna charta*, to raise and dispose of money for the public service, of their own free accord, without compulsion.

Thirdly, Because it must necessarily lessen the dignity and freedom of the house of representatives, in making acts, and raising and applying taxes, &c. and, consequently, cannot be thought a proper method to preserve that balance in the three branches of the legislature, which seems necessary to form, maintain, and uphold, the constitution.

Fourthly, Because the charter fully empowers the general assembly to make such laws and orders as they shall judge for the good and welfare of the inhabitants ; and if they, or any part of them, judge this not to be for their good, they neither ought nor could come into it, for, as to act beyond or without the powers granted in the charter might justly incur the King's displeasure, so not to act up and agreeable to those powers, might justly be deemed a betraying of the rights and privileges therein granted ; and if they should give up this right, they would open a door to many other inconveniences."

Many messages passed in quick succession between the governor and the house, in the course of which the arguments stated in the papers which have been mentioned, were enlarged and diversified. At length, the house repeated its request for an adjournment; but the governor replied that " unless his majesty's pleasure had due weight with them, their desires would have very little with him."

The council now interposed with a resolution declaring " that it is expedient for the court to ascertain a sum as a salary for his excellency's support, as also the term of time for its continuance." This resolution was transmitted to the house of representatives, and immediately rejected.

After much controversy, a small seeming advance towards an accommodation was made. Instead of voting a salary, as had been usual, for half a year, a grant was made to the governor of three thousand pounds, equal to one thousand pounds sterling, to enable him to manage the affairs of the province. This was generally understood to be a salary for a year. The governor having withheld his assent from this vote, the house intreated him to accept the grant; and added " we cannot doubt but that succeeding assemblies, according to the ability of the province, will be very ready to grant as ample a support; and if they should not, your excellency will then have an opportunity of showing your resentment." The governor

CHAP. VIII 1728. however persisted to withhold his assent from the vote.

The colony generally, and especially Boston, was opposed to a compliance with the instructions of the crown. At a general meeting of the inhabitants, the town passed a vote, purporting to be unanimous against fixing a salary on the governor. In couse-quence of this vote, and of an opinion that the members of the house were influenced by the inhabitants of the town, the governor determined to change the place at which the court should hold its session; and on the 24th of October, adjourned it to the 30th then to meet at Salem, in the county of Essex.

Adjourn-ment of the assembly to Salem.

Change of place did not change the temper of the house. This was not, as in the contests with governor Shute, an angry altercation, into which the representatives were precipitated by a restless and encroaching temper, but a solemn and deliberate stand, made in defence of a right believed to be unquestionable, and of a principle deemed essential to the welfare of the colony. The ground taken was considered well, and maintained with firmness. Votes and messages of the same tenor with those which had been often repeated, continued to pass between the representatives and the governor, until the subject was entirely exhausted. Each party being determined to adhere to its principles, the house met and adjourned daily, without entering on business.

In the mean time, the governor received no salary. To the members of Boston, who had not been accustomed to the expense of attending the legislature at a distant place, a compensation, above their ordinary wages, was made by that town.

The house, firmly persuaded of the propriety of its conduct, prepared a memorial to the King praying a change in the royal instructions to the governor. Agents were appointed to represent the general court in England, and a vote was passed for defraying the expenses attendant on the business. The council refused to concur in this vote, because the agents had been appointed by the house of representatives singly; and the measure must have been abandoned for want of money, had not the inhabitants of Boston raised the sum required, by subscription.

Letters were soon received from these agents, inclosing a report from the board of trade, before whom they had been heard by council, entirely disapproving the conduct of the house. The letters also indicated that, should the house persist in its refusal to comply with the King's instructions, the affair might be carried before parliament. But, should even this happen, the agents thought it more advisable that the salary should be fixed by the supreme legislature, than by that of the province. "It was better," they said, "that the liberties of the people should be taken from them, than given up by themselves."

The governor, at length, refused to sign a warrant on the treasury for the wages of the members. "One branch of the legislature, he said, might as well go without their pay as the other." The act,

CHAP. VIII
1729.

Death of governor Burnet.

1730. Arrival of governor Belcher.

and the reason for it, were alike unsatisfactory to the house.

After a recess from the 20th of December to the 2d of April, the general court met again at Salem. Repeated meetings at that place having produced no accommodation, the governor adjourned the legislature to Cambridge. A few days after the commencement of the session, he was seized with a fever, of which he died.

Mr. Burnet is said to have possessed many valuable qualities; and, had he not been engaged, by a sense of duty, in this long contest, he would, in all probability, have been a favourite of the province.*

Mr. Belcher, who succeeded Burnet, arrived at Boston early in August where he was cordially received. At the first meeting of the general court, he pressed the establishment of a permanent salary, and laid before them his instructions, in which it was declared that, in the event of the continued refusal of the assembly, " his majesty will find himself under the necessity of laying the undutiful behaviour of the province before the legislature of Great Britain, not only in this single instance, but in many others of the same nature and tendency, whereby it manifestly appears that this assembly, for some years last past, have attempted, by unwarrantable practices, to weaken, if not cast off, the obedience they owe to the crown, and the dependence which all colonies ought to have on the mother country."

* Hutchison.

At the close of these instructions, his majesty added his expectation, "that they do forthwith comply with this proposal, as the last signification of our royal pleasure to them on this subject, and if the said assembly shall not think fit to comply therewith, it is our will and pleasure, and you are required, immediately, to come over to this kingdom of Great Britain, in order to give us an exact account of all that shall have passed on this subject, that we may lay the same before our parliament."

The house proceeded, as in the case of governor Burnet, to make a grant to Mr. Belcher of one thousand pounds currency for defraying the expense of his voyage, and as a gratuity for his services while the agent of the colony in England; and, some time after, voted a sum equal to one thousand pounds sterling to enable him to manage the public affairs, &c.; but fixed no time for which the allowance was made. The council concurred in this vote, adding an amendment " and that the same sum be annually allowed for the governor's support." The house not agreeing to this amendment, the council carried it so as to read " that the same sum should be annually paid during his excellency's continuance in the government, and residence here." This also was disagreed to and the resolution fell.

The small-pox being in the town of Cambridge, the assembly was adjourned to Roxbury.

Two or three sessions passed with little more, on the part of the governor, than a repetition of his de-

CHAP. VIII
1730.

mand for a fixed salary, and an intimation that he should be obliged to return to England, and state the conduct of the house of representatives to the King. Some unsuccessful attempts were made by his friends to pass a bill fixing the salary during his administration, with a protest against the principle, and against that bill's being drawn into precedent. Failing in this expedient, and finding the house inflexible, he despaired of succeeding with that body, and turned his attention to the relaxation of his instructions.

1731.

He advised an address from the house to his majesty, praying that he might be permitted to receive the sum which the legislature had offered to grant him. This was allowed by the crown; with the understanding that he was still to insist on a compliance with his instructions. Leave to accept particular grants was obtained for two or three years successively; and, at length, a general permission was conceded to accept such sums as might be given by the assembly.*

Contest concerning the salary terminated.

Thus was terminated, the stubborn contest concerning a permanent salary for the governor. Its circumstances have been given more in detail than consists with the general plan of this work, because it is considered as exhibiting, in genuine colours, the character of the people engaged in it. It is regarded as an early and an honourable display of the same persevering temper in defence of principle, of the same unconquerable spirit of liberty, which at a later day,

* Hutchison.

and on a more important question, tore the British colonies from a country to which they had been strongly attached.

The immense quantity of depreciated paper which was in circulation throughout New England, had no tendency to diminish the complaints of the scarcity of money. Massachusetts and New Hampshire were restrained from farther emissions by the instructions to their governors, who received their appointments from the crown. Connecticut, engaged chiefly in agricultural pursuits, suffered less from this depreciated medium than her neighbours, and was less disposed to increase its evils. Rhode Island, equally commercial with Massachusetts, and equally fond of paper, chose her own governor, and might therefore indulge, without restraint, her passion for a system alike unfavourable to morals and to industry. That colony now issued one hundred thousand pounds on loan, to its inhabitants, for twenty years. The merchants of Boston, apprehensive that this capital would transfer the stock of Massachusetts to Rhode Island, associated against receiving the new emission; and many of them formed a company which issued one hundred and ten thousand pounds, redeemable with specie, in ten years, a tenth part annually, at the then current value of paper. The association against receiving the new emission of Rhode Island was not long observed.; and the bills of New Hampshire and Connecticut were also current. Silver immediately rose to twenty-seven shillings the ounce, and the notes

CHAP. VIII 1733. issued by the merchants soon disappeared, leaving in circulation only the government paper.

1739. Great uneasiness prevailed through Massachusetts on this subject. The last instalment of the bills would become due in 1741, and no power existed to redeem them by new emissions. Serious consequences were apprehended from calling in the circulating medium without substituting another in its place, and the alarm was increased by the circumstance that the taxes had been so lightly apportioned on the first years, as to require the imposition of heavy burdens for the redemption of what remained in circulation. The discontents excited by these causes were manifested in the elections, and were directed against the governor, who was openly hostile to the paper system.

Land bank. The projector of the bank again came forward; and, placing himself at the head of seven or eight hundred persons, some of whom possessed property, proposed to form a company which should issue one hundred and fifty thousand pounds in bills. By this scheme, every borrower of a sum larger than one hundred pounds, was to mortgage real estate to secure its re-payment. The borrowers of smaller sums might secure their re-payment either by mortgage, or by bond with two securities. Each subscriber, or partner was to pay, annually, three per centum interest on the sum he should take, and five per centum of the principal, either in the bills themselves, or in the produce and manufactures of the country, at such rates as the directors should, from time to time, establish.

CHAP V.
1739.

Although the favourers of this project were so successful at the elections as to obtain a great majority in the general court, men of fortune, and the principal merchants, refused to receive these bills. Many small traders, however, and other persons interested in the circulation of a depreciated currency, gave them credit. The directors themselves, it was said, became traders; and issued bills without limitation, and without giving security for their redemption. The governor, anticipating the pernicious effects of the institution, exerted all his influence against it. He displaced such executive officers as were members of it, and negatived the speaker, and thirteen members elected to the council, who were also of the company. General confusion being apprehended, application was made to parliament for an act to suppress the company. This being readily obtained, the company was dissolved, and the holders of the bills were allowed their action against its members, individually.*

1740.
Company dissolved.

About this time governor Belcher was re-called, and Mr. Shirley was appointed to succeed him. He found the land bank interest predominant in the house, and the treasury empty.

In this state of things, he deemed it necessary to depart from the letter of his instructions, in order to preserve their spirit. A bill was passed declaring that all contracts should be understood to be payable

1741.

* Hutchison.

CHAP. VIII
1741.

in silver at six shillings and eight pence the ounce, or in gold at its comparative value. Bills of a new form were issued, purporting to be for ounces of silver, which were to be received in payment of all debts, with this proviso, that if they should depreciate between the time of contract and of payment, a proportional addition should be made to the debt.

Affairs of New York.

While these transactions were passing in New England, symptoms of that jealousy which an unsettled boundary must produce between neighbours, began to show themselves in Canada and New York. The geographical situation of these colonies had, at an early period, directed the attention of both towards the commerce of the lakes. Mr. Burnet, the governor both of New York and New Jersey, impressed with the importance of acquiring the command of lake Ontario, had, in the year 1722, erected a trading house at Oswego in the country of the Senecas. This measure excited the jealousy of the French, who launched two vessels on the lake, and transported materials to Niagara for building a large store house, and for repairing the fort at that place. These proceedings were strongly opposed by the Senecas, and by the government of New York. Mr. Burnet remonstrated against them as encroachments on a British province, and also addressed administration on the subject. Complaints were made to the cabinet of Versailles; but the governor of Canada proceeded to complete the fort. To countervail the effects of a measure which he could not prevent, governor Burnet erected a fort at Oswego; soon after the building of which, while Mr. Vandam was governor of New York, the French took possession of Crown Point, which they fortified; and thus acquired the command of lake Champlain. Obviously as this measure was calculated to favour both the offensive and defensive operations of France in America, the English minister, after an unavailing remonstrance, submitted to it.

CHAPTER IX.

War with the southern Indians.—Dissatisfaction of Carolina with the proprietors.—Rupture with Spain. —Combination to subvert the proprietary government.—Revolution completed.—Expedition from the Havanna against Charleston.—Peace with Spain.— The proprietors surrender their interest to the crown. —The province divided.—Georgia settled.—Impolicy of the first regulations.—Intrigues of the Spaniards with the slaves of South Carolina.—Insurrection of the slaves.

1715.

IN Carolina, the contests between the inhabitants and the proprietors, added to the favour with which the Queen heard the complaints of the dissenters, had turned the attention of the people towards the crown, and produced a strong desire to substitute the regal, for the proprietary government. This desire was increased by an event which demonstrated the incompetency of their government.

War with the Indians.

The Yamassees, a powerful tribe of Indians on the north east of the Savanna, instigated by the Spaniards at St. Augustine, secretly prepared a general combination of all the southern Indians, against the province. Having massacred the traders settled among them, they advanced in great force against the southern frontier, spreading desolation and slaughter on their route. The inhabitants were driven into Charleston; and governor Craven proclaimed martial law. He also obtained an act of assembly empowering him to impress men; to seize arms, ammunition, and stores; to arm such negroes as could be trusted; and, generally, to prosecute the war with the utmost vigour. Agents were sent to Virginia and to England to solicit assistance, and bills were issued for the payment and subsistence of the army.

At the same time, the Indians entered the northern part of the province, and were within fifty miles of the capital. Thus surrounded by enemies, the governor took the course which was suggested equally by courage and by prudence. Leaving the less active part of the population to find security in the forts at Charleston, he marched with the militia, towards the southern frontier, which was invaded by the strongest body of Indians; and, at a place called Salt Catchers, attacked and totally defeated them. The victors pursued them into their own country, expelled them from it, and drove them over the Savanna river. The fugitives found protection in Florida, where they made a new settlement, from which they continued long afterwards, to make distressing incursions into Carolina.

The agent who had been sent by the legislature to England to implore the protection of the proprietors, had received ulterior instructions, should he not suc-

CHAP. IX.
1715.

ceed with them, to apply directly to the King. Being dissatisfied with his reception by the proprietors, he petitioned the house of commons, who addressed the King, praying his interposition, and immediate assistance to the colony. The King referred the matter to the lords commissioners of trade and plantations, whose report was unfavourable to the application, because the province of Carolina was a proprietary government. They were of opinion that, if the colony was to be protected at the expense of the nation, its government ought to be vested in the crown. On receiving this opinion, the proprietors, in a general meeting, avowed their inability to protect the province, and declared that, unless his majesty would graciously please to interpose, they could foresee nothing but the utter destruction of his faithful subjects in those parts.

A government unable to afford protection to the people, was ill adapted to the situation of Carolina.

The dissatisfaction growing out of this cause was still farther augmented by the unpopular, and, in some instances, unwise acts of the proprietors.

To relieve the distress produced by war, considerable sums of paper money had been issued; and the proprietors, on the complaint of the merchants, of London engaged in the trade of the province, had given instructions to reduce the quantity in circulation.

The assembly had appropriated the country of the Yamassees, to the use of such of his majesty's European subjects, as would settle it. Extracts from the law on this subject being published in England, and in Ireland, five hundred men from the latter kingdom emigrated to Carolina. The proprietors repealed this law; and, to the utter ruin of the emigrants, as well as to the destruction of this barrier against the savages, ordered the lands to be surveyed, and erected into baronies, for themselves.

While the population was confined to the neighbourhood of Charleston, all the members of the assembly had been elected at that place. As the settlements extended, this practice became inconvenient; and an act was passed, declaring that every parish should choose a certain number of representatives, and that the elections should be held, in each, at the parish church. As if to destroy themselves in the province, the proprietors repealed this popular law also.

Heavy expenses being still incurred for defence against the inroads of the southern Indians, the people complained loudly of the insufficiency of that government which, unable itself to protect them, prevented the interposition of the crown in their favour.

In this temper, governor Johnson, son of the former governor of that name, found the province. He met the assembly with a conciliatory speech, and received an answer expressing great satisfaction at his appointment. His original popularity was increased by the courage he displayed in two expeditions against a

H h

CHAP. IX. formidable band of pirates who had long infested the
1717. coast, which he entirely extirpated.

These expeditions occasioned still farther emissions of paper money. The governor, being instructed to diminish its quantity, had influence enough with the assembly to obtain an act for redeeming the bills of credit, in three years, by a tax on lands and negroes. This tax falling heavily on the planters, they sought to elude it by obtaining an act for a farther emission of bills. The proprietors, being informed of this design, and also of an intention to make the produce of the country a tender in payment of all debts, at a fixed value, enjoined the governor not to give his assent to any bill, until it should be laid before them.

About the same time, the King, by an order in council, signified his desire to the proprietors, that they would repeal an act passed in Carolina, for imposing a duty of ten per centum on all goods of British manufacture imported into the province. The repeal of this act, and of one declaring the right of the assembly to name a receiver of the public money, and of the election law, were transmitted to the governor, in a letter directing him to dissolve the assembly, and to hold a new election at Charleston, according to ancient usage.

1718. The assembly being employed in devising means for raising revenue, their dissolution was deferred; but the repeal of the law imposing duties, and the royal displeasure at the clause laying a duty on British manufactures, were immediately communicated, with a recommendation to pass another act, omitting that clause.

Meanwhile the governor's instructions were divulged. They excited great irritation; and produced a warm debate on the right of the proprietors to repeal a law enacted with the consent of their deputy in the province.

About this time, chief justice Trott, who had become extremely unpopular in the colony, was charged with many iniquitous proceedings; and the governor, the major part of the council, and the assembly, united in a memorial representing his mal-practices to the proprietors. Mr. Young was deputed their agent to enforce these complaints.

Soon after his arrival in London, he presented a memorial to the proprietors, detailing the proceedings of Carolina, and stating the objections of the assembly to the right of their lordships to repeal laws, which had been approved by their deputies.

This memorial was very unfavourably received, and the members of the council who had subscribed it, were displaced. The proprietors asserted their right to repeal all laws passed in the province, approved the conduct of the chief justice, censured that of the governor in disobeying their instructions respecting the dissolution of the assembly, and repeated their orders on this subject.

However the governor might disapprove the instructions given him, he did not hesitate to obey them. The new council was summoned, the assem-

CHAP IX
1719.

bly was dissolved, and writs were issued for electing another at Charleston.

The public mind had been gradually prepared for a revolution, and these irritating measures completed the disgust with which the people viewed the government of the proprietors. An opportunity to make the change so generally desired was soon afforded.

War with Spain.

A rupture having taken place between Great Britain and Spain, advice was received from England of a plan formed in the Havanna for the invasion of Carolina. The governor convened the council, and such members of the assembly as were in town, and laid his intelligence before them. He, at the same time, stated the ruinous condition of the fortifications, and proposed that a sum for repairing them should be raised, by voluntary subscription, of which he set the example by a liberal donation.

The assembly declared a subscription to be unnecessary, as the duties would afford an ample fund for the object. The repeal of the law imposing them was said to be utterly void, and would be disregarded.

The members of the new assembly, though they had not been regularly convened at Charleston, had held several private meetings in the country to con-

Combination to subvert the government.

cert measures of future resistance. They had drawn up an association for uniting the whole province in opposition to the proprietary government, which was proposed to the militia at their public meetings, and subscribed almost unanimously. This confederacy was formed with such secrecy and dispatch, that, before the governor was informed of it, almost every inhabitant of the province was engaged in it.

The members of the assembly, thus supported by the people, resolved to subvert the power of the proprietors.

The governor, who resided in the country, had no intimation of these secret meetings and transactions, until he received a letter from a committee of the representatives of the people, offering him the government of the province under the King; it having been determined to submit no longer to that of the proprietors.

Mr. Johnson resolved to suppress this spirit of revolt, and hastened to town in order to lay the letter before his council. They advised him to take no notice of it, until the legislature should be regularly convened. On meeting, the assembly declared, " that the laws, pretended to be repealed, continued to be in force; and that no power, other than the general assembly, could repeal them: That the writs under which they were elected were void, inasmuch as they had been issued by advice of an unconstitutional council: That the representatives cannot therefore, act as an assembly, but as a convention delegated by the people to prevent the utter ruin of the government: And, lastly, that the lords proprietors had unhinged the frame of the government, and forfeited their right thereto; and that an address be prepared to desire the honourable Robert Johnson, the present governor, to take on himself the government of the

CHAP. IX.
1719.
province in the name of the King." The address was signed by Arthur Middleton, as president of the convention, and by twenty-two members.

After several unavailing efforts, on the part of the assembly, to induce Mr. Johnson to accept the government under the King; and, on his part, to reinstate the government of the proprietors; he issued a proclamation dissolving the assembly, and retired into the country.

The proclamation was torn from the hands of the officer, and the assembly elected colonel James Moore chief magistrate of the colony.

Revolution completed.
After proclaiming him in the name of the King, and electing a council, the legislature published a declaration stating the revolution that had taken place, with the causes which produced it; and then proceeded, deliberately to manage the affairs of the province.

While Carolina was effecting this revolution, the agent of the colony obtained a hearing before the lords of the regency and council in England, (the King being then in Hanover) who were of opinion that the proprietors had forfeited their charter. They ordered the attorney general to take out a *scire facias* against it, and appointed Francis Nicholson provisioual governor of the province under the King. He was received with universal joy; and the people of Carolina passed, with great satisfaction, from the proprietary government to the immediate dominion of the crown. This revolution was completed by an

AMERICAN COLONIES.

agreement between the crown and seven of the pro- CHAP. IX.
prietors, whereby, for the sum of seventeen thousand 1719.
five hundred pounds sterling, they surrendered their The pro-
right and interest both in the government and soil. prietors
This agreement was confirmed by an act of parlia- surrender
ment; soon after which John Lord Carteret, the re- to the
maining proprietor, also surrendered all his interest in crown.
the government, but retained his rights of property.*

Carolina received with joy the same form of go- 1721.
vernment which had been bestowed on her sister colonies. The people pleased with their situation, and
secure of protection, turned their attention to domestic and agricultural pursuits; and the face of the country soon evidenced the happy effects which result
from contented industry, directed by those who are
to receive its fruits. For the convenience of the in- -1732.
habitants, the province was divided; and was, thence The pro-
forward, distinguished by the names of North and vince di-
South Carolina.† vided.

About this period, the settlement of a new colony
was planned in England. The tract of country lying
between the rivers Savanna and Alatamaha being unoccupied by Europeans. A company was formed
for the humane purpose of transplanting into this wilderness, the suffering poor of the mother country.
This territory, now denominated Georgia, was granted
to the company; and a corporation, consisting of
twenty-one persons, was created under the name of
" trustees for settling and establishing the colony of

* History of South Carolina.   † Idem,

CHAP IX
1732.

Georgia." Large sums of money were subscribed for transporting, and furnishing with necessaries, such poor people as should be willing to pass the Atlantic, and to seek the means of subsistence in a new world. One hundred and sixteen persons embarked at Gravesend, under the conduct of Mr. James Oglethorpe, one of the trustees, who, after landing at Charleston, proceeded to the tract of country allotted for the new colony, and laid the foundation of the town of Savanna, on the river which bears that name. A small fort was erected on its bank, in which some guns were mounted; and a treaty was held with the Creek Indians, from whom the cession of a considerable tract was obtained.

Georgia settled.

The trustees continued to make great efforts for the accomplishment of their object, and settled several companies of emigrants in Georgia. Unfortunately, the wisdom of their regulations did not equal the humanity of their motives. Totally unacquainted with the country they were to govern, they devised a system for it, rather calculated to impede than to promote its population.

1733. Considering each male inhabitant both as a soldier and a planter, to be provided with arms and ammunition for defence as well as with utensils for cultivation, they adopted the pernicious resolution of introducing such tenures for holding lands as were most favourable to a military establishment. Each tract granted, was considered as a military fief, for which the possessor was to appear in arms, and take the

Impolicy of the first regulations.

field, when required for the public defence. The grants were in *tail male;* and, on the termination of the estate, the lands were to revert to the trust, to be re-granted to such persons as would most benefit the colony. Any lands which should not be enclosed, cleared, and cultivated, within eighteen years, reverted to the trust. The importation of negroes, and of rum, was prohibited; and those only were allowed to trade with the Indians, to whom a license should be given.

However specious the arguments in support of these regulations might appear to the trustees, human ingenuity could scarcely have devised a system better calculated to defeat their hopes.

The tenure of lands drove the settlers into Carolina where that property might be acquired in fee simple. The prohibition of slavery rendered the task of opening the country, too heavy to be successfully undertaken in that burning climate; and the restriction on their trade to the West Indies, deprived them of the only market for lumber, an article in which they abounded.

Mr. Oglethorpe's first employment was the construction of fortifications for defence. He erected one fort on the Savanna, at Augusta, and another on an island of the Alatamaha, called Frederica, for defence against the Indians and the inhabitants of Florida. The Spaniards remonstrated against them; and a commissioner from the Havanna insisted on the evacuation of the country to the thirty-third degree of north lati-

CHAP. IX.
1734.

tude, which he claimed in the name of the King of Spain; but this remonstrance and claim were equally disregarded.

The restrictions imposed by the trustees, on the inhabitants of Georgia, were too oppressive to be endured in silence. They remonstrated, particularly, against the tenure by which their lands were held, and against the prohibition of the introduction of slaves. These complaints, the result of experience, were addressed to persons ignorant of the condition of the petitioners, and were neglected. The colony languished; while South Carolina, not unlike Georgia both in soil and climate, advanced with considerable rapidity. Although emigration was encouraged by paying the passage money of the emigrants, by furnishing them with clothes, arms, ammunition, and implements of husbandry, by maintaining their families for the first year, and, in some instances, by furnishing them with stock; yet the unwise policy, which has been mentioned, more than counterbalanced these advantages; and for ten years, during which time the exports from Carolina more than doubled, the settlers in Georgia could, with difficulty, obtain a scanty subsistence.

1737. The differences between Great Britain and Spain not admitting of adjustment, both nations prepared for war. The Spaniards strengthened East Florida; and the British government ordered a regiment, consisting of six hundred effective men, into Georgia. The

command of the troops, both of Georgia and Carolina, CHAP. IX.
was given to major general Oglethorpe, who fixed his 1739.
head quarters at Frederica.

Before hostilities had commenced, the Spaniards at St. Augustine engaged in criminal intrigues among the blacks of Carolina. Agents had been secretly employed in seducing the slaves of that province to escape to St. Augustine, where liberty was promised them, and where they were formed into a regiment officered by themselves. Hitherto these practices had been attended only with the loss of property; but, about this time, the evil assumed a much more alarming form. A large number of slaves assembled at Stono, where they forced a warehouse containing arms and ammunition, murdered the whites in possession of it, and, after choosing a captain, directed their march south westward, with drums beating and colours flying. On their march, they massacred the whites, seized all the arms they could find, and forced such blacks as did not voluntarily join them, to follow their party. Intoxicated with ardent spirits, and with their short lived success, they considered their work as already achieved, and halted in an open field, where the time which might have been employed in promoting their design, was devoted to dancing and exultation. Fortunately, the people of the neighbourhood had assembled on the same day, to attend divine service; and, as was then directed by law, all the men came armed. They marched immediately against the blacks, whom they completely surprised.

Insurrection of the slaves.

CHAP. IX.
1737.

Many were killed, and the residue dispersed or taken. Thus the insurrection was suppressed on the day of its commencement; and such of its leaders as survived the battle were immediately executed.

During the long repose, which the pacific temper of the duke of Orleans, Regent of France during the minority of Louis XV. and the equally pacific temper of sir Robert Walpole, minister of England, gave to their respective countries, the British colonies in America had increased rapidly in population and in wealth. Lands were cheap, and subsistence easily acquired. From New York to Virginia inclusive, no enemy existed to restrain new settlements, and no fears of inability to maintain a family, checked the natural propensity to early marriages. The people were employed in cultivating the earth, and in spreading themselves over the vast regions which were open to them; and, during this period, their history furnishes none of those remarkable events which interest posterity.

CHAPTER. X.

War declared against Spain.—Expedition againt St. Augustine.—Georgia invaded.—Spaniards land on an island in the Alatamaha.—Appearance of a fleet from Charleston.—Spanish army re-embarks. —Hostilities with France.—Expedition against Louisburg.—Louisburg surrenders.—Great plans of the belligerent powers.—Misfortunes of the armament under the duke D'Anville.—The French fleet dispersed by a storm.—Expedition against Nova Scotia.—Treaty of Aix la Chapelle.—Paper money of Massachusetts redeemed.—Contests between the French and English respecting boundaries.— Statement respecting the discovery of the Mississippi.—Scheme for connecting Louisiana with Canada.—Relative strength of the French and English colonies.—Defeat at the little meadows.—Convention at Albany.—Plan of union.—Objected to both in America and Great Britain.

THE increasing complaints of the merchants, and the loud clamours of the nation, at length forced the minister to abandon his pacific system; and war was declared against Spain. A squadron commanded by admiral Vernon was detached to the West Indies, with instructions to act offensively; and general Oglethorpe was ordered to annoy the settlements in Flo-

1739.
War with Spain.

rida. He planned an expedition against St Augustine, and requested the assistance of South Carolina. That colony, ardently desiring the expulsion of neighbours alike feared and hated, entered zealously into the views of the general, and agreed to furnish the men and money he requested. A regiment, commanded by colonel Vanderdussen, was immediately raised in Virginia and the two Carolinas. A body of Indians was also engaged, and captain Price, who commanded the small fleet on that station, promised his co-operation. These arrangements being made, and the mouth of St. John's river, on the coast of Florida, being appointed as the place of rendezvous, general Oglethorpe hastened to Georgia, to prepare his regiment for the expedition.

1740. Those unexpected impediments, which always embarrass military movements conducted by men without experience, having delayed the arrival of his northern troops, Oglethorpe entered Florida at the head of his own regiment, aided by a party of Indians; and invested Diego, a small fort about twenty-five miles from St. Augustine, which capitulated after a short resistance. He then returned to the place of rendezvous, where he was joined by colonel Vanderdussen, and by a company of Highlanders under the command of captain M'Intosh; a few days after which, he marched with his whole force, consisting of about two thousand men, to fort Moosa, in the neighbourhood of St. Augustine, which was evacuated on his approach. The general now perceived that the enterprise would be attended with more difficulty than had been anticipated. In the time which intervened between his entering Florida and appearing before the town, supplies of provisions had been received from the country, and six Spanish half gallies carrying long brass nine pounders, and two sloops laden with provisions, had entered the harbour. Finding the place better fortified than had been expected, he determined to invest it completely, and to advance by regular approaches. In execution of this plan, colonel Palmer, with ninety-five Highlanders, and forty-two Indians, remained at fort Moosa, while the army took different positions near the town, and began an ineffectual bombardment from the island of Anastasia. The general was deliberating on a plan for forcing the harbour and taking a nearer position, when colonel Palmer was surprised, and his detachment cut to pieces. At the same time some small vessels from the Havanna, with a reinforcement of men and supply of provisions, entered the harbour through the narrow channel of the Matanzas.

The army began to despair of success; and the provincials, enfeebled by the heat, dispirited by sickness, and fatigued by fruitless efforts, marched away in large bodies. The navy being ill supplied with provisions, and the season for hurricanes approaching, captain Price was unwilling to hazard his majesty's ships on that coast. The general, labouring under a fever, finding his regiment, as well as himself, worn out with fatigue, and rendered unfit for

CHAP. X.
1740.
action by disease; reluctantly abandoned the enterprise, and returned to Frederica.

The colonists, disappointed and chagrined by the failure of the expedition, attributed this misfortune entirely to the incapacity of the general, who was not less dissatisfied with them. Whatever may have been the true causes of the failure, it produced a mutual and injurious distrust between the general and the colonists.*

1742.
The events of the war soon disclosed the dangers resulting from this want of confidence in general Oglethorpe, and, still more, from the want of power to produce a co-operation of the common force for the common defence.

Spain had ever considered the settlement of Georgia as an encroachment on her territory, and had cherished the intention to seize every proper occasion to dislodge the English by force. With this view, an armament consisting of two thousand men, commanded by Don Antonio di Ridondo, embarked at the Havanna, under convoy of a strong squadron, and arrived at St. Augustine in May. The fleet having been seen on its passage, notice of its approach was given to general Oglethorpe, who communicated the intelligence to governor Glenn of South Carolina, and

* In the same year Charleston was reduced to ashes. A large portion of its inhabitants passed, in one day, from prosperity to indigence. Under the pressure of this misfortune, the legislature applied to parliament for aid; and that body, with a liberality reflecting honour on its members, voted twenty thousand pounds, to be distributed among the sufferers.

urged the necessity of sending the troops of that province to his assistance.

Georgia being a barrier for South Carolina, the policy of meeting an invading army on the frontiers of the former, especially one containing several companies composed of negroes who had fled from the latter, was too obvious not to be perceived: yet either from prejudice against Oglethorpe, or the disposition inherent in separate governments to preserve their own force for their own defence, Carolina refused to give that general any assistance. Its attention was directed entirely to the defence of Charleston; and the inhabitants of its southern frontier, instead of marching to the camp of Oglethorpe, fled to that city for safety. In the mean time, the general collected a few Highlanders, and rangers of Georgia, together with as many Indian warriors as would join him, and determined to defend Frederica.

Late in June, the Spanish fleet, consisting of thirty-two sail, carrying above three thousand men, crossed Simon's bar into Jekyl sound, and passing Simon's fort, then occupied by general Oglethorpe, procceeded up the Alatamaha, out of the reach of his guns; after which, the troops landed on the island, and erected a battery of twenty eighteen pounders.

Fort Simon's being indefensible, Oglethorpe retreated to Frederica. His whole force, exclusive of Indians, amounted to little more than seven hundred men, a force which could only enable him to act on the defensive until the arrival of re-inforcements which he

CHAP. X.
1742.
still expected from South Carolina. The face of the country was peculiarly favourable to this system of operations. Its thick woods and deep morasses opposed great obstacles to the advance of an invading enemy, not well acquainted with the paths which passed through them. Oglethorpe turned these advantages to the best account. In an attempt made by the Spanish general to pierce these woods in order to reach Frederica, several sharp rencounters took place; in one of which he lost a captain and two lieutenants killed, and above one hundred privates taken prisoners. He then changed his plan of operations; and, abandoning his intention of forcing his way to Frederica by land, called in his parties, kept his men under cover of his cannon, and detached some vessels up the river, with a body of troops on board, to reconnoitre the fort, and draw the attention of the English to that quarter.

About this time, an English prisoner escaped from the Spaniards, and informed general Oglethorpe that a difference existed between the troops from Cuba, and those from St. Augustine, which had been carried so far that they encamped in separate places. This intelligence suggested the idea of attacking them while divided; and his perfect knowledge of the woods favoured the hope of surprising one of their encampments. In execution of this design, he drew out the flower of his army, and marched in the night, unobserved, within two miles of the Spanish camp. There, his troops halted, and he advanced, himself, at the head of a select corps, to reconnoitre the situation of the enemy. While he was using the utmost circumspection to obtain the necessary information without being discovered, a French soldier of his party discharged his musket, and ran into the Spanish lines. Discovery defeating every hope of success, the general retreated to Frederica.

Oglethorpe, confident that the deserter would disclose his weakness, devised an expedient which turned the event to advantage. He wrote to the deserter as if in concert with him, directing him to give the Spanish general such information as might induce him to attack Frederica; hinting also at an attempt meditated by admiral Vernon on St. Augustine, and at late advices from Carolina, giving assurances of a re-inforcement of two thousand men. He then tampered with one of the Spanish prisoners, who, for a small bribe, promised to deliver this letter to the deserter, after which, he was permitted to escape. The prisoner, as was foreseen delivered the letter to his general, who ordered the deserter to be put in irons; and, was, in no small degree, embarrassed to determine whether the letter ought to be considered as a stratagem to save Frederica, and induce the abandonment of the enterprise; or as real instructions to direct the conduct of a spy. While hesitating on the course to be pursued, his doubts were removed by one of those incidents, which have so much influence on human affairs.

The assembly of South Carolina had voted a supply of money to general Oglethorpe; and the governor had ordered some ships of force to his aid. These appeared off the coast while the principal officers of the Spanish army were yet deliberating on the letter. They deliberated no longer. The whole army was seized with a panic; and, after setting fire to the fort, embarked in great hurry and confusion, leaving behind several pieces of heavy artillery, and a large quantity of provisions and military stores.

Spanish army re-embarks in confusion.

Thus was Georgia delivered from an invasion which threatened the total subjugation of the province.

The ill success of these reciprocal attempts at conquest, seems to have discouraged both parties; and the Spanish and English colonies, in the neighbourhood of each other, contented themselves, for the residue of the war, with guarding their own frontiers.

The connexion between the branches of the house of Bourbon was too intimate for the preservation of peace with France, during the prosecution of war against Spain. Both nations expected and prepared for hostilities. War had commenced in fact, though not in form, on the continent of Europe; but as they carried on their military operations as auxiliaries, in support of the contending claims of the elector of Bavaria, and the queen of Hungary, to the imperial throne, they preserved in America a suspicious and jealous suspension of hostility, rather than a real peace.

1744. This state of things was interrupted by a sudden incursion of the French into Nova Scotia.

The governor of Cape Breton having received information that France and Great Britain had become principals in the war, took possession of de Canseau. with a small military and naval force, and made the garrison, and inhabitants prisoners of war. This enterprise was followed by an attempt on Annapolis, which was defeated by the timely arrival of a re-inforcement from Massachusetts. These offensive operations stimulated the English colonists to additional efforts to expel such dangerous neighbours, and to unite the whole northern continent bordering on the Atlantic, under one common sovereign.

CHAP X.
1744.
Hostilities with France.

The island of Cape Breton, so denominated from one of its capes, lies between the 45th and 47th degree of north latitude, at the distance of fifteen leagues from cape Ray, the south western extremity of Newfoundland. Its position rendered the possession of it very material to the commerce of France; and the facility with which the fisheries might be annoyed from its ports, gave it an importance to which it could not otherwise have been entitled. Thirty millions of livres,* and the labour of twenty-five years, had been employed on its fortifications. From its strength, and still more from the numerous privateers that issued from its ports, it had been termed the Dunkirk† of America. On this place, governor Shirley meditated an attack.

The prisoners taken at Canseau, and others who had been captured at sea and carried to Louisbourg,

* About five and a half millions of dollars. † Belknap.

were sent to Boston. The information they gave, if it did not originally suggest this enterprise, contributed greatly to its adoption. They said that Duvivier had gone to France to solicit assistance for the conquest of Nova Scotia, in the course of the ensuing campaign; and that the store ships from France for Cape Breton, not having arrived on the coast until it was blocked up with ice, had retired to the West Indies.

In several letters addressed to administration, governor Shirley represented the danger to which Nova Scotia was exposed, and pressed for naval assistance. These letters were sent by captain Ryal, an officer of the garrison which had been taken at Causeau, whose knowledge of Louisbourg, of Cape Breton, and of Nova Scotia, enabled him to make such representations to the lords of the admiralty, as were calculated to promote the views of the northern colonies.

The governor was not disappointed. Orders were dispatched to commodore Warren, then in the West Indies, to proceed towards the north, early in the spring; and to employ such a force as might be necessary to protect the northern colonies in their trade and fisheries, as well as to distress the enemy. On these subjects, he was instructed to consult with Shirley, to whom orders of the same date were written, directing him to assist the King's ships with transports, men, and provisions.

Such deep impression had the design of taking Louisbourg made on the mind of Shirley, that he did not wait for intelligence of the reception given to his application for naval assistance. He was induced to decide on engaging in the enterprise, even without such assistance, by the representations of Mr. Vaughan, son of the lieutenant governor of New Hampshire, a man of a sanguine and ardent temper, who could think nothing impracticable which he wished to achieve. Mr. Vaughan had never been at Louisbourg, but had learned something of the strength of the place, from fishermen and others; and the bold turn of his mind suggested the idea of surprising it. There is something infectious in enthusiasm, whatever be its object; and Vaughan soon communicated his own convictions to Shirley.*

The governor informed the general court that he had a proposition of great importance to communicate, and requested that the members would take an oath of secrecy, previous to his laying it before them. This novel request being complied with, he submitted his plan for attacking Louisbourg. It was referred to a committee of both houses; the arguments for and against the enterprise were temperately considered; and the part suggested by prudence prevailed. The expedition was thought too great, too hazardous, and too expensive.

The report of the committee was approved by the house of representatives, and the expedition was supposed to be abandoned; but, notwithstanding the precaution taken to secure secrecy, the subject which

* Belknap.

had occupied the legislature was divulged,* and the people took a deep interest in it. Numerous petitions were presented, praying the general court to re-consider its vote, and to adopt the proposition of the governor. Among the several arguments urged in its favour, that which the petitioners pressed most earnestly, was the necessity of acquiring Louisbourg, to save the fisheries from ruin.

The subject being re-considered, a resolution in favour of the enterprise was carried by a single voice, in the absence of several members known to be against it. Yet all parties manifested equal zeal for its success. A general embargo was laid, and messengers were despatched to the several governments as far south as Pennsylvania, soliciting their aid. These solicitations succeeded only in the northern provinces. There being at that time no person in New England who had acquired any military reputation, the chief command was conferred on colonel Pepperel, a merchant, who was also a large land holder, and was highly respected throughout Massachusetts.†

All ranks of men combined to facilitate the enterprise, and those circumstances which are beyond human control, also concurred to favour the general wish.

The governors of Massachusetts and New Hamp-

---

* It is said the secret was kept until a member who performed family devotion at his lodgings, betrayed it by praying for the divine blessing on the attempt.

† Hutchison.

shire, whose orders forbad their assent to a farther emission of bills of credit, departed from their instructions to promote this favourite project; the people submitted to impressments of their property; and a mild winter gave no interruption to their warlike preparations.

The troops of Massachusetts,* New Hampshire, and Connecticut, amounting to rather more than four thousand men, assembled at Canseau about the middle of April; soon after which, to the great joy of the colonial troops, admiral Warren arrived, with a considerable part of his fleet. The army then embarked for Chapeaurouge bay, and the fleet cruised off Louisbourg.

After repulsing a small detachment of French troops, the landing was effected; and, in the course of the night, a body of about four hundred men led by Vaughan, marched round to the north east part of the harbour, and set fire to a number of warehouses containing spirituous liquors and naval stores. The smoke being driven by the wind into the grand battery, caused such darkness that the men placed in it were unable to distinguish objects; and, being apprehensive of an attack from the whole English army, abandoned the fort and fled into the town.

* The day before the armament sailed from Massachusetts, an express boat, which had been dispatched to admiral Warren to solicit assistance, returned with the unwelcome intelligence that he declined furnishing the aid required. This information could not arrest the expedition. Fortunately for its success, the orders from England soon afterwards reached the admiral, who immediately detached a part of his fleet; which he soon followed himself in the Superb, of sixty guns.

CHAP. X.
1745.

The next morning, as Vaughan was returning to camp with only thirteen men, he ascended the hill which over looked the battery, and observing that the chimneys in the barracks were without smoke, and the staff without its flag, he hired an Indian, with a bottle of rum, to crawl through an embrasure, and open the gate. Vaughan entered with his men and defended the battery against a party then landing to regain possession until the arrival of a reinforcement.

For fourteen nights successively, the troops were employed in dragging cannon from the landing place to the encampment, a distance of near two miles, through a deep morass. The army, being totally unacquainted with the art of conducting sieges, made its approaches irregularly, and sustained some loss on this account.

While these approaches were making by land, the ships of war which continued to cruise off the harbour, fell in with and captured the Vigilant, a French man of war of sixty-four guns, having on board a reinforcement of five hundred and sixty men, and a large quantity of stores for the garrison. Soon after this, an unsuccessful, and, perhaps, a rash attempt was made on the island battery by four hundred men; of whom sixty were killed, and one hundred and sixteen taken prisoners. All these prisoners, as if by previous concert, exaggerated the numbers of the besieging army, a deception which was favoured by the unevenness of the ground, and the dispersed state of the troops; and which probably contributed to the surrender of the place. The provincial army did indeed present a formidable front, but, in the rear, all was frolic and confusion.

The Vigilant had been anxiously expected by the garrison, and the information of her capture excited a considerable degree of perturbation. This event, with the erection of some works on the high cliff at the light house, by which the island battery was much annoyed, and the preparations evidently making for a general assault, determined Duchambon, the governor of Louisbourg, to surrender; and, in a few days, he capitulated.

[margin: Louisbourg surrenders.]

Upon entering the fortress, and viewing its strength, and its means of defence, all perceived how impracticable it would have been to carry it by assault.*

The joy excited in the British colonies by the success of the expedition against Louisbourg was unbounded. Even those who had refused to participate in its hazards and expense, were sensible of its advantages, and of the lustre it shed on the American arms. Although some disposition was manifested in England, to ascribe the whole merit of the conquest to the navy, colonel Pepperel received, with the title of baronet, the more substantial reward of a regiment in the British service, to be raised in America; and the same mark of royal favour was bestowed on governor Shirley. Reimbursements too were made by parliament for the expenses of the expedition. It

---

* Belknap. Hutchison.

was the only decisive advantage obtained by the English during the war.

The capture of Louisbourg, most probably, preserved Nova Scotia. Duvivier, who had embarked for France to solicit an armament for the conquest of that province, sailed, in July, 1745, with seven ships of war, and a body of land forces. He was ordered to stop at Louisbourg, and thence to proceed in the execution of his plan. Hearing, at sea, of the fall of that place, and that a British squadron was stationed at it, he relinquished the expedition against Nova Scotia, and returned to Europe.

The British empire on the American continent consisted, originally, of two feeble settlements unconnected with, and almost unknown to each other. For a long time the southern colonies, separated from those of New England by an immense wilderness, and by the possessions of other European powers, had no intercourse with them, except what was produced by the small trading vessels of the north, which occasionally entered the rivers of the south. Neither participated in the wars or pursuits of the other; nor were they, in any respect, actuated by common views, or united by common interest. The conquest of the country between Connecticut and Maryland, laid a foundation, which the settlement of the middle colonies completed, for connecting these disjoined members, and forming one consolidated whole, capable of moving, and acting in concert. This gradual change, unobserved in its commencement, had now become too perceptible to be longer overlooked; and, henceforward, the efforts of the colonies, were in a great measure combined, and directed to a common object.

CHAP X.
1745.

France, as well as England, had extended her views with her settlements; and, after the fall of Louisbourg, the governments of both nations meditated important operations for the ensuing campaign in America.

France contemplated, not only the recovery of Cape Breton and Nova Scotia, but the total devastation of the sea coast, if not the entire conquest of New England. Britain, on her part, calculated on the reduction of Canada, and the entire expulsion of the French from the American continent.

Great plans of the belligerents.

Shirley repaired to Louisbourg, after its surrender, where he held a consultation with Warren and Pepperel on the favourite subject of future and more extensive operations against the neighbouring possessions of France. From that place he wrote pressingly to administration, for reinforcements of men and ships to enable him to execute his plans. The capture of Louisbourg gave such weight to his solicitations that, in the following spring, the Duke of New Castle, then secretary of state, addressed a circular letter to the governors of the provinces as far south as Virginia, requiring them to raise as many men as they could spare, and hold them in readiness to act according to the orders that should be received. Before this letter was written, an extensive plan of operations had been digested in the British cabinet. It was proposed to detach a military and naval armament

1746.

CHAP X
1746.

which should, early in the season, join the troops to be raised in New England, at Louisbourg; whence they were to proceed up the St. Lawrence to Quebec. The troops from New York, and from the more southern provinces, were to be collected at Albany, and to march against Crown Point, and Montreal.

This plan, so far as it depended on the colonies, was executed with promptness and alacrity. The men were raised, and waited with impatience for employment; but neither troops, nor orders, arrived from England. The fleet destined for this service, sailed seven times from Spithead; and was compelled as often, by contrary winds, to return.

Late in the season, the military commanders in America, despairing of the succours promised by England, determined to assemble a body of provincials at Albany, and make an attempt on Crown Point. While preparing for the execution of this plan, they received accounts stating that Annapolis was in danger from a body of French and Indians assembled at Minas; upon which, orders were issued for the troops of Massachusetts, Rhode Island, and New Hampshire, to embark for Nova Scotia. Before these orders could be executed, intelligence was received which directed their attention to their own defence.

It was reported that a large fleet and army, under the command of the duke D'Anville, had arrived in Nova Scotia, and the views of conquest, which had been formed by the northern colonies, were converted into fears for their own safety. For six weeks, continual apprehensions of invasion were entertained; and the most vigorous measures were taken to repel it. From this state of anxious solicitude, they were at length relieved by the arrival of some prisoners set at liberty by the French, who communicated the extreme distress of the fleet.

CHAP. X.
1746.

This formidable armament consisted of near forty ships of war, seven of which were of the line; of two artillery ships; and of fifty-six transports laden with provisions and military stores, carrying three thousand five hundred land forces, and forty thousand stand of small arms, for the use of the Canadians and Indians. The fleet sailed in June, but was attacked by such furious and repeated storms, that many of the ships were wrecked, and others dispersed. In addition to this disaster, the troops were infected with a disease which carried them off in great numbers. While lying in Chebucto, under these circumstances, a vessel which had been dispatched by governor Shirley to admiral Townshend at Louisbourg, with a letter stating his expectation that a British fleet would follow that of France to America, was intercepted by a cruiser, and brought in to the admiral. These dispatches were opened in a council of war, which was considerably divided respecting their future conduct. This circumstance, added to the calamities already sustained, so affected the commander in chief, that he died suddenly. The vice-admiral fell by his own hand; and the command devolved on Monsieur le Jonguiere, governor of Canada, who had been declared *chef d'escadre* after the fleet sailed.

The French fleet dispersed by a storm.

CHAP X.
1746.

The design of invading New England was relinquished, and it was resolved to make an attempt on Annapolis. With this view the fleet sailed from Chebucto, but was again overtaken by a violent tempest which scattered the vessels composing it. Those which escaped shipwreck returned singly to France.*

"Never," says Mr. Belknap, "was the hand of divine providence more visible than on this occasion. Never was a disappointment more severe on the part of the enemy, nor a deliverance more complete, without human help, in favour of this country."

As soon as the fears excited by this armament were dissipated, the project of dislodging the French and Indians, who had invaded Nova Scotia, was resumed. Governor Shirley detached a part of the troops of Massachusetts on this service; and pressed the governors of Rhode Island and New Hampshire, to cooperate with him. The quotas furnished by these colonies were prevented by several accidents from joining that of Massachusetts, which was inferior to the enemy in numbers. The French and Indians, under cover of a snow storm, surprised the English at Minas; who, after an obstinate resistance, in which they lost upwards of one hundred men, were compelled to capitulate, and to engage not to bear arms against his most christian majesty, in Nova Scotia for one year. De Ramsay, who commanded the French, returned soon afterwards to Canada.

No farther transactions of importance took place in

* Hutchison. Belknap.

America during the war, which was terminated by the treaty of Aix la Chapelle. By this treaty, it was stipulated that all conquests made during the war should be restored; and the colonists had the mortification to see the French re-possess themselves of Cape Breton.

CHAP. X
1748.
Treaty of Aix la Chapelle.

The heavy expenses which had been incurred by the New England colonies, and especially by Massachusetts, had occasioned large emissions of paper money, and an unavoidable depreciation. Instead of availing themselves of peace, to discharge the debts contracted during war, they eagerly desired to satisfy every demand on the public treasury, by farther emissions of bills of credit, redeemable at future and distant periods. Every inconvenience under which commerce was supposed to labour, every difficulty encountered in the interior economy of the province, was attributed to a scarcity of money; and this scarcity was to be removed, not by increased industry, but by putting an additional sum in circulation. The rate of exchange, and the price of all commodities, soon disclosed the political truth that, however the quantity of the circulating medium may be augmented, its aggregate value cannot be arbitrarily increased; and that the effect of such a depreciating currency must necessarily be, to discourage the payment of debts, by holding out the hope of discharging contracts with less real value than that for which they were made; and to substitute cunning and speculation, for honest and regular industry. Yet the majority had perse-

CHAP. X.
1748.

vered in this demoralising system. The depreciation had reached eleven for one; and the evil was almost deemed incurable, when the fortunate circumstance of a reimbursement in specie, made by Parliament for colonial expenditures on account of the expeditions against Louisbourg and Canada, suggested to Mr. Hutchinson, speaker of the house of representatives in Massachusetts, the idea of redeeming the paper money in circulation, at its then real value.

This scheme, at first deemed Utopian, was opposed by many well meaning men who feared that its effect would be to give a shock to the trade and domestic industry of the province; and who thought that, as the depreciation had been gradual, justice required that the appreciation should be gradual also.

Paper money redeemed.

With great difficulty, the measure was carried; and the bills of credit in circulation, were redeemed at fifty shillings the ounce. The evils which had been apprehended were soon found to be imaginary. Specie, immediately took the place of paper. Trade, so far from sustaining a shock, flourished more than before this change in the domestic economy of the colony; and the commerce of Massachusetts immediately received an impulse, which enabled it to surpass that of her neighbours who retained their paper medium.*

Revival of contests with the French colonies respecting boundary.

The treaty of Aix la Chapelle did not remove the previously existing controversies between the colonies of France and England respecting boundary. These

* Hutchison.

AMERICAN COLONIES. 275

controversies, originating in the manner in which their CHAP. X
settlements had been made, and at first of small con- 1748.
sequence, were now assuming a serious aspect.
America was becoming an object of greater attention; and, as her importance increased, the question
concerning limits became important also.

In settling this continent, the powers of Europe,
estimating the right of the natives at nothing, adopted, for their own government, the principle, that those
who first discovered and took possession of any par- 1749.
ticular territory, became its rightful proprietors. But
as only a small portion of it could then be reduced
to actual occupation, the extent of country thus acquired was not well ascertained. Contests respecting
prior discovery, and extent of possession, arose
among all the first settlers. England terminated her
controversy with Sweden and with Holland, by the
early conquest of their territories; but her conflicting
claims with France and with Spain, remained un-
adjusted.

On the south, Spain had pretensions to the whole
province of Georgia, while England had granted the
country as far as the river St Matheo, in Florida.

On the north, the right of France to Canada was
undisputed; but the country between the St. Lawrence and New England had been claimed by both
nations, and granted by both. The first settlement
appears to have been made by the French; but its
principal town, called Port Royal, or Annapolis, had
been repeatedly taken by the English; and, by the

CHAP X.
1749.

treaty of Utrecht, the whole province, by the name of Nova Scotia, or Acadé, according to its ancient limits had been ceded to them.

But the boundaries of Nova Scotia, or Acadié, had never been ascertained. Though the treaty of Utrecht had provided that commissioners should be appointed by the two crowns, to adjust the limits of their respective colonies, the adjustment had never been made. France claimed to the Kennebec; and insisted " that only the peninsula which is formed by the bay of Fundy, the Atlantic ocean, and the gulph of St. Lawrence," was included in the cession of " Nova Scotia, or Acadié, according to its ancient limits." England, on the other hand, claimed all the country on the main land south of the river St. Lawrence. Under the treaty of Aix la Chapelle, commissioners were again appointed to settle these differences, who maintained the rights of their respective sovereigns with great ability, and laborious research; but their zeal produced a degree of asperity unfavourable to accommodation.

While this contest for the cold and uninviting country of Nova Scotia was carried on with equal acrimony and talents, a controversy arose for richer and more extensive regions in the south and west.

Discovery of the Mississippi.

So early as the year 1660, information was received, in Canada, from the Indians, that, west of that colony, was a great river, flowing neither to the north, nor to the east. The government, conjecturing that it must empty itself either into the gulph of

Mexico or the south sea, committed the care of ascertaining the fact to Joliet, an inhabitant of Quebec, and to the jesuit Marquette. These men proceeded from lake Michigan up the river of the Foxes, almost to its source, whence they travelled westward to the Ouisconsing, which they pursued to its confluence with the Mississippi. They sailed down this river to the 33d degree of north latitude, and returned by land, through the country of the Illinois, to Canada.

The mouth of the Mississippi was afterwards discovered by la Salle, an enterprising Norman, who, immediately after his return to Quebec, embarked for France, in the hope of inducing the cabinet of Versailles to patronise a scheme for proceeding by sea to the mouth of that river, and settling a colony on its banks.

Having succeeded in this application, he sailed for the gulph of Mexico, with a few colonists; but, steering too far westward, he arrived at the bay of St. Bernard, about one hundred leagues from the mouth of the Mississippi. In consequence of a quarrel between him and Beaujieu, who commanded the fleet, the colonists were landed at this place. La Salle was, soon afterwards, assassinated by his own men; and his followers were murdered or dispersed by the Spaniards and the Indians.

Several other attempts were made by the French to settle the country; but, by some unaccountable fatality, instead of seating themselves on the fertile borders of the Mississippi, they continually landed

CHAP X.
1749.

about the barren sands of Biloxi, and the bay of Mobile. It was not until the year 1722, that the miserable remnant of those who had been carried thither at various times, was transplanted to New Orleans; nor until the year 1731, that the colony began to flourish.

It had received the name of Louisiana, and soon extended itself by detached settlements, up the Mississippi and its waters, towards the great lakes.* As it advanced northward, the vast and interesting plan was formed of connecting it with Canada by a chain of forts.

Scheme for connecting Louisiana with Canada.

The fine climate and fertile soil of upper Louisiana enabling it to produce and maintain an immense population, rendered it an object which promised complete gratification to the views of France; while the extent given to it by that nation, excited the most serious alarm among the colonies of Britain.

The charters granted by the crown of England to the first adventurers, having extended from the Atlantic to the South Sea, their settlements had regularly advanced westward, in the belief that their title to the country in that direction, could not be controverted. The settlements of the French, stretching from north to south, necessarily interfered with those of the English. Their plan, if executed, would completely environ the English. Canada and Louisiana united, as has been aptly said, would form a bow, of which the English colonies would constitute the chord.

While Great Britain claimed, indefinitely, to the

* Abbe Raynal.

west, as appertaining to her possession of the sea coast; France insisted on confining her to the eastern side of the Apalachian, or Alleghany, mountains; and claimed the whole country drained by the Mississippi, in virtue of her right as the first discoverer of that river. The delightful region which forms the magnificent vale of the Mississippi was the object for which these two powerful nations contended; and it soon became apparent that the sword must decide the contest.

The white population of the English colonies was supposed to exceed one million of souls, while that of the French was estimated at only fifty-two thousand.*

* The following estimate is taken from "The History of the British empire in North America," and is there said to be an authentic account from the militia rolls, poll taxes, bills of mortality, returns from governors, and other authorities.

The colonies of	Inhabitants.
Halifax and Lunenberg in Nova Scotia	5,000
New Hampshire	30,000
Massachusetts Bay	220,000
Rhode Island and Providence	35,000
Connecticut	100,000
New York	100,000
The Jerseys	60,000
Pennsylvania (then including Delaware)	250,000
Maryland	85,000
Virginia	85,000
North Carolina	45,000
South Carolina	30,000
Georgia	6,000
Total	1,051,000

The white inhabitants of the French colonies were thus estimated:

The colonies of	Inhabitants.
Canada	45,000
Louisiana	7,000
Total	52,000

CHAP. X.
1749.

This disparity of numbers did not intimidate the governor of New France—a title comprehending both Canada and Louisiana; nor deter him from proceeding in the execution of his favourite plan. The French possessed advantages which, he persuaded himself, would counterbalance the superior numbers of the English. Their whole power was united under one governor, who could give it such a direction as his judgment should dictate. The genius of the people and of the government was military; and the inhabitants could readily be called into the field, when their service should be required. Great reliance too was placed on the Indians. These savages, with the exception of the Five Nations, were generally attached to France, and were well trained to war. To these advantages was added a perfect knowledge of the country about to become the theatre of action.

The British colonies, on the other hand, were divided into distinct governments, unaccustomed, except those of New England, to act in concert; were jealous of the power of the crown; and were spread over a large extent of territory, the soil of which, in all the middle colonies, was cultivated by men unused to arms.

The governors of Canada, who were generally military men, had, for several preceding years, judiciously selected and fortified such situations as would give them most influence over the Indians, and facilitate incursions into the northern provinces. The command of lake Champlain had been acquired by the erection of a strong fort at Crown Point; and a connected chain of posts was maintained from Quebec, up the St. Lawrence, and along the great lakes. It was intended to unite these posts with the Mississippi by taking positions which would favour the design of circumscribing and annoying the frontier settlements of the English.

The execution of this plan was, probably, accelerated by an act of the British government. The year after the conclusion of the war, several individuals both in England and Virginia who were associated under the name of the Ohio company, obtained from the crown a grant of six hundred thousand acres of land, lying in the country claimed by both nations. The objects of this company being commercial as well as territorial, measures were taken to derive all the advantages expected from their grant, in both these respects, by establishing trading houses, and by employing persons to survey the country.

The governor of Canada, who obtained early information of this intrusion, as he deemed it, into the dominions of his most christian majesty, wrote to the governors of New York and Pennsylvania, informing them that the English traders had encroached on the French territory by trading with their Indians; and giving notice that, if they did not desist, he should be under the necessity of seizing them wherever they should be found. At the same time the jealousy of the Indians was excited by impressing them with fears that the English were about to deprive them of their country.

His threat having been disregarded, the governor of Canada put it in execution by seizing the British traders among the Twightwees, and carrying them prisoners to Presque-isle, on lake Erie; where he was erecting a strong fort. About the same time, a communication was opened from Presque-isle, down French creek, and the Allegheny river, to the Ohio. This communication was kept up by detachments of troops, posted at proper distances from each other, in works capable of covering them from an attack made only with small arms.*

This territory having been granted as part of Virginia, to the Ohio company, who complained loudly of these aggressions, Dinwiddie, the lieutenant governor of that province, laid the subject before the assembly, and dispatched MAJOR WASHINGTON, the gentleman who afterwards led his countrymen to independence, with a letter to the commandant of the French forces on the Ohio; requiring him to withdraw from the dominions of his Britannic majesty.

This letter was delivered at a fort on the river Le Bœuf, the western branch of French creek, to Monsieur le Guarduer de St. Pierre, the commanding officer on the Ohio, who replied that he had taken possession of the country by the directions of his general, then in Canada, to whom he would transmit

* Minot Gazette.

the letter of the lieutenant governor, and whose orders he should implicitly obey.

CHAP. X.
1753.

Preparations were immediately made, in Virginia, to assert the rights of the British crown; and a regiment was raised for the protection of the frontiers. Early in the spring, Major Washington had advanced with a small detachment from this regiment into the country to be contended for, where he fell in with and defeated a party of French and Indians who were approaching him in a manner indicating hostile designs. On being joined by the residue of his regiment, the command of which had devolved on him, he made great exertions to pre-occupy the post at the confluence of the Alleghany and Monongahela rivers; but, on his march thither, was met by a much superior body of French and Indians, who attacked him in a small stockade hastily erected at the Little Meadows, and compelled him, after a gallant defence to capitulate. The French had already taken possession of the ground to which Washington was proceeding, and, having driven off some militia, and workmen sent thither by the Ohio company, had erected thereon a strong fortification called fort Du Quêsne.

1754.

Defeat at the Little Meadows.

The earl of Holderness, secretary of state, perceiving war to be inevitable, and aware of the advantages of union, and of securing the friendship of the Five Nations, had written to the governors of the respective colonies recommending these essential objects; and, at the same time, ordering them to repel force by

CHAP. X.
1754.

force; and to take effectual measures to dislodge the French from their posts on the Ohio.

Convention at Albany.

At the suggestion of the commissioners for the plantations, a convention of delegates from the several colonies met at Albany, to hold a conference with the five nations on the subject of French encroachments, and to secure their friendship in the approaching war. Availing himself of this circumstance governor Shirley had recommended to the other governors to instruct their commissioners on the subject of union. Ample powers for this object were given to the delegates of Massachusetts; and those of Maryland were instructed to observe what others should propose respecting it. But no direct authority for concerting any system to call out and employ the strength of the colonies, was given by any other of the governments.

The congress, consisting of delegates from New Hampshire, Massachusetts, Rhode Island, Connecticut, Pennsylvania, and Maryland, with the lieutenant governor and council of New York, after endeavouring to secure the friendship of the Five Nations by large presents, directed a committee, consisting of one member for each colony to draw and report a plan of union.

Plan of union.

A plan* was reported which was approved on the 4th of July. Its essential principles were, that application be made for an act of parliament authorising the formation of a grand council to consist of dele-

* See note No. 2, at the end of the volume.

gates from the several legislatures, and a president general, to be appointed by the crown, and to be invested with a negative power. This council was to enact laws of general import; to apportion their quotas of men and money on the several colonies; to determine on the building of forts; to regulate the operations of armies; and to concert all measures for the common protection and safety.

The delegates of Connecticut alone dissented from this plan. That cautious people feared that the powers vested in the president general might prove dangerous to their welfare.

In England, the objections were of a different character. The colonies had, in several instances, manifested a temper less submissive than was required; and it was apprehended that this union might be the foundation of a concert of measures opposing the pretensions of supremacy maintained by the mother country.

This confederation, therefore, notwithstanding the pressure of external danger, did not prevail. It was not supported in America, because it was supposed to place too much power in the hands of the King; and it was rejected in England from the apprehension that the colonial assemblies would be rendered still more formidable by being accustomed to co-operate with each other.

In its stead, the minister proposed that the governors, with one or two members of the councils of the respective provinces, should assemble to consult, and resolve on measures necessary for the common defence, and should draw on the British treasury for the sums to be expended, which sums should be afterwards raised by a general tax, to be imposed by parliament on the colonies.

This proposition being entirely subversive of all the opinions which prevailed in America, was not pressed for the present; and no satisfactory plan for calling out the strength of the colonies being devised, it was determined to carry on the war with British troops, aided by such reinforcements as the several provincial assemblies would voluntarily afford.*

* Minot.

CHAPTER XI.

General Braddock arrives.—Convention of governors and plan of the campaign.—French expelled from Nova Scotia, and inhabitants transplanted.—Expedition against fort Du Quêsne.—Battle of Monongahela.—Defeat and death of general Braddock.—Expedition against Crown Point.—Dieskan defeated.—Expedition against Niagara.—Frontiers distressed by the Indians.—Meeting of the governors at New York.—Plan for the campaign of 1756.—Lord Loudoun arrives.—Montcalm takes Oswego.—Lord Loudoun abandons offensive operations.—Small pox breaks out in Albany.—Campaign of 1757 opened.—Admiral Holbourne arrives at Halifax.—Is joined by the earl of Loudoun.—Expedition against Louisbourg relinquished.—Lord Loudoun returns to New York.—Fort William Henry taken.—Controversy between Lord Loudoun and the assembly of Massachusetts.

THE establishment of the post on the Ohio, and the action at the Little Meadows, being considered by the British government as the commencement of war in America, the resolution to send a few regiments to that country was immediately taken; and early in the year, general Braddock embarked at Cork, at the

1755.

General Braddock.

head of a respectable body of troops destined for the colonies.

An active offensive campaign being meditated, general Braddock convened the governors of the several provinces, on the 14th of April, in Virginia, who resolved to carry on three expeditions.

Plan of the campaign.

The first, and most important, was against fort Du Quêsne. This was to be conducted by general Braddock in person at the head of the British troops, with such aids as could be drawn from Maryland and Virginia.

The second, against Niagara and fort Frontignac, was to be conducted by governor Shirley. The American regulars, consisting of Shirley and Pepperel's regiments, constituted the principal force destined for the reduction of these places.

The third was against Crown Point. This originated with Massachusetts; and was to be prosecuted entirely with colonial troops, to be raised by the provinces of New England, and by New York. It was to be commanded by colonel William Johnson of the latter province.*

While preparations were making for these several enterprises, an expedition, which had been previously concerted by the government of Massachusetts, was carried on against the French in Nova Scotia.

It has been already stated that the limits of this province remained unsettled. While the commissioners of the two crowns were supporting the claims

* Minot.

of their respective sovereigns in fruitless memorials, the French occupied the country in contest, and established military posts for its defence. Against these posts this enterprise was to be conducted.

CHAP XL
1755.

On the 20th of May, the troops of Massachusetts, together with Shirley's and Pepperel's regiments, amounting in the whole to about three thousand men, embarked, at Boston, under the command of lieutenant colonel Winslow. The fleet anchored about five miles from fort Lawrence, where a reinforcement was received of three hundred British troops and a small train of artillery. The whole army, commanded by lieutenant colonel Monckton, immediately after landing, marched against Beau Sejour, the principal post held by the French in that country. At the river Mussaquack, which the French considered as the western boundary of Nova Scotia, some slight works had been thrown up with the intention of disputing its passage. After a short conflict, the river was passed with the loss of only one man; and, in five days, Beau Sejour capitulated. Other small places fell in succession, and, in the course of the month of June, with the loss of only three men killed, the English acquired complete possession of the whole province of Nova Scotia.

French expelled from Nova Scotia.

The recovery of this province was followed by one of those distressing measures which involve individuals in indiscriminate ruin, and aggravate the calamities of war.

Nova Scotia having been originally settled by

O o

France, its inhabitants were, chiefly, of that nation. In the treaty of Utrecht, it was stipulated for the colonists that they should be permitted to hold their lands on condition of taking the oaths of allegiance to their new sovereign. With this condition they refused to comply, unless permitted to qualify it with a proviso that they should not be required to bear arms in defence of the province. Though this qualification, to which the commanding officer of the British forces acceded, was afterwards disallowed by the crown, yet the French inhabitants continued to consider themselves as neutrals. Their devotion to France, however, would not permit them to conform their conduct to the character they had assumed. In all the contests for the possession of their country, they were influenced by their wishes rather than their duty; and three hundred of them were captured with the garrison of Beau Sejour.

Their continuance in the country, during the obstinate conflict which was commencing, would, it was feared, endanger the colony; and to expel them from it, leaving them at liberty to choose their place of residence, would be to re-enforce the French in Canada. A council was held by the executive of Nova Scotia aided by the admirals Boscawen and Morty, for the purpose of deciding on the destiny of these unfortunate people; and the severe policy was adopted of removing them from their homes, and dispersing them through the other British colonies. This harsh measure was immediately put in execution; and the miserable inhabitants of Nova Scotia were, in one instant, reduced from ease and contentment to a state of beggary. Their lands, and moveables, with the exception of their money and household furniture, were declared to be forfeited to the crown; and, to prevent their return, the country was laid waste, and their houses reduced to ashes.*

CHAP XI.
1755.

As soon as the convention of governors had separated, general Braddock proceeded from Alexandria to a fort at Wills' creek, afterwards called fort Cumberland, at that time the most western post in Virginia or Maryland; from which place the army destined against fort Du Quêsne was to commence its march. The difficulties of obtaining wagons, and other necessary supplies for the expedition, and delays occasioned by opening a road through an excessively rough country, excited apprehensions that time would be afforded the enemy to collect in such force at fort Du Quêsne, as to put the success of the enterprise into some hazard.

Under the influence of this consideration, it was determined to select twelve hundred men, who should be led by the general in person to the point of destination. The residue of the army, under the command of colonel Dunbar, was to follow, with the baggage, by slow and easy marches.

This disposition being made, Braddock pressed forward to his object, in the confidence that he could

* Minot.

CHAP XI.
1755.

find no enemy capable of opposing him; and reached the Monongahela on the eighth of July.

As the army approached fort Du Quêsne, the general was cautioned of the danger to which the character of his enemy, and the face of the country, exposed him; and was advised to advance the provincial companies in his front, for the purpose of scouring the woods, and discovering ambuscades. But he held both his enemy and the provincials in too much contempt, to follow this salutary council. Three hundred British troops comprehending the grenadiers and light infantry, commanded by colonel Gage, composed his van; and he followed, at some distance, with the artillery, and the main body of the army, divided into small columns.

Within seven miles of fort Du Quêsne, immediately after crossing the Monongahela the second time, in an open wood, thick set with high grass, as he was pressing forward without fear of danger, his front received an unexpected fire from an invisible enemy.

Battle of Mononga- hela.

The van was thrown into some confusion; but, the general having ordered up the main body, and the commanding officer of the enemy having fallen, the attack was suspended, and the assailants were supposed to be dispersed. This delusion was soon dissipated. The attack was renewed with increased fury; the van fell back on the main body; and the whole army was thrown into utter confusion.

The general possessed personal courage in an eminent degree; but was without experience in that species of war, in which he was engaged; and seems not CHAP XI. to have been endowed with that rare fertility of genius 1755. which adapts itself to the existing state of things, and invents expedients fitted to the emergency. In the impending crisis, he was peculiarly unfortunate in his choice of measures. Neither advancing nor retreating, he exerted his utmost powers to form his broken troops, under an incessant and galling fire, on the very ground where they had been attacked. In his fruitless efforts to restore order, every officer on horseback except Mr. Washington, one of his aids-de-camp, was killed or wounded. At length, after loosing three horses, the general himself received a mortal wound; upon which his regulars fled in terror and confusion. Fortunately, the Indian enemy was arrested by the plunder found on the field, and the pursuit was soon given over. The provincials exhibited an unexpected degree of courage, and were among the last to leave the field.

The defeated troops fled precipitately to the camp of Dunbar, where Braddock expired of his wounds. Their panic was communicated to the residue of the army. As if affairs had become desperate, all the stores, except those necessary for immediate use, were destroyed; and the British troops were marched to Philadelphia, where they went into quarters. The western parts of Pennsylvania, Maryland, and Virginia, were left exposed to the incursions of the savages; the frontier settlements were generally broken up; and the inhabitants were driven into the

Death of Braddock.

interior. So excessive was the alarm, that even the people of the interior entertained apprehensions for their safety, and many supposed that the sea-board itself was insecure.

The two northern expeditions, though not so disastrous as that against fort Du Quêsne, were, neither of them successful. That against Crown Point, was so retarded by those causes of delay to which military operations conducted by distinct governments are always exposed, that the army was not ready to move until the last of August. At length general Johnson reached the south end of lake George, on his way to Ticonderoga, of which he designed to take possession.

An armament fitted out in the port of Brest for Canada, had eluded a British squadron which was stationed off the banks of Newfoundland to intercept it; and, with the loss of two ships of war, had entered the St. Lawrence. After arriving at Quebec, the baron Dieskau, who commanded the French forces, resolved, without loss of time, to proceed against the English. At the head of about twelve hundred regulars, and about six hundred Canadians and Indians, he marched against Oswego. On hearing of this movement, general Johnson applied for reinforcements; and eight hundred men were ordered by Massachusetts to his assistance. An additional body of two thousand men was directed to be raised for the same object, and the neighbouring colonies also determined to furnish reinforcements.

Dieskau did not wait for their arrival. Perceiving that Johnson was approaching lake George, and being informed that the provincials were without artillery, he determined to postpone his designs upon Oswego, and to attack them in their camp.

CHAP. XI.
1755.

On being informed that Dieskau was approaching, Johnson detached colonel Williams, with about one thousand men, to reconnoitre and skirmish with him. This officer met the French about four miles from the American camp, and immediately engaged them. He fell early in the action; and his party was soon overpowered and put to flight. A second detachment, sent in aid of the first, experienced the same fate; and both were closely pursued to the main body, who were posted behind a breast-work of fallen trees. At this critical moment, within about one hundred and fifty yards of this work, the French halted for a short time. This interval having given the Americans an opportunity to recover from the first alarm, they determined on a resolute defence.

Dieskau defeated.

When the assailants advanced to the charge, they were received with firmness. The militia and savages fled; and Dieskau was under the necessity of ordering his regulars to retreat. A close and ardent pursuit ensued; and the general himself, being mortally wounded and left alone, was taken prisoner.

During the engagement, a scouting party from fort Edward, under captains Folsom and M'Gennis, fell in with the baggage of the enemy, and routed the guard which had been placed over it. Soon afterwards, the retreating army of Dieskau approached, and was gallantly attacked by the Americans. This unexpected attack from an enemy whose numbers were unknown, completed the confusion of the defeated army, which, abandoning its baggage, fled towards the posts on the lake.*

The repulse of Dieskau, magnified into a splendid victory, had some tendency to remove the depression of spirits occasioned by the defeat of Braddock, and to inspire the provincials with more confidence in themselves. General Johnson, who was wounded in the engagement, received very solid testimonials of the gratitude and liberality of his country. Five thousand pounds sterling, and the title of baronet, were the rewards of his service.

This success was not improved. The hopes and expectations of the public were not gratified; and the residue of the campaign was spent in fortifying the camp. Massachusetts pressed a winter campaign; but when her commissioners met those of Connecticut and the lieutenant governor and council of New York, it was unanimously agreed that the army under general Johnson should be discharged, except six hundred men to garrison fort Edward, on the great carrying place between the Hudson and lake George, and fort William Henry on that lake.

The French took possession of Ticonderoga, and fortified it.

* Minot. Belknap. Entic.

The expedition against Niagara and fort Frontignac, was also defeated by delays in making the preparations necessary for its prosecution. Shirley did not reach Oswego till late in August. After ascertaining the state of the garrison, he determined to abandon that part of the enterprise which respected fort Frontignac, and to proceed against Niagara. While employed in the embarkation of his troops on the lake, the rains set in with such violence as to suspend his operations until the season was so far advanced that the attempt against Niagara was also relinquished, and Shirley returned to Albany.*

CHAP XI
1755
Expedition against Niagara.

Thus terminated the campaign of 1755. It opened with so decided a superiority of force on the part of the English, as to promise the most important advantages. But, if we except the expulsion of the French from Nova Scotia, no single enterprise was crowned with success. Great exertions were made by the northern colonies, but their efforts were productive of no benefit. From the want of one general superintending authority in their councils, which could contemplate and control the different parts of the system, which could combine all their operations, and direct them with effect towards the attainment of the object pursued, every thing failed. Such delays and deficiencies were experienced that, though a considerable force was in motion, it could not be brought to the point against which it was to act, until the season for action was over; nor execute the plans

* Minot. Belknap. Entic.

which were concerted until the opportunity had passed away.

The system adopted by the British cabinet, for conducting the war in America, left to the colonial governments to determine, what number of men each should bring into the field; but required them to support their own troops, and to contribute to the support of those sent from Great Britain to their assistance. But this system could not be enforced. The requisitions of the minister were adopted, rejected, or modified, at the discretion of the government on which they were made; and, as no rule of apportionment had been adopted, each colony was inclined to consider itself as having contributed more than its equal share towards the general object, and as having received, less than its just proportion, of the attention and protection of the mother country. This temper produced a slow and reluctant compliance on the part of some, which enfeebled and disconcerted enterprises, for the execution of which the resources of several were to be combined.

Distress of the frontiers. In the mean time the whole frontier, as far as North Carolina, was exposed to the depredations of the savages, who were, almost universally, under the influence of the French. Their bloody incursions were made in all directions, and many settlements were entirely broken up.

It is a curious and singular fact that, while hostilities were thus carried on by France and England against each other in America, the relations of peace and amity were preserved between them in Europe. Each nation had, in consequence of the military operations in 1754, determined to fit out a considerable armament to aid the efforts made in its colonies; and, when it was understood that admiral Boscawen was ordered to intercept that of France, the Duc de Mirepoix, the French ambassador at London, complained of the proposed measure, and gave formal notice that the King his master would consider the first gun fired at sea, as a declaration of war. On receiving intelligence of the capture of a part of the squadron by Boscawen, the French minister at the court of St. James was recalled without asking an audience of leave; upon which, letters of marque and reprisal were issued by the British government. This prompt and vigorous measure had much influence on the war, which was declared, in form, the following spring.

General Shirley, on his return to Albany after the close of the campaign in 1755, received a commission appointing him commander in chief of the King's forces in North America. A meeting of all the governors was immediately called at New York, for the purpose of concerting a plan for the ensuing campaign. Operations equally extensive with those proposed for the preceding campaign were again contemplated. To ensure their success, it was determined to raise ten thousand men, for the expedition against Crown Point; six thousand, for that against Niagara; and three thousand, for that against fort Du Quêsne. To favour the operations of this formidable force, it was farther

CHAP XL.
1755.

determined that two thousand men should advance up the Kennebec, destroy the settlement on the Chaudiere, and, descending to the mouth of that river, keep all that part of Canada in alarm.

In the mean time, it was proposed to take advantage of the season when the lake should be frozen, to seize Ticonderoga, in order to facilitate the enterprise against Crown Point. This project was defeated by the unusual mildness of the winter; and, about the middle of January, general Shirley repaired to Boston in order to make the necessary preparations for the ensuing campaign.

Such was the solicitude to accomplish the objects in contemplation, and so deep an interest did the colonists take in the war, that every nerve was strained, to raise and equip the number of men required.

1756.

Command bestowed on Lord Loudoun.

Having made in Massachusetts all the preparations for the next campaign, so far as depended on the government, Shirley repaired to Albany, where he was superseded* by major general Abercrombie; who, soon afterwards, yielded the command to the earl of Loudoun. Early in the year, that nobleman had been appointed to the command of all his majesty's forces in North America; and extensive powers, civil as well as military, had been conferred on him. But he did not arrive at Albany until midsummer.

In the spring, the provincial troops destined for the expedition against Crown Point, were assembled in the neighbourhood of lake George. They were found

* He was also recalled from his government.

not much to exceed seven thousand men; and even this number was to be reduced in order to garrison posts in the rear. This army being too weak to accomplish its object, major general Winslow, who commanded it, declared himself unable to proceed on the expedition without reinforcements. The arrival of a body of British troops, with general Abercrombie, removed this difficulty; but another occurred which still farther suspended the enterprise.

The regulations respecting rank had given great disgust in America; and had rendered it disagreeable and difficult to carry on any military operations which required a junction of British and provincial troops. When consulted on this delicate subject, Winslow assured general Abercrombie of his apprehensions that, if the result of the junction should be to place the provincial troops under British officers, it would produce general discontent, and perhaps desertion. His officers concurred in this opinion; and it was finally agreed that British troops should succeed the provincials in the posts then occupied by them, so as to enable the whole colonial force to proceed under Winslow, against Crown Point.

On the arrival of the earl of Loudoun, this subject was revived. The question was seriously propounded, " whether the troops in the several colonies of New England, armed with his majesty's arms, would, in obedience to his commands signified to them, act in conjunction with his European troops; and under the command of his commander in chief?" The

CHAP. XI
1756.

colonial officers answered this question in the affirmative; but entreated it as a favour of his lordship, as the New England troops had been raised on particular terms, that he would permit them, so far as might consist with his majesty's service, to act separately. This request was acceded to; but before the army could be put in motion, the attention both of the Europeans and provincials, was directed to their own defence.

Montcalm takes Oswego.

Monsieur de Montcalm, an able officer, who succeeded Dieskau in the command of the French troops in Canada, sought to compensate by superior activity, for the inferiority of his force. While the British and Americans were adjusting their difficulties respecting rank, and deliberating whether to attack Niagara or fort du Quêsne, Montcalm advanced at the head of about five thousand Europeans, Canadians, and Indians, against Oswego. In three days he brought up his artillery, and opened a battery which played on the fort with considerable effect. Colonel Mercer, the commanding officer, was killed; and, in a few hours, the place was declared by the engineers to be no longer tenable. The garrison, consisting of the regiments of Shirley and Pepperel, amounting to sixteen hundred men, supplied with provisions for five months, capitulated, and became prisoners of war. A respectable naval armament, then on the lake, was also captured.

The fort at Oswego had been erected in the country of the Five Nations, and had been viewed by them with some degree of jealousy. Montcalm, actuated by a wise policy, destroyed it in their presence; declaring at the same time, that the French wished only to enable them to preserve their neutrality, and would, therefore, make no other use of the rights of conquest, than to demolish the fortresses which the English had erected in their country to overawe them.

The British general, disconcerted at this untoward event, abandoned all his plans of offensive operations. General Winslow was ordered to relinquish his intended expedition, and to fortify his camp, and endeavour to prevent the enemy from penetrating into the country by the way of South bay, or Wood creek. Major general Webb, with fourteen hundred men, was posted at the great carrying place; and, to secure his rear, sir William Johnson, with one thousand militia, was stationed at the German flats.

These dispositions being made, the colonies were strenuously urged to reinforce the army. It was represented to them that, should any disaster befal Winslow, the enemy might be enabled to overrun the country, unless opposed by a force much superior to that in the field.*

During this state of apprehensive inactivity, the *Small-pox in Albany.*

---

* The northern colonies had been enabled to attend to these representations, and, in some degree to comply with the requisitions made on them, by having received from the British government, in the course of the summer, a considerable sum of money as a reimbursement for the extraordinary expenses of the preceding year. One hundred and fifteen thousand pounds sterling had been apportioned among them, and this sum gave new vigour and energy to their councils.

CHAP VI
1756.

small-pox broke out in Albany. This enemy was more dreaded by the provincials than Montcalm himself. So great was the alarm, that it was found necessary to garrison the posts in that quarter, entirely with British troops, and to discharge all the provincials except a regiment raised in New York.

Thus terminated for a second time, in defeat and utter disappointment, the sanguine hopes which the colonists had formed of a brilliant and successful campaign. After all their expensive and laborious preparations, not an effort had been made to drive the invaders of the country even from their out-post at Ticonderoga.

The expedition to lake Ontario had not been commenced; and no preparations had been made for that against fort Du Quêsne. The colonies of Pennsylvania, Maryland, and Virginia, far from contemplating offensive operations, had been unable to defend themselves; and their frontiers were exposed to all the horrors of Indian warfare.

The expedition up the Kennebec was also abandoned. Thus, no one enterprise contemplated at the opening of the campaign, was carried into execution.*

1757. About the middle of January, the governors of the northern provinces were convened in a military council at Boston. The earl of Loudoun opened his propositions to them with a speech in which he attributed all the disasters that had been sustained, to the colonies; and in which he proposed that New England

* Minot. Belknap. Entic.

should raise four thousand men for the ensuing campaign. Requisitions proportionably large were also made on New York and New Jersey.

The ill success which had, thus far, attended the combined arms of Great Britain and her colonies, did not discourage them. Their exertions to bring a powerful force into the field were repeated; and the winter was employed in preparations for the ensuing campaign. The requisitions of lord Loudoun were complied with; and he found himself, in the spring, at the head of a respectable army. Some important enterprise against Canada, when the armament expected from Europe should arrive, was eagerly anticipated; and the most sanguine hopes of success were again entertained.

In the beginning of July, admiral Holbourne reached Halifax with a powerful squadron, and reinforcement of five thousand British troops commanded by George Viscount Howe, and, on the 6th of the same month, the earl of Loudoun sailed from New York with six thousand regulars. A junction of these formidable armaments was effected without opposition, and the colonists looked forward with confidence for a decisive blow which would shake the power of France in America.

The plan of this campaign varied from that which had been adopted in the preceding years. The vast and complex movements heretofore proposed, were no longer contemplated, and offensive operations were to be confined to a single object. Leaving the posts

Q q

on the lakes strongly garrisoned, the British general determined to direct his whole disposable force against Louisbourg; and fixed on Halifax as the place of rendezvous for the fleet and army.

After assembling the land and naval forces at this place, information was received that a fleet had lately arrived from France, and that Louisbourg was so powerfully defended as to render any attempt upon it hopeless. In consequence of this intelligence the enterprise was deferred until the next year; the general and admiral returned to New York in August; and the provincials were dismissed.

The French general, feeling no apprehension for Louisbourg, determined to avail himself of the absence of a large part of the British force, and to obtain complete possession of lake George. With an army collected chiefly from the garrisons of Crown Point, Ticonderoga, and the adjacent forts; amounting, with the addition of Indians, and Canadians, to nine thousand men, the marquis de Montcalm laid siege to fort William Henry. That place was well fortified, and garrisoned by three thousand men; and derived additional security from an army of four thousand men at fort Edwards, under the command of major general Webb. Notwithstanding the strength of the place and its means of defence, Montcalm urged his approaches with so much vigour, that articles of capitulation, surrendering the fort, artillery, and stores, and stipulating that the garrison should not serve against his most christian majesty or his allies for the space of eighteen months, were signed within six days after its investment.

When this important place was surrendered, the commander in chief had not returned from Halifax. General Webb, alarmed for fort Edward, applied for reinforcements; and the utmost exertions were made to furnish the aids he required. The return of the army to New York on the last of August, dispelled all fear of an invasion, and enabled the general, who contemplated no farther active operations, to dismiss the provincials.

Unsuccessful in all his attempts to gather laurels from the common enemy, the earl of Loudoun engaged in a controversy with Massachusetts; in the commencement of which, he displayed a degree of vigour which had been kept in reserve for two campaigns. This controversy is thus stated by Mr. Minot.

Upon information from the governor that a regiment of Highlanders was expected in Boston, the general court provided barracks for the accommodation of one thousand men at Castle Island. Soon afterwards, several officers arrived from Nova Scotia to recruit their regiments. Finding it impracticable to perform this service while in the barracks at the castle, they applied to the justices of the peace to quarter and billet them, as provided by act of parliament. The justices refused to grant this request, on the principle that the act did not extend to the colonies. When informed of this refusal, lord Loudoun addressed a letter to the justices, insisting peremptorily on the right, as the act did, in his opinion, extend to America, and to every part of the King's dominions, where the necessities of the people should oblige him to send his troops. He concluded a long dissertation on the question in the following decisive terms, " that having used gentleness and patience, and confuted their arguments, without effect, they having returned to their first mistaken plan, their not complying would lay him under the necessity of taking measures to prevent the whole continent from being thrown into a state of confusion. As nothing was wanting to set things right, but the justices doing their duty (for no act of the assembly was necessary or wanting for it) he had ordered the messenger to remain only forty-eight hours in Boston; and if on his return he found things not settled, he would instantly order into Boston the three battalions from New York, Long Island, and Connecticut; and if more were wanting, he had two in the Jerseys at hand, beside those in Pennsylvania. As public business obliged him to take another route, he had no more time left to settle this material affair, and must take the necessary steps before his departure, in case they were not done by themselves."

The general court passed a law for the purpose of removing the inconveniences of which the officers complained; but, this law not equalling the expectations of lord Loudoun, he communicated his dissatisfaction in a letter to the governor, which was laid before the assembly, who answered by an address to his excellency in which the spirit of their forefathers seemed to revive. They again asserted that the act of parliament did not extend to the colonies; and that they had for this reason enlarged the barracks at the castle, and passed a law for the benefit of recruiting parties, as near the act of parliament as the circumstances of the country would admit; that such a law was necessary to give power to the magistrates, and they were willing to make it, whenever his majesty's troops were necessary for their defence. They asserted their natural rights as Englishmen; that by the royal charter, the powers and privileges of civil government were granted to them; that their enjoyment of these was their support under all burdens, and would animate them to resist an invading enemy to the last. If their adherence to their rights and privileges should, in any measure, lessen the esteem which his lordship had conceived for them, it would be their great misfortune; but that they would have the satisfaction of reflecting that, both in their words and actions, they had been governed by a sense of duty to his majesty, and faithfulness to the trust committed to them.

This address being forwarded to lord Loudoun, he affected to rely on their removing all difficulties in future, and not only countermanded the march of the troops, but condescended to make some conciliatory observations respecting the zeal of the province in his majesty's service. For these the two houses made an ample return in a message to the governor, in which they disavowed any intention of lessening their dependence on parliament; and expressly acknowledged the authority of all acts which concerned, and extended to, the colonies.

This explicit avowal of sentiments so different from those which Massachusetts had long cherished respecting her connexion with the mother country, would induce a belief that she had recently become more colonial in her opinions. This was probably the fact; but Mr. Minot, who may be presumed to have been personally acquainted with the transaction, does not attribute to that cause entirely, the conciliating temper manifested at the close of a contest, which had commenced with such appearances of asperity. Massachusetts had made large advances for the prosecution of the war, for which she expected re-imbursements from parliament; and was not willing, at such a juncture, to make impressions unfavourable to the success of her claims.

CHAPTER XII.

Preparations for the campaign of 1758.—*Admiral Boscawen and general Amherst arrive at Halifax.—Plan of the campaign.—Expedition against Louisbourg, Ticonderoga, and Crown Point.—General Abercrombie repulsed under the walls of Ticonderoga.—Fort Frontignac taken.—Expedition against fort Du Quêsne.—Preparations for the campaign of* 1759.—*General Amherst succeeds general Abercrombie.—Plan of the campaign.—Ticonderoga and Crown Point taken.—Army goes into winter quarters.—French repulsed at Oswego.—Defeated at Niagara.—Niagara taken.—Expedition against Quebec.—Check to the English army.—Battle on the Plains of Abraham.—Death of Wolf and Montcalm.—Quebec capitulates.—Garrisoned by the English under the command of general Murray.—Attempt to recover Quebec.—Battle near Sillery.—Quebec besieged by Monsieur Levi.—Siege raised.—Montreal capitulates.—War with the southern Indians.—Battle near the town of Etchoe.—Grant defeats them and burns their towns.—Treaty with the Cherokees.—War with Spain.—Success of the English.—Peace.*

The affairs of great Britain in North America wore a more gloomy aspect, at the close of the campaign

1758.

CHAP. XII. of 1757, than at any former period. By the acquisi-
1758.
tion of fort William Henry, the French had obtained
complete possession of the lakes Champlain, and
George. By the destruction of Oswego, they had acquired the dominion of those lakes which connect the
St. Lawrence with the waters of the Mississippi, and
unite Canada to Louisiana. By means of fort Du
Quêsne, they maintained their ascendency over the
Indians, and held undisturbed possession of the country west of the Allegheny mountains; while the English settlers were driven to the blue ridge. The great
object of the war in that quarter was gained, and
France held the country for which hostilities had been
commenced. With inferior numbers, the French had
been victorious in every campaign, and had uniformly gained ground on the English colonies. Nor were
they less successful elsewhere. The flame of war
which was kindled in America, had communicated
itself to Europe and Asia. In every quarter of the
world where hostilities had been carried on, the British arms were attended with defeat and disgrace.

But this inglorious scene was about to be succeeded by one of unrivalled brilliancy. From the point
of extreme depression to which their affairs had sunk,
the brightest era of British history was to commence.
Far from being broken by misfortune, the spirit of the
nation was high; and more of indignation than dismay
was inspired by the ill success of their arms. The
public voice had, at length, made its way to the throne,
and had forced, on the unwilling monarch, a minister

who has been justly deemed one of the greatest men of the age in which he lived.

Mr. Pitt had been long distinguished in the house of commons, for the boldness and the splendour of his eloquence. His parliamentary talents, and the independent grandeur of his character, had given him a great ascendancy in that body, and had made him the idol of the nation. In 1756, he had been introduced into the cabinet, but could not long retain his place. The public affection followed him out of office ; and, the national disasters continuing, it was found impracticable to conduct the complicated machine of government without his aid. In the summer of 1757, an administration was formed, which conciliated the great contending interests in parliament ; and Mr. Pitt was placed at its head. The controling superiority of his character gave him the same ascendancy in the cabinet which he had obtained in the house of commons; and he seemed to dictate the measures of the nation. Only a short time was required to show that qualities, seldom united in the same person, were combined in him ; and his talents for action seemed to eclipse even those he had displayed in debate. His plans partaking of the proud elevation of his own mind, and the exalted opinion he entertained of his countrymen, were always grand ; and the means he employed for their execution, were always adequate to the object. Possessing the public confidence without limitation, he commanded all the resources of the nation, and drew liberally from the public purse; but the money was always faithfully and judiciously applied to the public service. Too great in his spirit, too lofty in his views, to become the instrument of faction; when placed at the head of the nation, he regarded only the interest of the nation; and, overlooking the country or the party, which had given birth to merit, he searched for merit only, and employed it wherever it was found. From the elevation of the house of Brunswick to the British throne, a great portion of the people, under the denomination of tories, had been degraded, persecuted, and oppressed. Superior to this narrow and short sighted policy, Mr. Pitt sought to level these enfeebling and irritating distinctions, and to engage every British subject in the cause of his country. Thus commanding both the strength and the wealth of the kingdom, with perhaps greater talents, he possessed certainly greater means, than any of his predecessors.*

In no part of his majesty's dominions was the new administration more popular than in his American colonies. Deeply and peculiarly interested in the events of the war, they looked for a change of fortune from this change of men, and cheerfully made every exertion, of which they were capable, for the ensuing campaign. The circular letter of Mr. Pitt assured the several governors that, to repair the losses and disappointments of the last inactive campaign, the cabinet was determined to send a formidable force, to operate by sea and land, against the French in

* Russel.

America; and he called upon them to raise as large bodies of men, within their respective governments, as the number of inhabitants might allow. Arms, ammunition, tents, provisions, and boats, would, he said, be f rnished by the crown; and he required the colonies to clothe and pay their men; assuring them, at the same time, that it should be recommended to parliament to make them compensation.

The legislature of Massachusetts agreed to furnish seven thousand men; Connecticut five thousand; and New Hampshire three thousand. These troops, great as were their numbers, when compared with the population of the country, were in the field early in May; and the transports for carrying those of Massachusetts to Halifax, were ready to sail in fifteen days after they were engaged. Near one-third of the effective men of that province, are said to have been in military service; and the taxes were so heavy that, in the capital, they amounted to two-thirds of the income of real estate.*

In the mother country too, the utmost activity was transfused into every department. Her fleets blocked up in the French ports the men and stores designed for Canada, and captured, on the seas, most of those which had been able to make their way into the ocean. At the same time, a powerful armament, equipped with unusual expedition, sailed from her ports. Early in the spring, admiral Boscawen arrived at Halifax with a formidable fleet, and twelve

---

* Minot.

CHAP XII
1758.

thousand British troops, under the command of general Amherst.

The earl of Loudoun had returned to England, and the command of the British and American forces in the colonies, had devolved on general Abercrombie. That officer found himself at the head of the most powerful army ever seen in the new world. His whole numbers, comprehending troops of every description, have been computed by Mr. Belsham at fifty thousand men, of whom twenty thousand were provincials.

The objects of the campaign were no longer defeated by delays. The preparations for action were made during the winter, and military operations commenced in the spring.

Plan of the campaign.

Three expeditions were proposed. The first was against Louisbourg; the second against Ticonderoga and Crown Point; and the third against fort du Quêsne.*

Expedition against Louisbourg.

The army destined against Louisbourg, consisting of fourteen thousand men, was commanded by major general Amherst; and the fleet, consisting of twenty ships of the line and eighteen frigates, by admiral Boscawen. On the 24th of May, the troops embarked at Halifax; and, on the 2d of June, arrived before Louisbourg.

The use made by Great Britain of her naval superiority was felt in no part of the possessions of his most christian majesty more sensibly than in Louisbourg.

* Minot. Belknap.

The garrison of that important place was composed of only two thousand five hundred regulars, aided by six hundred militia. The harbour was defended by five ships of the line; one ship of fifty guns; and five frigates, three of which were sunk across the mouth of the basin.

CHAP XII
1758.

Soon after investment of the place, one of the large ships was set on fire by a bomb from a battery on the light house point, and blown up. The flames were communicated to two others which shared the same fate. The English admiral then sent a detachment of six hundred seamen, in boats, into the harbour, under captains La Forcey and Balfour, to make an attempt on the two remaining ships of the line, which still kept possession of the basin. This service was executed with great gallantry. One, which was aground, was destroyed, and the other was towed off in triumph.

The harbour being in possession of the English, and several practicable breaches made in the works, the place was no longer deemed defensible, and the governor was under the necessity of capitulating. The garrison became prisoners of war, and Louisbourg, with its artillery, provisions, and military stores; and also Island Royal, St. Johns, and their dependencies, were surrendered to the English, who encountered no farther difficulty in taking possession of the whole island.*

This important acquisition was made with the loss

---

* Minot. Belknap. Belsham. Russel.

CHAP. XII
1758.

of between five and six hundred men, killed and wounded. The joy it diffused throughout the colonies, long familiarised to disaster, was in proportion to their former disappointments.

Against Ticonderoga.

The expedition against Ticonderoga and Crown Point was conducted by general Abercrombie in person. His army, consisting of near sixteen thousand effectives, of whom nine thousand were provincials, was attended by a formidable train of artillery, and possessed every requisite to ensure success.

On the 5th of July, he embarked on lake George, and reached the landing place early the next morning. A disembarkation being effected without opposition, the troops were immediately formed into four columns, the British in the centre, and the Provincials on the flanks; in which order they marched towards the advanced guard of the French, composed of one battalion posted in a log camp, which, on the approach of the English, made a precipitate retreat.

Abercrombie continued his march towards Ticonderoga, with the intention of investing that place; but, the woods being thick, and the guides unskilful, his columns were thrown into confusion, and, in some measure, entangled with each other. In this situation lord Howe, at the head of the right centre column, fell in with a part of the advanced guard of the French, which, in retreating from lake George, was likewise lost in the wood. He immediately attacked and dispersed them; killing several, and taking one hundred and forty-eight prisoners, among whom were five officers.

This small advantage was purchased at a dear rate. Though only two officers, on the side of the British, were killed, one of these was lord Howe himself, who fell on the first fire. This gallant young nobleman had endeared himself to the whole army. The British and provincials alike lamented his death; and the assembly of Massachusetts passed a vote for the erection of a superb cenotaph to his memory, in the collegiate church of Westminster, among the heroes and patriots of Great Britain.

Without farther opposition, the English army took possession of the post at the Saw Mills, within two miles of Ticonderoga. This fortress, which commands the communication between the two lakes, is encompassed on three sides by water, and secured in front by a morass. The ordinary garrison amounting to four thousand men, was stationed under the cannon of the place, and covered by a breast-work, the approach to which had been rendered extremely difficult by trees felled in front, with their branches outward, many of which were sharpened so as to answer the purpose of chevaux-de-frize. This body of troops was rendered still more formidable by its general than by its position. It was commanded by the marquis de Montcalm.

Having learned from his prisoners the strength of the army under the walls of Ticonderoga, and that a reinforcement of three thousand men was daily ex-

CHAP XII
1758.

pected, general Abercrombie thought it advisable to storm the place before this reinforcement should arrive. Being informed by an engineer directed to reconnoitre the works, that they were unfinished, and were practicable, he resolved, without waiting for his artillery, to storm the lines; and the dispositions for an assault were instantly made.

The rangers, the light infantry, and the right wing of the provincials, were ordered to form a line out of cannon shot of the intrenchments, with their right extending to lake George, and their left to lake Champlain. The regulars who were to storm the works, were formed in the rear of this line. The piquets were to begin the attack, and to be sustained by the grenadiers; and the grenadiers by the battalions. The whole were ordered to march up briskly, to rush upon the enemy's fire, and to reserve their own until they had passed the breast-work.

The troops marched to the assault with great intrepedity; but their utmost efforts could make no impression on the works. The impediments in front of the intrenchments retarded their advance, and exposed them, while entangled among the boughs of the trees, to a very galling fire. The breast work itself was eight or nine feet high, and much stronger than had been represented; so that the assailants, who do not

General Abercrombie repulsed under the walls of Ticonderoga.

appear to have been furnished with ladders, were unable to pass it. After a contest of near four hours, and several repeated attacks, general Abercrombie ordered a retreat.

The army retired to the camp from which it had marched in the morning; and, the next day, resumed its former position on the south side of lake George.*

CHAP XII
1758.

In this rash attempt, the killed and wounded of the English amounted to near two thousand men, of whom not quite four hundred were provincials. The French were covered during the whole action, and their loss was inconsiderable.†

Entirely disconcerted by this unexpected and bloody repulse, general Abercrombie relinquished his designs against Ticonderoga and Crown Point. Searching however for the means of repairing the misfortune, if not the disgrace, sustained by his arms, he readily acceded to a proposition made by colonel Bradstreet, for an expedition against fort Frontignac. This fortress stands on the north side of Ontario, at the point where the St. Lawrence issues from that lake; and though a post of real importance, had been left, in a great degree, undefended.

The detachment designed for this service was commanded by colonel Bradstreet. It consisted of three thousand men, of whom two hundred were British, and was furnished with eight pieces of cannon, and three mortars.

Colonel Bradstreet embarked on the Ontario at Oswego, and on the 25th of August, landed within one mile of the fort. In two days, his batteries were opened at so short a distance that almost every shell took effect; and the governor, finding the place ab-

Fort Frontignac taken.

* Letter of general Abercrombie.   † Minot. Belknap.

solutely untenable, surrendered at discretion. The Indians having deserted, the prisoners amounted only to one hundred and ten men. A great quantity of military stores, together with nine armed vessels, mounting from eight to eighteen guns, also fell into the hands of the English.*

After destroying the fort and vessels, and such stores as could not be brought off, colonel Bradstreet returned to the army which undertook nothing farther during the campaign.

Expedition against fort du Quêsne. The demolition of fort Frontignac and of the stores which had been collected there, contributed materially, to the success of the expedition against fort du Quêsne. The conduct of this enterprise had been entrusted to general Forbes, who marched from Philadelphia, about the beginning of July, at the head of the main body of the army, destined for this service, in order to join colonel Bouquet at Raystown. So much time was employed in preparing to move from this place, that the Virginia regulars, commanded by colonel Washington, were not ordered to join the British troops until the month of September. It had been determined not to use the road made by Braddock, but to cut a new one from Raystown to fort du Quêsne. About the time this resolution was formed, and before the army was put in motion, major Grant was detached from the advanced post at Loyal Hannan with eight hundred men, to reconnoitre the fort and the adjacent country. This gentleman

* Letter of colonel Bradstreet.

invited an attack from the garrison, the result of which was that upwards of three hundred of the detachment were killed and wounded, and major Grant himself was made a prisoner.*

CHAP. XII
1758.

Early in October general Forbes moved from Raystown; but the obstructions to his march were so great that he did not reach fort du Quêsne until late in November. The garrison, being deserted by the Indians, and too weak to maintain the place against the formidable army which was approaching, abandoned the fort the evening before the arrival of the British, and escaped down the Ohio in boats. The English placed a garrison in it, and changed its name to Pittsburg, in compliment to their popular minister. The acquisition of this post was of great importance to Pennsylvania, Maryland, and Virginia. Its possession had given the French an absolute control over the Indians of the Ohio, who were accustomed to assemble at that place, for the purpose of making their destructive incursions into those colonies. Their route was marked by fire and the scalping knife; and neither age nor sex could afford exemption from their ferocity. The expulsion of the French gave the English entire possession of the country, and produced a complete revolution in the disposition of the Indians inhabiting it. Finding the current of success to be running against their ancient friends, they were willing to reconcile themselves to the most

Fort du Quêsne evacuated.

* MSS.

CHAP. XII
1758.

powerful; and all the Indians between the lakes and the Ohio concluded a peace with the English.

Although the events of 1758 did not equal the expectations which had been formed from the force brought into the field, the advantages were decisive. The whole country constituting the original cause of the war, had changed masters, and was in possession of the English. The acquisition of the island of Cape Breton opened the way to Quebec; and their success in the west enabled them to direct all their force against Canada. The colonies, encouraged by this revolution in their affairs, and emboldened, by the conquests already made, to hope for others still more extensive, prepared vigorously on the application of Mr. Pitt, for the farther prosecution of the war.

General Amherst succeeds general Abercrombie.

Late in the year 1758, general Abercrombie was succeeded in the command of the army by major general Amherst, who formed the bold plan of conquering Canada in the course of the ensuing campaign.

1759.

The decided superiority of Great Britain at sea, and the great exertions of France in other quarters of the world, still prevented the arrival of such reinforcements as were necessary for the preservation of his most christian majesty's possessions in North America. To take advantage of this weakness, the English proposed to enter Canada by three different routes, with three powerful armies; and to attack all the strong holds by which that country was defended.

Plan of the campaign.

It was determined that one division of the army, to

be commanded by brigadier general Wolf, a young officer who had signalised himself in the siege of Louisbourg, should ascend the St. Lawrence, and lay siege to Quebec. A strong fleet was to escort the troops destined for this enterprise, and to co-operate with them.

Major general Amherst was to lead the central and main army against Ticonderoga and Crown Point. After making himself master of these places, he was to proceed over lake Champlain, and by the way of Richlieu, to the St. Lawrence, and down that river, so as to effect a junction with general Wolfe before the walls of Quebec. From their combined force, the conquest of the capital of Canada was expected.

The third army was to be commanded by general Prideaux. Its first destination was against Niagara. After the reduction of this place, Prideaux was to embark on lake Ontario, and proceed down the St. Lawrence against Montreal. Should Montreal fall into his hands before the surrender of Quebec, he was to join the grand army at that place.*

It could not be expected that a plan so extensive and so complex, should succeed in all its parts; and it was greatly to be apprehended, that the failure of one part might defeat the whole. But it suited the daring spirit which eminently distinguished the officers then commanding the British forces, and was entered upon with zeal and activity.

As the other two expeditions, expecially that against

* Minot. Belknap. Belsham. Russel. Entic.

CHAP XII.
1759.

Quebec, were supposed to depend greatly on the celerity with which the movements of the main army should be made, general Amherst began his preparations in the commencement of winter, for the enterprise he was to undertake. Early in the spring, he transferred his head quarters from New York to Albany, where his troops were assembled by the last of May. Notwithstanding his continued exertions, the summer was far advanced before he could cross lake George; nor did he reach Ticonderoga until the 22d of July. The lines drawn around that place were immediately abandoned, and the English took possession of them.

Ticonderoga abandoned.

The French troops in this quarter being unequal to the defence of the posts they held, their object seems to have been, to embarrass and delay the invading army; but not to hazard any considerable diminution of strength, by persevering in the defence of places until the retreat of the garrison should become impracticable. The hope was entertained, that by retreating from post to post, and making a show of intending to defend each, the advance of the English might be retarded, until the season for action on the lakes should pass away; while the French would be gradually strengthened by concentration, and thus enabled to maintain some point, which would arrest the progress of Amherst down the St. Lawrence.

In pursuance of this plan, as soon as the English had completed their arrangements for taking possession of lake Champlain, the garrison of Ticonderoga retreated to Crown Point.

Early in the month of August, Amherst advanced to Crown Point, which was abandoned on his approach; and the garrison retired to isle Aux Noix, at the northern extremity of lake Champlain. The French had collected between three and four thousand men at this place, in an entrenched camp, defended by artillery, and protected by several armed vessels on the lake. After making great exertions to obtain a naval superiority, General Armherst embarked his army on lake Champlain; but, a succession of storms compelling him to abandon the farther prosecution of the enterprise, he returned to Crown Point, where the troops were put into winter quarters.*

In the beginning of July, general Prideaux, embarked on lake Ontario with the army destined against Niagara. Immediately after his departure from Oswego, that place, which was defended by twelve hundred men under the command of colonel Haldiman, was vigorously attacked by a body of French and Indians, who were repulsed with some loss.

In the mean time, Prideaux proceeded towards Niagara, and landed without opposition, about three miles from the fort. The place was invested in form, and the siege was carried on by regular approaches. In its progress, general Prideaux was killed by the bursting of a cohorn, and the command devolved on general Johnson. Great efforts were made

* Minot. Belknap. Belsham. Russel. New York Gazette.

CHAP. XII
1759.

to relieve this important place. A considerable body of troops drawn from the neighbouring garrisons, aided by some Indian auxiliaries, advanced on the English army, with the determination to risk a battle, in order to raise the siege. Early in the morning of the 24th, the approach of this party was announced, and a strong detachment marched out to meet it. The action, which immediately commenced, was not of long duration. The French were forsaken by their savage allies, and victory soon declared in favour of the English.

Niagara capitulates.

This battle decided the fate of Niagara. The works of the besiegers had been pushed within one hundred yards of the walls, and a farther attempt to defend the place being hopeless, a capitulation was signed, by which the garrison, amounting to rather more than six hundred men, became prisoners of war.

Although important advantages were gained by the British arms in Upper Canada, yet, as neither division of the army, in that quarter, succeeded so completely as to co-operate with general Wolfe, serious fears were entertained for the fate of that officer. The enterprise conducted by him being of the greatest hazard and of the deepest interest, its success was to decide, whether the whole campaign would terminate in a manner favourable to the future conquest of Canada.

Expedition against Quebec.

As soon as the waters were sufficiently freed from ice to be navigable, Wolfe embarked eight thousand men with a formidable train of artillery, at Louisbourg, under convoy of admirals Saunders and Holmes.

Late in June, he anchored about half way up the island of Orleans, on which he landed, without opposition.

From this position, he could take a near and accurate view of the obstacles to be surmounted, before he could hope for success in his enterprise. These were so great, that even his bold and sanguine temper perceived more to fear than to hope; and, in a celebrated letter written to Mr. Pitt, and afterwards published, he declared that he could not flatter himself with being able to reduce the place.*

Quebec stands on the north side of the St. Lawrence, and on the west of the St. Charles, which rivers unite immediately below the town. It consists of an upper and a lower town; the latter is built upon the strand, which stretches along the base of the lofty rock, on which the former is situated. This rock continues, with a bold and steep front, far to the westward, parallel to, and near the river St. Lawrence. On this side, therefore, the city might well be deemed inaccessible. On the other, it was protected by the river St. Charles, in which were several armed vessels, and floating batteries, deriving additional security from a strong boom drawn across its mouth. The channel of this river is rough and broken, and its borders intersected with ravines. On its left, or eastern bank, was encamped a French army, strongly entrenched, and amounting, according to the English

* Belsham.

accounts, to ten thousand men.* The encampment extended from St. Charles, eastward, to the Montmorency, and its rear was covered by an almost impenetrable wood. To render this army still more formidable, it was commanded by a general, who had given signal proofs of active courage, and consummate prudence. The marquis de Montcalm, who, when strong enough to act offensively, had so rapidly carried Oswego, and fort William Henry, and who, when reduced to the defensive, had driven Abercrombie with such slaughter from the walls of Ticonderoga, was now at the head of the army which covered Quebec, and was an antagonist, in all respects, worthy of Wolfe.

The British general perceived these difficulties in their full extent, but, his ardent mind glowing with military enthusiasm, sought only how to subdue them.

He took possession of Point Levi, on the southern side of the St. Lawrence, where he erected several heavy batteries, which opened on the town, but were at too great a distance to make any considerable impression on the works. Nor could his ships be employed in this service. The elevation of the principal fortifications placed them beyond the reach of the guns of the fleet; and the river was so commanded

---

* These accounts must be exaggerated. According to the letter of general Townshend, the force engaged on the Plains of Abraham amounted to three thousand five hundred men; and not more than fifteen hundred are stated to have been detached under Bougainville.

by the batteries on shore, as to render a station near the town ineligible.

The English general, sensible of the impracticability of reducing Quebec, unless he should be enabled to erect his batteries on the north side of the St. Lawrence, determined to use his utmost endeavours to bring Montcalm to an engagement. After several unavailing attempts to draw that able officer from his advantageous position, Wolfe resolved to pass the Montmorency, and to attack him in his entrenchments.

In consequence of this resolution, thirteen companies of British grenadiers, and part of the second battalion of royal Americans, were landed near the mouth of the Montmorency, under cover of the cannon of the ships; while two divisions, under generals Townshend and Murray, prepared to cross that river higher up. The original plan was to make the first attack on a detached redoubt close to the water's edge, apparently unprotected by the fire from the entrenchments, in the hope that Montcalm might be induced to support this work, and thereby enable Wolfe to bring on a general engagement.*

On the approach of the British troops, this redoubt was evacuated. Observing some confusion in the French camp, Wolfe determined to avail himself of the supposed impression of the moment, and to storm the lines. With this view, he directed the grenadiers and royal Americans to form on the beach, where

* Belsham.

CHAP XII they were to wait until the whole army could be ar-
1759. ranged to sustain them. Orders were at the same
time dispatched to Townshend and Murray to be in
readiness for fording the river.

The grenadiers and royal Americans, disregarding
their orders, rushed forward, with impetuous valour
on the entrenchments of the enemy. They were received with so steady and well supported a fire,
that they were thrown into confusion, and compelled
to retreat. The general advancing in person with the
remaining brigades, the fugitives formed again in the
The Eng- rear of the army; but the plan of the attack was
lish army
repulsed. effectually disconcerted, and the English commander
gave orders for re-passing the river, and returning to
the island of Orleans.

Convinced by this disaster of the impracticability
of approaching Quebec on the side of the Montmorency, Wolfe again turned his whole attention to the
St. Lawrence. To destroy some ships of war lying
in the river, and at the same time to distract the attention of Montcalm by descents at different places,
twelve hundred men were embarked in transports under the command of general Murray, who made two
vigorous, but unsuccessful attempts, to land on the
northern shore. In the third he was more fortunate.
In a sudden descent on Chambaud, he burnt a valuable magazine filled with military stores, but was still
unable to accomplish the main object of the expedition. The ships were secured in such a manner as
not to be approached by the fleet or army. Murray

was recalled; and on his return brought with him the intelligence that Niagara was taken, that Ticonderoga and Crown Point had been abandoned, and that general Amherst was making preparations to attack the isle Aux Noix.*

This intelligence, though joyfully received, promised no immediate assistance; and the season for action was rapidly wasting away.† Nor was it easy for Wolfe to avoid contrasting the success of the British arms under other auspices, with the ill fortune attending his own.

A council of war having determined that all their future efforts should be directed towards effecting a landing above the town, the troops were withdrawn from the island of Orleans, and embarked on board the fleet. Some of them were landed at Point Levi, and the residue carried higher up the river.‡

Montcalm could not view this movement without alarm. That part of Quebec, which faces the country, had not been well fortified; and he was apprehensive that a landing might be effected high up the river, and the town approached on its weak side. At the same time, he could not safely relinquish his position, because the facility of transportation which the command of the water gave the English, would enable them to seize the ground he then occupied, should his army be moved above the town.

Thus embarrassed, he detached Monsieur de Bou-

* Belsham. Russel. † Belsham ‡ Belsham.

gainville with fifteen hundred men, to watch the motions of the English, and to prevent their landing.

In this state of things Wolfe formed the bold and hazardous plan of landing in the night, a small distance above the city, on the northern bank of the river; and, by scaling a precipice, accessible only by a narrow path, and therefore but weakly guarded, to gain the heights in the rear of the town.

This resolution being taken, the admiral moved up the river, several leagues above the place where the landing was to be attempted, and made demonstrations of an intention to disembark a body of troops at different places. During the night, a strong detachment, in flat bottomed boats, fell silently down with the tide to the place fixed on for the descent. This was made an hour before day-break, about a mile above cape Diamond, Wolfe being the first man who leaped on shore. The Highlanders and light infantry, who composed the van, under the particular command of colonel Howe, had been directed to secure a four gun battery defending an intrenched path by which the heights were to be ascended, and to cover the landing of the remaining troops. The violence of the current forced them rather below the point of disembarkation; a circumstance which increased their difficulties. However, scrambling up the precipice, they gained the heights, and quickly dispersed the guard. The whole army followed up this narrow pass; and, having encountered only a scattering fire from some Canadians and Indians, gained the summit by the break of day, when the several corps were formed under their respective leaders.*

The intelligence that the English had gained the heights of Abraham was soon conveyed to Montcalm, who comprehended at once the full force of the advantage obtained by his adversary, and prepared for the engagement which could no longer be avoided. Leaving his camp at Montmorency, he crossed the St. Charles, for the purpose of attacking the English army.†

This movement was made in the view of Wolfe, who immediately formed his order of battle. His right wing was commanded by general Monckton, and his left by general Murray. The right flank was covered by the Louisbourg grenadiers, and the rear and left by the light infantry of Howe. The reserve consisted of Webb's regiment, drawn up in eight subdivisions, with large intervals between them.

Montcalm had formed his two wings of European and colonial troops in nearly equal numbers. A column of Europeans composed his centre; and two small field pieces were brought up to play on the English line. In this order he marched to the attack, advancing in his front about fifteen hundred militia and Indians, who kept up an irregular and galling fire under cover of the bushes.

The movements of the French indicating an intention to flank his left, general Wolfe ordered the bat-

* Belsham. Russel. † Townshend's letter.

CHAP XII talion of Amherst, and the two battalions of royal
1759. Americans, to that part of his line; where they were
formed *en potence* under general Townshend, presenting a double front. Disregarding the fire of the militia and Indians, he ordered his troops to reserve themselves for the column advancing in the rear of these irregulars.

Battle on the plains of Abraham. Moncalm had taken post on the left of the French army, and Wolfe on the right of the British; so that the two generals met each other, at the head of their respective troops; and there the battle was most severe. The French advanced briskly to the charge, and commenced the action with great animation. The English reserved their fire until the enemy were within forty yards of them, when they gave it with immense effect. The action was kept up for some time with great spirit. Wolfe, advancing at the head of his grenadiers with charged bayonets, received a

Death of Wolfe, mortal wound and soon afterwards expired. Undismayed by the loss of their general, the English continued their exertions under Monckton, on whom the command devolved. He also received a ball through his body, and general Townshend took command of

and of Montcalm. the British army. About the same time Montcalm received a mortal wound, and general Senezergus, the second in command, also fell. The left wing and centre of the French began to give way; and, being pressed close by the British, were driven from the field.

On the left and rear of the English, the action was

less severe. The light infantry had been placed in houses; and colonel Howe, the better to support them, had taken post still farther to the left, behind a copse. As the right of the French attacked the English left, he sallied from this position, upon their flanks, and threw them into disorder. In this critical moment, Townshend advanced several platoons against their front, and completely frustrated the attempt to turn the left flank.

HAP XII
C 1759.

In this state of the action, Townshend was informed that the command had devolved on him. Proceeding instantly to the centre, he found that part of the army thrown into some disorder by the ardour of pursuit; and his immediate efforts were employed in restoring the line. Scarcely was this effected, when Monsieur de Bougainville, who had been detached as high as cape Rouge to prevent a landing above, and who, on hearing that the English had gained the plains of Abraham, hastened to the assistance of Montcalm, appeared in the rear at the head of fifteen hundred men. Fortunately for the English, the right wing of the French, as well as their left and centre, had been entirely broken, and driven off the field. Two battalions and two pieces of artillery being advanced towards Bougainville, he retired; and Townshend did not think it advisable to risk the important advantages already gained, by pursuing this fresh body of troops through a difficult country.*

Victory of the English.

In this decisive battle, nearly equal numbers ap-

* Townshend's letter. Belsham. Russel. Gazette

pear to have been engaged. The English however possessed this immense advantage;—they were all veterans; while not more than half the French were of the same description. This circumstance would lead to an opinion that some motive, not well explained, must have induced Montcalm to hazard an action before he was assured of being joined by Bougainville.

The French regulars were almost entirely cut to pieces. The loss of the English was not so considerable as the fierceness of the action would indicate. The killed and wounded were less than six hundred men; but among the former, was the commander in chief. This gallant officer, whose rare merit, and lamented fate, have presented a rich theme for panegyric to both the poet and historian, received a ball in his wrist in the commencement of the action; but, wrapping a handkerchief around his arm, he continued to encourage his troops. Soon afterwards he received a shot in the groin, which he also concealed; and was advancing at the head of the grenadiers, when a third bullet pierced his breast. Though expiring, it was with reluctance he permitted himself to be carried into the rear, where he displayed, in the agonies of death, the most anxious solicitude concerning the fate of the day. Being told that the enemy was visibly broken, he reclined his head, from extreme faintness, on the arm of an officer standing near him; but was soon roused with the distant cry of " they fly, they fly." " Who fly ?" exclaimed the dying hero. On being answered "the French." "Then," said he, "I depart content;" and, almost immediately expired. "A death more glorious," adds Mr. Belsham, "and attended with circumstances more picturesque and interesting, is no where to be found in the annals of history."

The less fortunate, but not less gallant Montcalm expired on the same day. The same love of glory, and the same fearlessness of death, which so remarkably distinguished the British hero, were equally conspicuous in his competitor for victory and for fame. He expressed the highest satisfaction on hearing that his wound was mortal; and when told that he could survive only a few hours, quickly replied, "so much the better, I shall not then live to see the surrender of Quebec."*

The first days after the action were employed by general Townshend in making preparations for the siege of Quebec. But before his batteries were opened, the town capitulated; on condition that the inhabitants should, during the war, be protected in the free exercise of their religion, and the full enjoyment of their civil rights, leaving their future destinies to be decided by the treaty of peace.

Quebec was garrisoned by about five thousand English, under the command of general Murray; and the fleet sailed from the St. Lawrence.

The English minister, aware of the importance of completing the work thus fortunately begun, was not

* Russel.

of a temper to relax his exertions. His letters to the governors of the several colonies contained declarations of his intention to employ a strong military force for the ensuing year, and exhortations to them to continue their efforts for the annihilation of the French power in Canada. These exhortations were accompanied with assurances that he would again apply to parliament to reimburse their future extraordinary expenses; and were productive of the desired effect. The several assemblies voted the same number of troops, and amount of supplies, as had been furnished the preceding year.

In the mean time the governor of New France, and the general of the army, made great exertions to retrieve their affairs, and to avert the ruin which threatened them.

The remaining European troops were collected about Montreal; where they were reinforced with six thousand militia, and a body of Indians. Monsieur de Levi, on whom the command had devolved, determined to attempt the recovery of Quebec, before the opening of the St. Lawrence should enable the English to reinforce the garrison, and to afford it the protection of their fleet. But the out-posts being found too strong to admit of his carrying the place by *a coup de main*, he was under the necessity of postponing the execution of this design, until the upper part of the St. Lawrence should open, and afford a transportation by water, for his artillery and military stores.

In the month of April these were embarked at Montreal, under convoy of six frigates; which, sailing down the St. Lawrence, while the army marched by land, reached Point au Tremble in ten days.

CHAP XII
1760
Attempt to recover Quebec.

To avoid the hardships and dangers of a siege in a town too extensive to be defended by his sickly garrison, and inhabited by persons known to be hostile, Murray took the bold resolution of hazarding a battle. Having formed this determination, he led out his garrison to the heights of Abraham, and attacked the French near Sillery. He was received with unexpected firmness; and, perceiving that his utmost efforts could make no impression, he called off his army, and retired into the city. In this fierce encounter, the English loss amounted to near one thousand men; and they represent that of the French to have been not less considerable.

Battle near Sillery.

Monsieur de Levi improved his victory to the utmost. His trenches were opened before the town, on the same evening; but such was the difficulty of bringing up his heavy artillery, that near a fortnight elapsed before he could mount his batteries, and bring his guns to bear on the city. The batteries had been opened but a few days, when the garrison was relieved from its perilous situation, by the arrival of a British fleet.

Quebec besieged.

Quebec being secure, Monsieur de Levi raised the siege, and retired to Montreal.

During these transactions, general Amherst was taking measures for the annihilation of the remnant of

CHAP. XII
1760.

French power in Canada. He determined to employ the immense force under his command for the accomplishment of this object, and made arrangements, during the winter, to bring the armies from Quebec, lake Champlain, and lake Ontario, to act against Montreal.

The preparations being completed, the commander in chief marched at the head of upwards of ten thousand British and provincials, from the frontiers of New York to Oswego, where he was joined by sir William Johnson, with one thousand Indians. He embarked his army at that place, and proceeded down the St. Lawrence to Montreal.

Murray, who had been directed to advance up the river to the same point, with as many men as could be spared from Quebec, appeared below the town on the very day that Amherst approached it from above. The two generals found no difficulty in disembarking their troops, and the whole plan of co-operation had been so well concerted that, in a short time, they were joined by colonel Haviland with the detachment from Crown Point.

Montreal capitulates.

The junction of these armies presenting before Montreal a force not to be resisted, the governor offered to capitulate. In the month of September, Montreal, and all other places within the government of Canada, then remaining in the possession of France, were surrendered to his Britannic majesty. The troops were to be transported to France, and the Canadians to be protected in their property, and the full enjoyment of their religion.*

That colossal power, which France had been long erecting in America, with vast labour and expense; which had been the motive for one of the most extensive and desolating wars of modern times; was thus entirely overthrown. The causes of this interesting event are to be found in the superior wealth and population of the colonies of England, and in her immense naval strength; an advantage, in distant war, not to be counterbalanced by the numbers, the discipline, the courage, and the military talents, which may be combined in the armies of an inferior maritime power.

The joy diffused throughout the British dominions by this splendid conquest, was mingled with a proud sense of superiority which did not estimate with exact justice, the relative means employed by the belligerents. In no part of those dominions was this joy felt, in a higher degree, or with more reason, than in America. In that region, the wars between France and England had assumed a form, happily unknown to other parts of the civilised world. Not confined, as in Europe, to men in arms; women and children were its common victims. It had been carried by the savage to the fire side of the peaceful peasant, where the tomahawk and scalping knife were applied indiscriminately to every age, and to either sex. The hope was now fondly indulged that these scenes, at

* Minot. Belknap. Belsham. Russel.

least in the northern and middle colonies, were closed for ever.

The colonies of South Carolina and Georgia had been entirely exempted from the sharp conflicts of the north. France having been unable to draw Spain into the war, their neighbours in Florida remained quiet: and the Indians on their immediate frontiers were in the English interest. As the prospect of establishing peace in the north seemed to brighten, this state of repose in the south sustained a short interruption.

When the garrison of fort Du Quêsne retired down the Ohio into Louisiana, the French employed their address in the management of Indians, to draw the Cherokees from their alliance with Great Britain. Their negotiations with these savages were favoured by the irritations given to their warriors in Virginia, where they had been employed against the French, and the Indians in the French interest.

Their ill humour began to show itself in 1759. Upon its first appearance, governor Lyttleton prepared to march into their country at the head of a respectable military force. Alarmed at these hostile appearances, they dispatched thirty-two of their chiefs to Charleston, for the purpose of deprecating the vengeance with which their nation was threatened. Their pacific representations did not arrest the expedition. The governor not only persisted in the enterprise, but, under the pretext of securing the safe return of the Indian messengers, took them into the train of his army, where they were, in reality, confined as prisoners. To add to this indignity, they were, when arrived at the place of destination, shut up together in a single hut.

CHAP.XII
1760.

Notwithstanding the irritation excited by this conduct, a treaty was concluded, in which it was agreed that the chiefs detained by the governor should remain with him as hostages, until an equal number of those who had committed murder on the frontiers, should be delivered in exchange for them; and that, in the meantime, the Indians should seize and deliver up every white or red man coming into their country, who should endeavour to excite them to war against the English. After making this accommodation, the governor returned to Charleston, leaving his hostages prisoners in fort Prince George.

Scarcely had the army retired, when the Cherokees began to contrive plans for the relief of their chiefs. In an attempt to execute these plans, they killed the captain of the fort and wounded two officers. Orders were immediately given to put the hostages in irons; an indignity so resented by these fierce savages, that the first persons who attempted to execute the orders were stabbed. The soldiers enraged at this resistance, fell on the hostages and massacred them.

Inflamed to madness by this event, the whole nation flew to arms; and, according to their established mode of warfare, wreaked their fury on the inhabitants of the country in indiscriminate murder.

War with the southern Indians.

Mr. Bull, on whom the government of the province

had devolved, represented the distresses of South Carolina in such strong terms to general Amherst, that colonel Montgomery was ordered into that colony with a detachment of regular troops. He arrived in April; but, as all the forces would be required in the north, in order to complete the conquest of Canada, he was directed to strike a sudden blow, and to return to New York in time for the expedition against Montreal.

The utmost exertions were made by the colony in aid of colonel Montgomery, and he entered the Cherokee country with all the forces that could be collected. Their lower towns were destroyed; but, near the village of Etchoe, the first of their middle settlements, in an almost impenetrable wood, he was met by a large body of savages, and a severe action ensued. The English claimed the victory, but without much reason. They were so roughly handled, that colonel Montgomery withdrew his army, and retired to fort Prince George, at which place he prepared to embark for New York.

The consternation of the province was the greater, as serious fears were entertained that the Creeks and Choctaws, might be induced by the French to join the Cherokees. Colonel Montgomery was pressed in the most earnest manner, not to leave the province; and was, with difficulty, prevailed on to permit four companies to remain, while, with the main body of his detachment, he returned to New York.

1761. Mean while, the war continued to rage. The savages surrounded fort Loudoun; and the garrison amounting to four hundred men, was compelled by famine to surrender, on condition of being permitted to march into the settlements. The Indians, who regard conventions no longer than they are useful, attacked the garrison on its march, killed a number, and made the residue prisoners. Carolina again applied to general Amherst for assistance, who having completed the conquest of Canada, had leisure to attend to the southern colonies. Late in May, a strong detachment, commanded by colonel Grant, arrived at fort Prince George; and the colony raised a body of provincials, and of friendly Indians, to join him.

Early in June, he marched for the Cherokee towns. Near the place where the action had been fought the preceding year by Montgomery, the Indians again assembled in force, and gave battle in defence of their country. The action commenced about eight in the morning, and was maintained with spirit until eleven, when the Cherokees began to give way. They were pursued for two or three hours, after which Grant marched to the adjacent village of Etchoe, which he reduced to ashes. All the towns of the middle settlement shared the same fate. Their houses and corn fields were destroyed, and the whole country laid waste. Reduced to extremity, they sued sincerely for peace; and, in the course of the summer, the war was terminated by a treaty.*

Indians defeated.

It was not in America only that the vigour presiding in the councils of Britain shed lustre on the British

---

* History of South Carolina and Georgia.

CHAP XII arms. Splendid conquests were also made in Asia
1761. and Africa; and in Europe, her aids of men and
money enabled the greatest monarch of his age to
surmount difficulties which only Frederick and Mr.
Pitt could have dared to encounter.

1762. At length, Spain, alarmed at the increase of British
power in America, and apprehensive for the safety of
her own dominions, determined to take part against
Great Britain; and, early in the year 1762, the two
crowns declared war against each other. It was prosecuted, on the part of Great Britain, with signal success; and, in the course of the year, Martinique, Granada, St. Lucia, St. Vincent, and all the Caribbee
Islands were wrested from France; and the very important city of Havanna, which in a great degree
commands the gulph of Mexico, was taken from
Spain.

This course of conquest, which no force in possession of France and Spain seemed capable of checking,
while any of their distant possessions remained to be
subdued, was arrested by preliminary articles of
peace signed at Paris.

By this treaty, his christian majesty ceded to Britain, all the conquests made by that power on the continent of North America, together with the river and
port of Mobile; and all the territory to which France
was entitled on the left bank of the Mississippi, reserving only the island of New Orleans. And it was
agreed that, for the future, the confines between the
dominions of the two crowns, in that quarter of the

world, should be irrevocably fixed by a line drawn along the middle of the Mississippi, from its source as far as the river Iberville, and thence, by a line drawn along the middle of that river, and of the lakes Maurepas and Pont Chartrain.

The Havanna was exchanged with Spain for the Floridas. By establishing these great natural boundaries to the British empire in North America, all causes of future contest respecting that continent, with any potentate of Europe, were supposed to be removed.

CHAPTER XIII.

Opinions on the supremacy of parliament, and its right to tax the colonies.—The stamp act.—Congress at New York.—Violence in the towns.—Change of administration.—Stamp act repealed.—Opposition to the mutiny act.—Act imposing duties on tea, &c. resisted in America.—Letters from the assembly of Massachusetts to members of the administration.—Petition to the King.—Circular letter to the colonial assemblies.—Letter from the Earl of Hillsborough.—Assembly of Massachusetts dissolved.—Seizure of the Sloop Liberty.—Convention at Fanueil Hall.—Moderation of its proceedings.—Two British regiments arrive at Boston.—Resolutions of the house of Burgesses of Virginia.—Assembly dissolved.—The members form an association.—General measures against importation.—General court convened in Massachusetts.—Its proceedings.—Is prorogued.—Duties, except that on tea, repealed.—Circular letter of the earl of Hillsborough.—New York recedes from the non-importation agreement in part.—Her example followed.—Riot in Boston.—Trial and acquittal of Capain Preston.

1763.   THE attachment of the colonies to the mother country was never stronger than at the signature of the treaty of Paris.* The union of that tract of country which extends from the Atlantic to the Mississippi, and from the gulph of Mexico to the north pole, was deemed a certain guarantee of future peace, and an effectual security against the return of those bloody scenes from which no condition in life could afford an exemption.

This state of things, long and anxiously wished for by British America, had, at length, been effected by the union of British and American arms. The soldiers of the parent state and her colonies had co-operated in the same service, their blood had mingled in the same plains, and the object pursued was common to both people.

While the British nation was endeared to the Americans by this community of danger, and identity of interest, the brilliant achievements of the war had exalted to enthusiasm their admiration of British valour. They were proud of the land of their ancestors, and gloried in their descent from Englishmen.

---

* After the expulsion of the French from Canada, a considerable degree of ill humour was manifested in Massachusetts with respect to the manner in which the laws of trade were executed. A question was agitated in court, in which the colony took a very deep interest. A custom house officer applied for what was termed " a writ of assistance," which was an authority to search any house for dutiable articles suspected to be concealed in it. The right to grant special warrants was not contested; but this grant of a general warrant was deemed contrary to the principles of liberty, and an engine of oppression equally useless and vexatious, which would enable every petty officer of the customs to gratify his resentments by harrassing the most respectable men in the province. The ill temper excited on this occasion was shown by a reduction of the salaries of the Judges; but no diminution of attachment to the mother country appears to have been produced by it.

But this sentiment was not confined to the military character of the nation. While the excellence of the English constitution was a rich theme of declamation, every colonist believed himself entitled to its advantages; nor could he admit that, by crossing the Atlantic, his ancestors had relinquished the essential rights of British subjects.

The degree of authority which might rightfully be exercised by the mother country over her colonies, had never been accurately defined. In Britain, it had always been asserted that Parliament possessed the power of binding them in all cases whatever. In America, at different times, and in different provinces, different opinions had been entertained on this subject.

In New England, originally settled by republicans, habits of independence had nourished the theory that the colonial assemblies possessed every legislative power not surrendered by compact; that the Americans were subjects of the British crown, but not of the nation; and were bound by no laws to which their representatives had not assented. From this high ground they had been compelled reluctantly to recede. The Judges, being generally appointed by the governors with the advice of council, had determined that the colonies were bound by acts of parliament which concerned them, and which were expressly extended to them; and the general court of Massachusetts had, on a late occasion, explicitly recognised the same principle. This had probably become the opinion of many of the best informed men of the province; but the doctrine seems still to have been extensively maintained, that acts of parliament possessed only an external obligation; that they might regulate commerce, but not the internal affairs of the colonies.

In the year 1692, the general court of Massachusetts passed an act, denying the right of any other legislature to impose any tax whatever on the colony; and also asserting those principles of national liberty, which are found in Magna Charta. Not long afterwards, the legislature of New York, probably with a view only to the authority claimed by the governor, passed an act in which its own supremacy, not only in matters of taxation, but of general legislation, is expressly affirmed. Both these acts however were disapproved in England; and the parliament asserted its authority, in 1696, by declaring "that all laws, bye laws, usages, and customs, which shall be in practice in any of the plantations, repugnant to any law made or to be made in this kingdom relative to the said plantations, shall be void and of none effect." And three years afterwards, an act was passed for the trial of pirates in America, in which is to be found the following extraordinary clause. " Be it farther declared that, if any of the governors, or any person or persons in authority there, shall refuse to yield obedience to this act, such refusal is hereby declared to be a forfeiture of all and every the charters granted for the government and propriety of such plantations."

The English statute book furnishes many instances

CHAP XIII in which the legislative power of parliament over the
1763.
colonies was extended to regulations completely internal; and it is not recollected that their authority was in any case, openly controverted.

In the middle and southern provinces, no question respecting the supremacy of parliament, in matters of general legislation, ever existed. The authority of such acts of internal regulation as were made for America, as well as of those for the regulation of commerce, even by the imposition of duties, provided those duties were imposed for the purpose of regulation, had been at all times admitted. But these colonies, however they might acknowledge the supremacy of parliament in other respects, denied the right of that body to tax them internally.

Their submission to the act for establishing a general post office, which raised a revenue on the carriage of letters, was not thought a dereliction of this principle; because that regulation was not considered as a tax, but as a compensation for a service rendered, which every person might accept or decline. And all the duties on trade were understood to be imposed, rather with a view to prevent foreign commerce, than to raise a revenue. Perhaps the legality of such acts was the less questioned, because they were not rigorously executed, and their violation was sometimes designedly overlooked. A scheme for taxing the colonies by authority of parliament had been formed so early as the year 1739, and recommended to government by a club of American merchants, at whose head was sir William Keith, governor of Pennsylvania. In this scheme, it was proposed to raise a body of regulars, to be stationed along the western frontier of the British settlements, for the protection of the Indian traders; the expense of which establishment was to be paid with monies arising from a duty on stamped paper and parchment in all the colonies. This plan, however, was not countenanced by those in power; and seems never to have been seriously taken up by the government until the year 1754. The attention of the minister was then turned to a plan of taxation by authority of Parliament; and it will be recollected that a system was devised and recommended by him, as a substitute for the articles of union proposed by the convention at Albany. The temper and opinion of the colonists, and the impolicy of irritating them at a crisis which required all the exertions they were capable of making, suspended this delicate and dangerous measure; but it seems not to have been totally abandoned. Of the right of Parliament, as the supreme legislature, of the nation, to tax as well as govern the colonies, those who guided the councils of Britain seem not to have entertained a doubt; and the language of men in power, on more than one occasion through the war, indicated a disposition to put this right in practice when the termination of hostilities should render the experiment less dangerous. The failure of some of the colonies, especially those in which a proprietary government was established, to furnish, in time,

CHAP. XIII 1763. the aids required of them, contributed to foster this disposition. This opposition of opinion on a subject the most interesting to the human heart, was about to produce a system of measures which tore asunder all the bonds of relationship and affection that had subsisted for ages, and planted almost inextinguishable hatred in bosoms where the warmest friendship had long been cultivated.

1764. The unexampled expenses of the war required a great addition to the regular taxes of the nation. Considerable difficulty was found in searching out new sources of revenue, and great opposition was made to every tax proposed. Thus embarrassed, administration directed its attention to the continent of North America. The system which had been laid aside was renewed; and, on the motion of Mr. Grenville, first commissioner of the treasury, a resolution passed without much debate, declaring that it would be proper to impose certain stamp duties in the colonies and plantations, for the purpose of raising a revenue in America, payable into the British exchequer. This resolution was not carried into immediate effect, and was only declaratory of an intention to be executed the ensuing year.*

Other resolutions were passed at the same time, laying new duties on the trade of the colonies, which being in the form of commercial regulations, were not generally contested on the ground of right, though imposed expressly for the purpose of raising revenue.

* Belsham.

Great disgust, however, was produced by the increase of the duties, by the new regulations which were made, and by the manner in which those regulations were to be executed. The gainful commerce long carried on clandestinely with the French and Spanish colonies, in the progress of which an evasion of the duties imposed by law had been overlooked by the government, was to be rigorously suppressed by taxes amounting to a prohibition of fair trade; and their exact collection was to be enforced by measures not much less offensive in themselves, than on account of the object to be effected.*

Completely to prevent smuggling, all the officers in the sea service, who were on the American station, were converted into revenue officers; and directed to take the custom house oaths. Many vexatious seizures were made, for which no redress could be obtained, but in England. The penalties and forfeitures too accruing under the act, as if the usual tribunals could not be trusted, were made recoverable in any court of vice-admiralty in the colonies. It will be readily conceived, how odious, a law, made to effect an odious object, must have been rendered by such provisions as these.

The resolution concerning the duties on stamps excited a great and general ferment in America. The right of parliament to impose taxes on the colonies for the purpose of raising a revenue, became the subject of universal conversation, and was almost uni-

* Belsham. Minot.

CHAP. XIII
1765.

versally denied. Petitions to the King, and memorials to both houses of parliament against the measure, were transmitted by several of the provincial assemblies to the board of trade in England, to be presented to his majesty immediately; and to parliament, when that body should be convened. The house of representatives of Massachusetts instructed their agent to use his utmost endeavours to prevent the passage of the stamp act, or any other act levying taxes or impositions of any kind on the American provinces. A committee was appointed to act in the recess of the general court, with instructions to correspond with the legislatures of the several colonies, to communicate to them the instructions given to the agent of Massachusetts, and to solicit their concurrence in similar measures. These legislative proceedings were, in many places, seconded by associations entered into by individuals, for diminishing the use of British manufactures.*

The administration, perceiving the opposition to be encountered by adhering to the vote of the preceding session, informed the agents of the colonies in London that, if they would propose any other mode of raising the sum required†, their proposition would be accepted, and the stamp duty laid aside. The agents replied that they were not authorised to propose any substitute, but were ordered to oppose the bill when it should be brought into the house, by petitions questioning the right of parliament to tax

* Minot. † 100,000*l.* sterling.

the colonies. This reply placed the controversy on ground which admitted of no compromise. Determined to persevere in the system he had adopted, and believing successful resistance to be impossible, Mr. Grenville brought into parliament his celebrated act for imposing stamp duties in America; and it passed both houses by great majorities, but not without animated debate. So little weight does the human mind allow to the most conclusive arguments, when directed against the existence of power in ourselves, that general Conway is said to have stood alone* in denying the right claimed by parliament.

CHAP XIII.
1765.

This act excited serious alarm throughout the colonies. It was sincerely believed to wound vitally the constitution of the country, and to destroy the most sacred principles of liberty. Combinations against its execution were formed; and the utmost exertions were used to diffuse among the people a knowledge of the pernicious consequences which must flow from admitting that the colonists could be taxed by a legislature in which they were not represented.

The assembly of Virginia was in session when the intelligence was received; and, by a small majority, passed several resolutions introduced by Mr. Henry, and seconded by Mr. Johnson,† one of which asserts

---

* Mr. Pitt was not in the house; and Mr. Ingersoll, in his letter, states that Alderman Beckford joined general Conway. Mr. Belsham, therefore, who makes this statement, was probably mistaken.

† See note No. 3, at the end of the volume.

the exclusive right of that assembly to lay taxes and impositions on the inhabitants of that colony.*

On the passage of these resolutions, the governor dissolved the assembly; and writs for new elections were issued. In almost every instance, the members who had voted in favour of the resolutions were re-elected, while those who had voted against them were generally excluded.

The legislatures of several other colonies passed resolutions similar to those of Virginia. The house of representatives of Massachusetts, contemplating a still more solemn and effectual expression of the general sentiment, recommended a congress of deputies from all the colonial assemblies, to meet at New York the first Monday in October. Circular letters communicating this recommendation, were addressed to the respective assemblies wherever they were in session. New Hampshire alone, although concurring in the general opposition, declined sending members to the congress; and the legislatures of Virginia and North Carolina were not in session.†

In the meantime, the press teemed with the most animating exhortations to the people, to unite in defence of their liberty and property; and the stamp officers were, almost universally, compelled to resign.

At the time appointed, the commissioners from the assemblies of Massachusetts, Rhode Island, Connecticut, New York, New Jersey, Pennsylvania, the three lower counties on the Delaware, Maryland, and

* Prior documents. Virginia Gazette. † Minot.

South Carolina assembled at New York ; and, having chosen Timothy Ruggles, of Massachusetts, their chairman, proceeded on the important objects for which they had convened. The first measure of congress was a declaration* of the rights and grievances of the colonists. This paper asserts their title to all the rights and liberties of natural born subjects within the kingdom of Great Britain; among the most essential of which are, the exclusive power to tax themselves, and the trial by jury.

The act granting certain stamp and other duties in the British colonies was placed first on the list of grievances. Its direct tendency they said, was, by taxing the colonists without their consent, and by extending the jurisdiction of courts of admiralty, to subvert their rights and liberties. They also addressed a petition to the King, and a memorial to each house of parliament.

These papers were drawn with temperate firmness. They express, unequivocally, the attachment of the colonists to the mother country ; and assert the rights they claim in the earnest language of conviction.

Having, in addition to these measures, recommended to the several colonies to appoint special agents, with instructions to unite their utmost endeavours in soliciting a redress of grievances ; and directed their clerk to make out a copy of their proceedings for each colony, congress adjourned.†

---

* See note No. 4, at the end of the volume.   † Minot. Prior documents.

CHAP XIII
1765.

To interest the people of England against the measures of administration, associations were formed for the encouragement of domestic manufactures, and against the use of those imported from Great Britain. To increase their quantity of wool, the colonists determined to kill no lambs, and to use all the means in their power to multiply their flocks of sheep. To avoid the use of stamps, proceedings in the courts of justice were suspended; and a settlement of all controversies by arbitration was strongly recommended.

Violence in the large towns.

While this determined and systematic opposition was made by the thinking part of the community, some riotous and disorderly meetings took place, especially in the large towns, which threatened serious consequences. Many houses were destroyed, much property injured, and several persons, highly respectable in character and station, were grossly abused.

Change of administration.

While these transactions were passing in America, causes entirely unconnected with the affairs of the colonies, produced a total revolution in the British cabinet. The Grenville party was succeeded by an administration unfriendly to the plan for taxing the colonies without their consent. General Conway, one of the principal secretaries of state, addressed a circular letter to the several governors, in which he censured, in mild terms, the violent measures that had been adopted, and recommended to them, while they maintained the dignity of the crown and of parliament, to observe a temperate and conciliatory conduct towards the colonists, and to endeavour, by persuasive means, to restore the public peace.

Parliament was opened by a speech from the throne, in which his majesty declared his firm confidence in their wisdom and zeal, which would, he doubted not, guide them to such sound and prudent resolutions, as might tend at once to preserve the constitutional rights of the British legislature over the colonies, and to restore to them that harmony and tranquillity which had lately been interrupted by disorders of the most dangerous nature."

In the course of the debate in the house of commons, on the motion for the address, Mr. Pitt, in explicit terms, condemned the act for collecting stamp duties in America; and avowed the opinion that parliament had no right to tax the colonies. He asserted, at the same time, "the authority of that kingdom to be sovereign and supreme in every circumstance of government and legislation whatever." He maintained the difficult proposition "that taxation is no part of the governing, or legislative power; but that taxes are a voluntary gift and grant of the commons alone;" and concluded an eloquent speech, by recommending to the house, "that the stamp act be repealed, *absolutely*, *totally*, and *immediately*."

The opinions expressed by Mr. Pitt were warmly opposed by the late ministers. Mr. Grenville said, "that the disturbances in America were grown to tumults and riots; he doubted, they bordered on open rebellion; and, if the doctrine he had heard that day should be confirmed, he feared they would lose that name to take that of revolution. The government over them being dissolved, a revolution would take place in America." He contended that taxation was a part of the sovereign power;—one branch of legislation; and had been exercised over those who were not represented. He could not comprehend the distinction between external and internal taxation; and insisted that the colonies ought to bear a part of the burdens occasioned by a war for their defence.

Stamp act repealed. The existing administration, however, concurred in sentiment with Mr. Pitt, and the act was repealed; but its repeal was accompanied with a declaratory act, asserting the right of Great Britain to bind the colonies in all cases whatsoever.

The intelligence of this event was received in America with general manifestations of joy. The assertion of the abstract principle of right gave many but little concern, because they considered it merely as a salvo for the wounded pride of the nation, and believed confidently that no future attempt would be made to reduce it to practice. The highest honours were conferred on those parliamentary leaders who had exerted themselves to obtain a repeal of the act; and, in Virginia, the house of Burgesses voted a statue to his majesty, as an acknowledgment of their high sense of his attention to the rights and petitions of his people.

Though all the colonies rejoiced at the repeal of the stamp act, the same temper did not prevail in all of them. In the commercial cities of the north, the regulations of trade, were nearly as odious as the stamp act itself. Political parties too had been formed, and had assumed a bitterness in some of the colonies, entirely unknown in others. These dispositions were not long concealed. The first measures of Massachusetts and of New York demonstrated that, in them, the reconciliation with the mother country was not cordial.

The letter of secretary Conway, transmitting the repeal of the act imposing a duty on stamps, enclosed also a resolution of parliament declaring that those persons who had suffered injuries in consequence of their assisting to execute that act, ought to be compensated by the colony in which such injuries were sustained. This was chiefly in Massachusetts. The resolution of parliament was laid before the general court of that province, by governor Bernard, in a speech rather in the spirit of the late, than the present administration;—rather calculated to irritate than assuage the angry passions that had been excited. The house of representatives resented his manner of addressing them; and appeared more disposed to inquire into the riots, and to compel those concerned in them to make indemnities, than to compensate the sufferers out of the public purse. But, after a second session, and some intimation that parliament would enforce its requisition, an act of pardon to the offenders, and of indemnity to the sufferers, was passed; but was rejected by the King, because the colonial assembly had no power, by their charter, to pass an act of general pardon, but at the instance of the crown.*

In New York, where general Gage was expected with a considerable body of troops, a message was transmitted by the governor to the legislature, desiring their compliance with an act of parliament called " the mutiny act," which required that the colony in which any of his majesty's forces might be stationed, should provide barracks for them, and necessaries in their quarters. The legislature postponed the consideration of this message until the troops were actually arrived; and then, after a second message from the governor, reluctantly and partially complied with the requisitions of the act.

At a subsequent session, the governor brought the subject again before the assembly, who determined that the act of parliament could be construed only to require that provision should be made for troops on a march, and not while permanently stationed in the country.† The reason assigned for not furnishing the accommodations required by the governor, implies the opinion that the act of parliament was rightfully obligatory; and yet the requisitions of the mutiny act were unquestionably a tax; and no essential distinction is perceived between the power of parliament to levy a tax by its own authority, and to levy it through the medium of the colonial legislatures; they having no right to refuse obedience to the act. It is remarkable that such inaccurate ideas should still have pre-

* Minot.   † Minot. Prior documents. Belsham.

vailed, concerning the controling power of parliament over the colonies.

In England it was thought to manifest a very forbearing spirit, that this instance of disobedience was punished with no positive penalties; and that the ministers contented themselves with a law prohibiting the legislature of the province from passing any act, until it should comply, in every respect, with the requisitions of parliament. The persevering temper of Massachusetts not having found its way to New York, this measure produced the desired effect.

Two companies of artillery, driven into the port of Boston by stress of weather, applied to the governor for supplies. He laid the application before his council, who advised that, " in pursuance of the act of parliament" the supplies required should be furnished. They were furnished, and the money to procure them was drawn from the treasury by the authority of the executive.

On the meeting of the legislature, the house of representatives expressed in pointed terms their disapprobation of the conduct of the governor. Particular umbrage was given by the expression " *in pursuance of an act of parliament.*" " After the repeal of the stamp act, they were surprised to find that this act, equally odious and unconstitutional, should remain in force. They lamented the entry of this reason for the advice of council the more, as it was an uuwarrantable and unconstitutional step which totally disabled them from testifying the same cheerfulness they had always shown in granting to his majesty, of their free accord, such aids as his service has from time to time required."* Copies of these messages were transmitted by governor Bernard to the minister, accompanied by letters not calculated to diminish the unpleasantness of the communication.

The idea of raising revenue in America, was so highly favoured in England, especially by the landed interest, that not even the influence of administration could have obtained a repeal of the stamp act, on the naked principle of right. Few were hardy enough to question the supremacy of parliament; and the act receding from the practical assertion of the power to tax the colonists, deeply wounded the pride of the King, and of the nation.

The temper discovered in some of the colonies was ill calculated to assuage the wound, which this measure had inflicted, on the haughty spirit of the country; and is supposed to have contributed to the revival of a system, which had been reluctantly abandoned.

Charles Townshend, chancellor of the exchequer, said boastingly in the house of commons, " that he knew how to draw a revenue from the colonies without giving them offence."† Mr. Grenville eagerly caught at the declaration, and urged this minister to pledge himself to bring forward the measure, at which he had hinted. During the sickness and absence of lord Chatham, the cabinet had decided on introduc-

* Minot. † Belsham.

ing a bill for imposing certain duties on tea, glass, paper, and painter's colours, imported into the colonies from Great Britain; and appropriating the money in the first instance, to the salaries of the officers of government. This bill was brought into parliament, and passed almost without opposition.

The friends of America, in England, had distinguished between internal and external taxation; and the same distinction had been made in the colonies. But the discussions originating in the stamp act, while they diffused among the colonists a knowledge of their political rights, had inspired also more accurate ideas respecting them.

These duties were plainly intended, not to regulate commerce, but to raise revenue, which would be as certainly collected from the colonists, as the duties on stamps could have been. The principle of the two measures was the same. Many of the Americans were too intelligent to be misguided by the distinction between internal and external taxation, or by the precedents quoted in support of the right, for which parliament contended. This measure was considered as establishing a precedent of taxation for the mere purpose of revenue, which might afterwards be extended at the discretion of parliament; and was spoken of as the *entering wedge*, designed to make way for impositions too heavy to be borne. The appropriation of the money did not lessen the odium of the tax. The colonists considered the dependence of the officers of government, on the colonial legislature, for

CHAP XIII. their salaries, as the best security for their attending
1767. to the interests, and cultivating the affections of the
provinces.* Yet the opinion that this act was unconstitutional, was not adopted so immediately, or so generally, as in the case of the stamp act. Many able political essays appeared in the papers, demonstrating that it violated the principles of the English constitution and of English liberty, before the conviction became general, that the same principle which had before been successfully opposed, was again approaching in a different form.

The general court of Massachusetts, perceiving plainly that the claim to tax America was revived, and being determined to oppose it, addressed an elaborate letter to Dennis de Berdt, agent for the house of representatives, detailing at great length, and with much weight of argument, all the objections to the late acts of parliament. Letters were also addressed to the earl of Shelburne and general Conway, secretaries of state, to the marquis of Rockingham, lord Camden, the earl of Chatham, and the lords commissioners of the treasury. These letters, while they breathe a spirit of ardent attachment to the British constitution, and to the British nation, manifest a perfect conviction that their complaints were just.

1768.

Letters from the general court to several members of administration.

Conclusive as the arguments they contained might have appeared to Englishmen, if urged by themselves in support of their own rights, they had not much weight, when used to disprove the existence of their

* Prior documents.

authority over others. The deep and solemn tone of conviction, however, conveyed in all these letters, ought to have produced a certainty that the principles assumed in them had made a strong impression, and would not be lightly abandoned. It ought to have been foreseen that with such a people, so determined, the conflict must be stern and hazardous: and, it was well worth the estimate, whether the object would compensate the means used to obtain it.

The assembly also voted a petition to the King, replete with professions of loyalty and attachment; but stating, in explicit terms, their sense of the acts against which they petitioned.

Petition to the King.

A proposition was next made for an address to the other colonies on the power claimed by parliament, which, after considerable debate, was carried in the affirmative; and a circular letter to the assemblies of the several provinces, setting forth the proceedings of the house of representatives, was prepared and adopted.*

To rescue their measures from the imputation of systematic opposition to the British government, the house, without acknowledging the obligation of the mutiny act, complied with a requisition of the governor to make a farther provision for one of the King's garrisons within the province. The governor, soon afterwards, prorogued the general court with an angry speech, not calculated to diminish the resentments of the house directed against himself; resentments

---

* See note 5, at the end of the volume.

occasioned as much by the haughtiness of his manners, and a persuasion that he had misrepresented their conduct and opinions to ministers, as by the unpopular course his station required him to pursue.*

The circular letter of the house of representatives of Massachusetts was well received in the other colonies. They approved the measures which had been taken, and readily united in them. They, too, petitioned the King against the obnoxious acts of parliament, and instructed their several agents to use all proper means to obtain their repeal. Virginia transmitted a statement of her proceedings† to her sister colonies; and her house of Burgesses, in a letter to Massachusetts, communicating the representation made to parliament, say, " that they do not affect an independency of their parent kingdom, the prosperity of which they are bound, to the utmost of their abilities, to promote; but cheerfully acquiesce in the authority of parliament to make laws for the preserving a necessary dependence, and for regulating the trade of the colonies; yet they cannot conceive, and humbly insist, it is not essential to support a proper relation between the mother country, and colonies transplanted from her, that she should have a right to raise money from them without their consent, and presume they do not aspire to more than the rights of British subjects, when they assert that no power on earth has a right to impose taxes on the people, or take the

* Minot. † Prior documents.

smallest portion of their property without their consent given by their representatives in parliament.*

On the first intimation of the measures taken by Massachusetts, the earl of Hillsborough, who had been appointed to the newly created office of secretary of state for the department of the colonies, addressed a circular to the several governors, to be laid before the respective assemblies, in which he treated the circular letter of Massachusetts, as being of the most dangerous tendency, calculated to inflame the minds of his majesty's good subjects in the colonies, to promote an unwarrantable combination, to excite an open opposition to the authority of parliament, and to subvert the true principles of the constitution.†

His first object was to prevail on the several assemblies openly to censure the conduct of Massachusetts; his next, to prevent their approving the proceedings of that colony. The letter, far from producing the desired effect, rather served to strengthen the determination of the colonies to unite in their en-

---

* In this letter the house of Burgesses express their opinion of the mutiny act in the following terms. "The act suspending the legislative power of New York, they consider as still more alarming to the colonies, though it has that single province in view. If parliament can compel them to furnish a single article to the troops sent over, they may, by the same rule, oblige them to furnish clothes, arms, and every other necessary, even the pay of the officers and soldiers; a doctrine replete with every mischief, and utterly subversive of all that's dear and valuable; for what advantage can the people of the colonies derive from choosing their own representatives, if those representatives, when chosen, be not permitted to exercise their own judgments, be under a necessity (on pain of being deprived of their legislative authority) of enforcing the mandates of a British parliament."

† Prior documents.

deavours to obtain a repeal of laws universally detested. On manifesting this disposition, the assemblies were generally dissolved;—probably in pursuance of instructions from the crown.

When the general court of Massachusetts was again convened, governor Bernard laid before the house of representatives, an extract of a letter from the earl of Hillsborough, in which, after animadverting in harsh terms on the circular letter to the colonies, he declared it to be " the King's pleasure" that the governor " should require of the house of representatives, in his majesty's name, to rescind the resolution on which the circular letter was founded, and to declare their disapprobation of, and dissent from, that rash and hasty proceeding."

This message excited considerable agitation; but the house, without coming to any resolution on it, requested the governor to lay before them the whole letter of the earl of Hillsborough, and also copies of such letters as had been written by his excellency to that nobleman, on the subject to which the message referred.

The copies were haughtily refused; but the residue of the letter from the earl of Hillsborough was laid before them. That minister said, " if, notwithstanding the apprehensions which may justly be entertained of the ill consequence of a continuance of this factious spirit, which seems to have influenced the resolutions of the assembly at the conclusion of the last session, the new assembly should refuse to comply with his majesty's reasonable expectation, it is the King's pleasure that you immediately dissolve them."

This subject being taken into consideration, a letter to the earl was reported, and agreed to by a majority of ninety-three to thirteen, in which they defended their circular letter in strong and manly, but respectful terms; and concluded with saying, " the house humbly rely on the royal clemency, that to petition his majesty will not be deemed by him to be inconsistent with a respect to the British constitution as settled at the revolution by William III., and that to acquaint their fellow subjects involved in the same distress, of their having so done, in full hopes of success, even if they had invited the union of all America in one joint supplication, would not be discountenanced by their gracious sovereign, as a measure of an inflammatory nature. That when your lordship shall in justice lay a true state of these matters before his majesty, he will no longer consider them as tending to create unwarrantable combinations, or excite an unjustifiable opposition to the constitutional authority of parliament; that he will then truly discern who are of that desperate faction which is continually disturbing the public tranquillity; and that, while his arm is extended for the protection of his distressed and injured subjects, he will frown upon all those who, to gratify their own passions, have dared to attempt to deceive him."*

* Prior documents.

CHAP XIII
1768.

Legislature of Massachusetts dissolved.

Seizure of the Sloop Liberty.

A motion to rescind the resolution on which their circular letter was founded, passed in the negative, by a majority of ninety-two to seventeen; and a letter to the governor was prepared, stating their motives for refusing to comply with the requisition of the earl of Hillsborough. Immediately after receiving it, he prorogued the assembly, with an angry speech; and, the next day, dissolved it by proclamation.*

While the opposition was thus conducted by the legislature with temperate firmness, and legitimate means, the general irritation occasionally displayed itself at Boston, in acts of violence denoting evidently that the people of that place, were prepared for much stronger measures than their representatives had adopted.

The seizure of the sloop Liberty belonging to Mr. Hancock, by the collector of the customs, occasioned the assemblage of a tumultuous mob, who beat the officers and their assistants, took possession of a boat belonging to the collector, burnt it in triumph, and patrolled the streets for a considerable time. The revenue officers fled for refuge, first to the Romney man of war, and afterwards to Castle William. After the lapse of some time, the governor moved the council to take into consideration some measure for restoring vigour and firmness to government. The council replied "that the disorders which happened were occasioned by the violent and unprecedented manner in which the sloop Liberty had been seized

* Minot.

by the officers of the customs. And the inhabitants of Boston, in a justificatory memorial, supported by affidavits, insisted that the late tumults were occasioned, principally, by the haughty conduct of the commissioners and their subordinate officers, and by the illegal and offensive conduct of the Romney man of war.*

The legislature however did not think proper to countenance this act of violence. A committee of both houses, appointed to inquire into the state of the province, made a report which, after reprobating the circumstances attending the seizure, to which the mob was ascribed, declared their abhorrence of a procedure which they pronounced criminal; desired the governor to direct a prosecution against all persons concerned in the riot; and to issue a proclamation offering a reward to any person who should make discoveries by which the rioters or their abettors should be brought to condign punishment.

This report, however, seems to have been intended, rather to save appearances, than to produce any real effect. It was perfectly understood that no person would dare to inform; or even to appear, as a witness, in any prosecution which might be instituted. Suits were afterwards brought against Mr. Hancock and others, owners of the vessel and cargo; but they were never prosecuted to a final decision.†

This riot accelerated a measure, which tended, in

---

* Minot. Prior documents.   † Minot.

CHAP XIII
1768.

no inconsiderable degree, to irritate still farther the angry dispositions already prevalent in Boston.

The governor had pressed on administration the necessity of stationing a military force in the province, for the protection of the officers employed in collecting the revenue, and of the magistrates, in preserving the public peace. In consequence of these representations, orders had already been given to general Gage to detach, at least, one regiment on this service, and to select for the command of it, an officer on whose prudence, resolution, and integrity, he could rely. The transactions respecting the sloop Liberty rendered any attempt to produce a countermand of these orders entirely abortive; and, probably occasioned two regiments, instead of one, to be detached by general Gage.*

It seems to have been supposed that a dissolution of the assembly of Massachusetts would dissolve also the opposition to the measures of administration; and that the people, having no longer constitutional leaders, being no longer excited and conducted by their representatives, would gradually become quiet, and return to, what was termed, their duty to government. But the opinions expressed by the house of representatives were the opinions of the great body of the people, and had been adopted with too much ardour to be readily suppressed. The most active and energetic part of society had embraced them with enthusiasm; and the dissolution of the assembly, by creat-

* Minot.

ing a necessity for devising other expedients, hastened a mode of conducting opposition at least as efficacious, and afterwards universally adopted.

CHAP. XIII
1768.

At a town meeting of the inhabitants of Boston, a committee was deputed for the purpose of praying the governor to convene another general assembly. He replied that no other could be convened until his majesty's commands to that effect should be received. This answer being reported, the meeting resolved " that to levy money within that province by any other authority than that of the general court, was a violation of the royal charter, and of the undoubted natural rights of British subjects.

" That the freeholders, and other inhabitants of the town of Boston would, at the peril of their lives and fortunes, take all legal and constitutional measures to defend all and singular the rights, liberties, privileges, and immunities, granted in their royal charter.

" That as there was an apprehension in the minds of many of an approaching war with France, those inhabitants who were not provided with arms should be requested duly to observe the laws of the province, which required that every freeholder should furnish himself with a complete stand."

But the important resolution was " that, as the governor did not think proper to call a general court for the redress of their grievances, the town would then make choice of a suitable number of persons to act for them as a committee in a convention, to be held

CHAP XIII 1768. at Faneuil Hall in Boston, with such as might be sent to join them from the several towns in the province."

These votes were communicated by the select men, in a circular letter to the other towns in the province, which were requested to concur, and to elect committee men, to meet those of Boston in convention.

Convention assembles in Boston. The measure was generally adopted; and a convention met, which was regarded with all the respect that could have been paid to a legitimate assembly.*

The country in general, though united on the great constitutional question of taxation, was probably not so highly exasperated as the people of Boston; and the convention acted with unexpected moderation.

Its moderation. They disclaimed all pretensions to any other character than that of mere individuals, assembled by deputation from the towns, to consult and advise on such measures as might tend to promote the peace of his majesty's subjects in the province, but without power to pass any acts possessing a coercive quality.

They petitioned the governor to assemble a general court, and addressed a letter to the agent of the province in England, stating the character in which they met, and the motives which brought them together. After expressing their opinions with temper and firmness on the subjects of general complaint, and recommending patience and order to the people, they dissolved themselves, and returned to their respective homes.†

* Minot. † Idem.

The day before the convention rose, the two regiments which had been detached by general Gage arrived, under convoy, in Nantasket road. The council had rejected an application of the governor to provide quarters for them, because the barracks in the castle were sufficient for their accommodation; and, by act of parliament, the British troops were not to be quartered elsewhere until those barracks were full. General Gage had directed one regiment to be stationed in Boston; but, on hearing a report that the people were in a state of open revolt, he gave additional orders, which left the whole subject to the discretion of the commanding officer; who was induced, by some rash threats of opposing the disembarkation of the troops to land both regiments in that place. The ships took a station which commanded the whole town, and lay with their broad sides towards it, ready to fire, should any resistance be attempted. The troops landed under cover of their cannon, and marched into the common with loaded muskets and fixed bayonets;* a display of military pomp, which was believed by the inhabitants to have been intended for the purpose either of intimidation, or of irritation.

CHAP. XIII
1768.
Two regiments arrive.

The select men, as well as the council, having refused to provide quarters for the troops, the governor ordered the state house to be opened for their reception; and they took possession of all the apartments in it, except that which was reserved for the council. The people were filled with indignation at seeing the

* Gazette.

chamber of their representatives crowded with regular soldiers, their counsellors surrounded with foreign troops, and their whole city exhibiting the appearance of a garrisoned town. With the difference of manners between the soldiers and the inhabitants, and the strong prejudices reciprocally felt against each other, it is not wonderful that personal broils should frequently occur, and that mutual antipathies should be still farther increased.*

While these measures were pursuing in America, every session of parliament was opened with a speech from the King, stating that a disposition to refuse obedience to the laws, and to resist the authority of the supreme legislature of the nation, still prevailed among his misguided subjects in some of the colonies. In the addresses to the throne, both houses uniformly expressed their abhorrence of the rebellious spirit manifested in the colonies, and their approbation of the measures taken by his majesty for the restoration of order and good government.

To give a more solemn expression to the sense of parliament on this subject, the two houses entered into joint resolutions, condemning the measures pursued by the Americans; and agreed to an address, approving the conduct of the crown, giving assurances of effectual support to such farther measures as might be found necessary to maintain the civil magistrates in a due execution of the laws within the province of Massachusetts Bay, and beseeching his

* Minot

majesty to direct the governor of that colony to obtain and transmit information of all treasons committed in Massachusetts since the year 1767, with the names of the persons who had been most active in promoting such offences, that prosecutions might be instituted against them within the realm, in pursuance of the statute of the 35th of Henry VIII.*

The impression made by these threatening declarations, which seem to have been directed particularly against Massachusetts, in the hope of deterring the other provinces from involving themselves in her dangers, was far from being favourable to the views of the mother country. The determination to resist the exercise of the authority claimed by Great Britain not only remained unshaken, but was manifested in a still more decided form.

Not long after these votes of parliament, the assembly of Virginia was convened by lord Botetourt, a nobleman of conciliating manners, who had lately been appointed governor of that province. The house took the state of the colony into their immediate consideration, and passed unanimously several resolutions asserting the exclusive right of that assembly to impose taxes on the inhabitants within his majesty's dominion of Virginia, and their undoubted right to petition for a redress of grievances, and to obtain a concurrence of the other colonies in such petitions. That all persons charged with the commission of any offence within that colony, were entitled to a trial be-

Resolutions of the house of Burgesses of Virginia.

* Belsham. Prior documents.

fore the tribunals of the country, according to the fixed and known course of proceeding therein, and that to sieze such persons, and transport them beyond sea for trial, derogated in a high degree from the rights of British subjects, as thereby the inestimable privilege of being tried by a jury from the vicinage, as well as the liberty of summoning and producing witnesses on such trial, will be taken from the party accused."

An address to his majesty was also agreed on, which states in the style of loyalty and real attachment to the crown, the deep conviction of the house of Burgesses of Virginia, that the complaints of the colonists were well founded.*

Assembly dissolved. Intelligence of these proceedings having reached the governor, he suddenly dissolved the assembly. This measure did not produce the desired effect. The members convened at a private house, and, having chosen their speaker, moderator, proceeded to form a non-importing association, which was signed by every person present, and afterwards, almost universally throughout the province.†

From the commencement of the controversy, the opinion seems to have prevailed in all the colonies, that the most effectual means of succeeding in the struggle in which they were engaged, were those which would interest the merchants and manufacturers of Great Britain in their favour. Under the influence of this opinion, associations had been proposed in

*, Gazette. Prior documents.   † Idem.

Massachusetts, as early as May 1765, for the non-importation of goods from that country. The merchants of some of the trading towns in the other colonies, especially those of Philadelphia, refused, at that time, to concur in a measure which they thought too strong for the existing state of things; and it was laid aside. But, in the beginning of August, it was resumed in Boston; and the merchants of that place entered into an agreement not to import from Great Britain any articles whatever, except a few of the first necessity, between the first of January 1769, and the first of January 1770; and not to import tea, glass, paper, or painter's colours, until the duties imposed on those articles should be taken off. This agreement was soon afterwards adopted in the town of Salem, the city of New York, and the province of Connecticut; but was not generally entered into through the colonies, until the resolutions and address of the two houses of parliament which have already been mentioned, seemed to cut off the hope that petitions and memorials alone, would effect the object for which they contended.*

The proceedings of the house of Burgesses of Virginia had been transmitted to the speakers of the several assemblies throughout the continent. In the opinion of the neighbouring colonies, the occasion required efficacious measures; and an association, similar to that which had been formed by their elder sister, was entered into by Maryland, and the Carolinas.

<small>Measures against the importation of British goods.</small>

* Minot.

The inhabitants of Charleston went so far as to break off all connexion with Rhode Island and Georgia, which had refused to adopt the non-importation agreement. This vigorous measure was not without its influence; and those provinces, soon afterwards, entered into the association.*

In Portsmouth in New Hampshire, where governor Wentworth possessed great influence, some repugnance to this measure was also discovered; but, being threatened with a suspension of their intercourse with the other colonies, the merchants of that place concurred in the general system.

All united in giving effect to this agreement. The utmost exertions were used to improve the manufactures of the country; and the fair sex, laying aside the late fashionable ornaments of England, exulted, with patriotic pride, in appearing dressed in the produce of their own looms. Committees chosen by the people superintended importations; and the force of public opinion went far to secure the agreement from violation.

General court in Massachusetts. The necessities of government requiring a supply of money, the general court of Massachusetts was again convened. The members of the former house of representatives were generally re-elected, and brought with them the temper which had occasioned their dissolution. Instead of entering on the business for which they were called together, they engaged in a controversy with the governor concerning the re-

* Gazette. Prior documents.

moval of the ships of war from the harbour, and of the troops from the town of Boston, to which they contended, his power, as the representative of the crown was adequate.

The governor, ascribing this temper to the influence of the metropolis, adjourned the general court to Cambridge; but this measure served to increase the existing irritation. The business recommended to them remained unnoticed; their altercations with the governor continued; and they entered into several warm resolutions enlarging the catalogue of their grievances, in terms of greater exasperation than had appeared in the official acts of any legislature on the continent.*

Not long after the passage of these resolutions, the house explicitly refused to make the provision required by the mutiny act for the troops stationed in Massachusetts; upon which, the legislature was prorogued until the first of January.†

The committees, appointed to examine the cargoes of vessels arriving from Great Britain, continued to execute the trust reposed in them. Votes of censure were passed on such as refused to concur in the association, or violated its principles; and the names of the offenders were published, as enemies to their country. In some cases, the goods imported in contravention of it, were locked up in warehouses; and, in some few instances, they were re-shipped to Great Britain.

* Prior documents. Minot.   † Minot.

CHAP XIII.
1769.

Administration resolved on a partial repeal of duties.

Circular letter of the earl of Hillsborough.

Not long after the strong resolutions already noticed had been agreed to by parliament, while their effect was unfolding itself in every part of the American continent, an important revolution took place in the British cabinet. The duke of Grafton was placed at the head of a new administration. He supported, with great earnestness, a proposition to repeal the duties imposed for the purpose of raising revenue in the colonies; but his whole influence was insufficient to carry this measure completely. It was deemed indispensable to the maintenance of the legislative supremacy of Great Britain, to retain the duty on some one article; and that on tea was reserved while the others were relinquished.

Seldom has a wise nation adopted a more ill judged measure than this. The contest with America was plainly a contest of principle, and had been conducted entirely on principle by both parties. The amount of taxes proposed to be raised was too inconsiderable to interest the people of either country. But the principle was, in the opinion of both, of the utmost magnitude. The measure now proposed, while it encouraged the colonists to hope that their cause was gaining strength in Britain, had no tendency to conciliate them.

In pursuance of this resolution of the cabinet, a circular letter was written by the earl of Hillsborough to the several governors, informing them "that it was the intention of his majesty's ministers to propose, in the next session of parliament, taking off the duties

on glass, paper, and painter's colours, in considera- CHAP XIII.
tion of such duties having been laid contrary to the 1769.
true spirit of commerce; and assuring them that, at
no time, had they entertained the design to propose
to parliament to lay any further taxes on America for
the purpose of raising a revenue."*

This measure was soon communicated in letters
from private individuals in England to their correspondents in Massachusetts. The merchants of Boston, apprehensive that an improper opinion concerning its operation might be formed, resolved that the
partial repeal of the duties did not remove the difficulties under which their trade laboured, and was
only calculated to relieve the manufacturers of Great
Britain; and that they would still adhere to their nonimportation agreement.†

The communication of the earl of Hillsborough to
the several governors, was laid before the respective
assemblies as they convened, in terms implying an
intention to renounce the imposition, in future, of any
taxes in America. But this communication seems
not to have restored perfect content in any of the colonies.

The Virginia legislature was in session on its arrival, and governor Botetourt laid it before them.
Their dissatisfaction with it was manifested by a petition to the King re-asserting the rights previously
maintained; and by an association, signed by the
members as individuals, renewing their non importa-

* Prior documents. † Minot.

tion agreement, until the duty on tea should be repealed.*

Yet several causes combined to prevent a rigid observance of these associations. The sacrifice of interest made by the merchants could be continued only under the influence of powerful motives. Suspicions were entertained of each other in the same towns; and committees to superintend the conduct of importers were charged with gross partiality. The different towns too watched each other with considerable jealousy; and accusations were reciprocally made of infractions of the association to a great extent. Letters were published purporting to be from England, stating that large orders for goods had been received; and the inconvenience resulting from even a partial interruption of commerce, and from the want of those manufactures which the inhabitants had been accustomed to use, began to be severely and extensively felt. In Rhode Island, and Albany, it was determined to import as usual, with the exception of such articles as should be dutiable. On the remonstrances of other commercial places, especially of Boston, these resolutions were changed; and the hope was entertained that the general system on which the colonies relied, would still be maintained.

These hopes were blasted by New York. That city soon manifested a disposition to import as usual, with the exception of those articles only which were subject to a duty. At first, the resolution thus to

* Gazette.

limit the operation of the non-importation agreement, was made to depend on its being acceded to by Boston and Philadelphia. These towns refused to depart from the association as originally formed, and strenuously urged their brethren of New York to persevere with them in the glorious struggle. This answer was communicated to the people, and their opinion on the question of rescinding, or adhering to, the non-importation agreement, was taken in their respective wards. A decided majority was found in favour of rescinding, with the single exception of dutiable articles. This determination excited the most lively chagrin in New England and Philadelphia. Their remonstrances against it were, however, ineffectual; and the example was soon followed throughout the colonies.*

The people of New York alleged, in justification of themselves, that the towns of New England had not observed their engagements fairly; and that the merchants of Albany had been in the practice of receiving goods from Quebec. But no sufficient evidence in support of these assertions was ever produced.

About this time a circumstance occurred, which produced the most serious agitation. The two regiments stationed in Boston, to support, as was said, the civil authority, and preserve the peace of the town, were viewed by the inhabitants with very prejudiced eyes. Frequent quarrels arose between them; and, at length, an affray took place in the night, near the

marginalia: CHAP XIII. 1769. New York recedes in part from the non-importation agreement. 1770. March. Riot in Boston.

---

* Minot. Prior documents. Gazette.

CHAP XIII 1770. gates of the barracks, which brought out captain Preston, the officer of the day, with a part of the main guard, between whom and the townsmen blows ensued; on which some of the soldiers fired, and four of the people were killed.

The alarm bells were immediately rung, the drums beat to arms, and an immense multitude assembled. Inflamed to madness by the view of the dead bodies, they were with difficulty restrained from rushing on the 29th regiment, which was then drawn up under arms in King street. The exertions of the lieutenant governor, who promised that the laws should be enforced on the perpetrators of the act, and the efforts of several respectable and popular individuals, prevented their proceeding to extremities, and prevailed on them, after the regiment had been marched to the barracks, to disperse without farther mischief. Captain Preston, and the soldiers who had fired, were committed to prison for trial. On the next day, upwards of four thousand citizens of Boston assembled at Faneuil Hall; and, in a message to the lieutenant governor, stated it to be " the unanimous opinion of the meeting, that the inhabitants and soldiers can no longer live together in safety; that nothing can rationally be expected to restore the peace of the town, and prevent farther blood and carnage, but the immediate removal of the troops; and they therefore most fervently prayed his honour that his power and influence might be exerted for their instant removal."

The lieutenant governor expressed his extreme sorrow at the melancholy event which had occurred; and declared that he had taken measures to have the affair inquired into, and justice done. That the military were not under his command, but received their orders from the general at New York, which orders it was not in his power to countermand. That, on the application of the council for the removal of the troops, colonel Dalrymple, their commanding officer, had engaged that the twenty-ninth regiment, which had been concerned in the affair, should be marched to the castle, and there placed in barracks until farther orders should be received from the general; and that the main guard should be removed, and the fourteenth regiment laid under such restraints, that all occasions of future disturbance should be prevented. This answer was voted to be unsatisfactory; and a committee was deputed to wait on the lieutenant governor, and inform him that nothing could content them but an immediate and total removal of the troops.

This vote was laid before the council by Mr. Hutchinson, who had succeeded Mr. Bernard in the government of the province. The council declared themselves unanimously of opinion " that it was absolutely necessary for his Majesty's service, the good order of the town, and the peace of the province, that the troops should be immediately removed out of the town of Boston."

This opinion and advice being communicated to colonel Dalrymple, he gave his honour that measures should be immediately taken for the removal of both regiments. Satisfied with this assurance, the meeting secured the tranquillity of the town by appointing a strong military watch, and immediately dissolved itself.

This transaction was very differently related by the different parties. Mr. Gordon, whose history was written when the resentments of the moment had subsided, and who has collected the facts of the case carefully, states it in such a manner as nearly, if not entirely, to exculpate the soldiers. It appears that an attack upon them had been pre-concerted; and that, after being long insulted with the grossest language, they were repeatedly assaulted by the mob with balls of ice and snow, and with sticks, before they were induced to fire. This representation is strongly supported by the circumstances, that captain Preston, after a long and public trial, was acquitted by a Boston jury; and that six of the eight soldiers who were prosecuted, were acquitted, and the remaining two found guilty of manslaughter only. Mr. Quincy, and Mr. John Adams, two eminent lawyers, and distinguished leaders of the patriotic party, defended the accused, without sustaining any diminution of popularity. Yet this event was very differently understood through the colonies. It was generally believed to be a massacre, equally barbarous and unprovoked; and it increased the detestation in which the soldiers were universally held.

CHAPTER XIV.

Insurrection in North Carolina.—Dissatisfaction of Massachusetts.—Corresponding committees.—Governor Hutchinson's correspondence communicated by Dr. Franklin.—The assembly petition for his removal.—He is succeeded by general Gage.—Measures to enforce the act concerning duties.—Ferment in America.—The tea thrown into the sea at Boston.—Measures of Parliament.—General enthusiasm in America.—A general congress proposed.—General Gage arrives.—Troops stationed on Boston neck.—New counsellors and judges.—Obliged to resign.—Boston neck fortified.—Military stores seized by general Gage.—Preparations for defence.—King's speech.—Proceedings of Parliament.—Battle of Lexington.—Massachusetts raises men.—Meeting of Congress.—Proceedings of that body.—Transactions in Virginia.—Provincial congress of South Carolina.—Battle of Breed's hill.

In the middle and southern colonies, the irritation against the mother country appears to have gradually subsided and no disposition was manifested to extend opposition farther than to the importation of tea. Their attention was a good deal directed to an insurrection in North Carolina, where a number of igno-

1770.

Insurrection in North Carolina.

rant people, supposing themselves to be aggrieved by the fee bill, rose in arms for the purpose of shutting up the courts of justice, destroying all officers of government, and all lawyers, and of prostrating government itself. Governor Tryon marched against them, defeated them in a decisive battle, quelled the insurrection, and restored order.

Dissatisfaction of Massachusetts. In Massachusetts, where the doctrine that parliament could not rightfully legislate for the colonies was maintained as a corollary from the proposition that parliament could not tax them, a gloomy discontent was manifested. That the spirit of opposition seemed to be expiring, without securing the rights they claimed, excited apprehensions of a much more serious nature in the bosoms of that inflexible people, than the prospect of any conflict, however terrible. This temper displayed itself in all their proceedings.

The legislature, which the governor continued to convene at Cambridge, remonstrated against this removal as an intolerable grievance; and, for two sessions, refused to proceed on business. In one of their remonstrances, they asserted the right of the people to appeal to heaven in disputes between them and persons in power, when power shall be abused.

Corresponding committees. From the commencement of the contest, Massachusetts had been peculiarly solicitous to unite all the colonies in one system of measures. In pursuance of this favourite idea, a committee of correspondence was elected by the general court, to communicate with such committees as might be appointed by other legislatures.* Similar committees were soon afterwards chosen by the towns† throughout the province, for the purpose of corresponding with each other; and the example was soon followed by other colonies.

While this system of vigilance was in progress, a discovery was made which greatly increased the ill temper of New England. Doctor Franklin, the agent of Massachusetts, by some unknown means, obtained possession of the letters which had been addressed by governor Hutchinson, and by lieutenant governor Oliver, to the department of state. He transmitted these letters to the general court. They were obviously designed to induce government to persevere in the system which was alienating the affections of the colonists. The opposition was represented as being confined to a few factious men, whose conduct was not generally approved, and who had been emboldened by the weakness of the means used to restrain them. More vigorous measures were recommended; and several specific propositions were made, which were peculiarly offensive. Among these was a plan for altering the charters of the colonies, and rendering the high officers dependent solely on the crown for their salaries.‡

The assembly, inflamed by these letters, unanimously resolved, " that their tendency and design

---

* Almost at the same time, and without concert, the same measure was adopted in Virginia.

† See note No. 6, at the end of the volume. ‡ Minot.

CHAP. XIV.
1773.

Petition for the removal of the governor and lieutenant governor.

were to overthrow the constitution of the government, and to introduce arbitrary power into the province." At the same time, a petition to the King was voted, praying him to remove governor Hutchinson and lieutenant governor Oliver, for ever, from the government of the colony. This petition was transmitted to Doctor Franklin, and laid before the King in council. After hearing it, the lords of the council reported " that the petition in question was founded upon false and erroneous allegations, and that the same is groundless, vexatious, and scandalous, and calculated only for the seditious purposes of keeping up a spirit of clamour and discontent in the provinces." This report, his majesty was pleased to approve.

Hutchinson succeeded by Gage.

Governor Hutchinson however was soon afterwards removed, and general Gage appointed to succeed him.

Measures to enforce the duties.

The fears of Massachusetts, that the spirit which had been roused in the colonies might gradually subside, were not of long continuance. The determination not to import tea from England, had so lessened the demand for that article, that a considerable quantity had accumulated in the magazines of the East India company. They urged the minister to take off the import American duty of three pence per pound, and offered, in lieu of it, to pay double that sum on exportation. Instead of acceding to this proposition, drawbacks were allowed on tea exported to the colonies; and the export duty on that article was taken off. These encouragements induced the company to make shipments on their own account; and large quantities were consigned to agents in Boston, New York, Philadelphia, Charleston, and other principal places on the continent.*

The crisis was arrived; and the conduct of the colonies was now to determine whether they would submit to be taxed by parliament, or meet the consequences of a practical assertion of the opinions they had maintained. The tea, if landed, would be sold; the duties would, consequently, be paid; and the precedent for taxing them established. The same sentiment on this subject appears to have pervaded the whole continent at the same time. This ministerial plan of importation was considered by all, as a direct attack on the liberties of the people of America, which it was the duty of all to oppose. A violent ferment was excited in all the colonies; the corresponding committees were extremely active; and it was almost universally declared that whoever should, directly or indirectly, countenance this dangerous invasion of their rights, was an enemy to his country. The consignees were, generally, compelled to relinquish their consignments; and, in most instances, the ships bringing the tea were obliged to return with it.

At Boston, a town meeting appointed a committee to wait on the consignees to request their resignation. This request not being complied with, another large

* Minot. Belsham.

meeting* assembled at Faneuil Hall, who voted, with acclamation, "that the tea shall not be landed, that no duty shall be paid, and that it shall be sent back in the same bottoms." With a foreboding of the probable consequences of the measure about to be adopted, and a wish that those consequences should be seriously contemplated, a leading member† thus addressed the meeting.

"It is not, Mr. Moderator, the spirit that vapours within these walls that must stand us in stead. The exertions of this day will call forth events which will make a very different spirit necessary for our salvation. Whoever supposes that shouts and hosannahs will terminate the trials of the day, entertains

---

* The language said by Mr. Gordon to have been used at this meeting proves that many of the people of Boston were already ripe for the revolution. To the more cautious among "*the sons of liberty,*" who had expressed some apprehensions lest they should push the matter too far, and involve the colony in a quarrel with Great Britain, others answered "It must come to a quarrel between Great Britain and the colony sooner or later; and if so what can be a better time than the present? Hundreds of years may pass away before parliament will make such a number of acts in violation as it has done of late years, and by which it has excited so formidable an opposition to the measures of administration. Beside, the longer the contest is delayed, the more administration will be strengthened. Do not you observe how the government at home are increasing their party here by sending over young fellows to enjoy appointments, who marry into our best families, and so weaken the opposition? By such means, and by multiplying posts and places, and giving them to their own friends, or applying them to the corruption of their antagonists, they will increase their own force faster in proportion, than the force of the country party will increase by population. If then we must quarrel ere we can have our rights secured, now is the most eligible period. Our credit also is at stake; we must venture, and unless we do, we shall be discarded by the sons of liberty in the other colonies, whose assistance we may expect upon emergencies, in case they find us steady, resolute, and faithful."

† Mr. Quincy.

a childish fancy. We must be grossly ignorant of the importance and value of the prize for which we contend; we must be equally ignorant of the power of those who have combined against us; we must be blind to that malice, inveteracy, and insatiable revenge, which actuate our enemies, public and private, abroad and in our bosoms, to hope that we shall end this controversy without the sharpest, sharpest conflicts;—to flatter ourselves that popular resolves, popular harangues, popular acclamations, and popular vapour, will vanquish our foes. Let us consider the issue. Let us look to the end. Let us weigh and consider, before we advance to those measures, which must bring on the most trying and terrible struggle this country ever saw."*

The question was again put, and passed unanimously in the affirmative. The captain of the vessel, aware of the approaching danger, was desirous of returning, and applied to the governor for a clearance. Affecting a rigid regard to the letter of his duty, he declined giving one, unless the vessel should be properly qualified at the custom house. This answer being reported, the meeting was declared to be dissolved; and an immense crowd repaired to the quay, where a number of the most resolute, disguised as Mohawk Indians, boarded the vessel, broke open three hundred and forty-two chests of tea, and discharged their contents into the ocean.† *Tea thrown into the sea.*

These proceedings were laid before parliament in

* Minot.   † Idem.

CHAP XIV. 1774.

Measures of parliament.

a message from the crown, and excited a high and general indignation against the colonies. Both houses expressed, almost unanimously, their approbation of the measures adopted by his Majesty; and gave explicit assurances that they would exert every means in their power, to provide effectually for the due execution of the laws, and to secure the dependence of the colonies upon the crown and parliament of Great Britain. The temper both of the parliament and of the nation was entirely favourable to the high-handed system of coercion proposed by ministers; and that temper was not permitted to pass away unemployed. A bill was brought in " for discontinuing the lading and shipping of goods, wares, and merchandises, at Boston or the harbour thereof, and for the removal of the custom-house with its dependencies to the town of Salem." This bill was to continue in force, not only until compensation should be made to the East India company for the damage sustained, but until the King in council should declare himself satisfied as to the restoration of peace and good order in Boston. It passed both houses without a division, and almost without opposition.*

Soon afterwards, a bill was brought in " for better regulating the government of the province of Massachusetts Bay." This act entirely subverted the charter, and vested in the crown the appointment of the counsellors, magistrates, and other officers of the colony, who were to hold their offices during the royal

* Belsham.

pleasure. This bill also was carried through both houses by great majorities; but not without a vigorous opposition, and an animated debate.*

The next measure proposed was a bill " for the impartial administration of justice in the province of Massachusetts Bay. It provided that in case any person should be indicted, in that province, for murder or any other capital offence, and it should appear by information given on oath to the governor, that the fact was committed in the exercise or aid of magistracy in suppressing riots, and that a fair trial could not be had in the province, he should send the person so indicted to any other colony, or to Great Britain to be tried." This act was to continue in force for four years.†

A bill was also passed for quartering soldiers on the inhabitants; and the system was completed, by " an act making more effectual provision for the government of the province of Quebec." This bill extended the boundaries of that province so as to comprehend the territory between the lakes, the Ohio, and the Mississippi; and established a legislative council to be appointed by the crown, for its government.‡

Amidst these hostile measures, one single conciliatory proposition was made. Mr. Rose Fuller moved that the house resolve itself into a committee to take into consideration the duty on the importation of tea into America, with a view to its repeal. This

* Belsham. † Idem. ‡ Idem.

motion was seconded by Mr. Burke, and supported with all the power of reasoning, and all the splendour of eloquence which distinguished that consummate statesman; but reason and eloquence were of no avail. It was lost by a great majority. The earl of Chatham, who had long been too ill to attend parliament, again made his appearance in the house of lords. He could have been drawn out, only by a strong sense of the fatal importance of those measures into which the nation was hurrying. But his efforts were unavailing. Neither his weight of character, his sound judgment, nor his manly eloquence, could arrest the hand of fate which seemed to propel this lofty nation, with irresistible force, to measures which terminated in its dismemberment.*

It was expected, and this expectation was encouraged by Mr. Hutchinson, that, by directing these measures particularly against Boston, not only the union of the colonies would be broken, but Massachusetts herself would be divided. Never was expectation more completely disappointed. All perceived that Boston was to be punished for having resisted, only with more violence, the principle which they had all resisted; and that the object of the punishment was to coerce obedience to a principle they were still determined to resist. They felt therefore that the cause of Boston was the cause of all, that their destinies were indissolubly connected with those of that devoted town, and that they must submit to

* Belsham.

be taxed by a parliament, in which they were not and could not be represented, or support their brethren who were selected to sustain the first shock of a power which, if successful there, would overwhelm them all. The neighbouring towns, disdaining to avail themselves of the calamities inflicted on a sister for her exertions in the common cause, clung to her with increased affection; and that spirit of enthusiastic patriotism, which, for a time, elevates the mind above all considerations of individual acquisition, became the ruling passion in the American bosom.

CHAP XIV
1774.

General enthusiasm.

On receiving intelligence of the Boston port bill, a meeting of the people of that town was called. They perceived that " the sharpest, sharpest conflict" was indeed approaching, but were not dismayed by its terrors. Far from seeking to shelter themselves from the threatening storm by submission, they grew more determined as it increased.

Resolutions were passed, expressing their opinion of the impolicy, injustice, inhumanity, and cruelty of the act, from which they appealed to God, and to the world; and also inviting the other colonies to join with them in an agreement to stop all imports and exports to and from Great Britain, Ireland, and the West Indies, until the act should be repealed.*

It was not in Boston only that this spirit was roused. Addresses were received from every part of the continent, expressing sentiments of sympathy in their afflictions, exhorting them to resolution and perseve-

* Minot.

CHAP XIV 1774. rance, and assuring them that they were considered as suffering in the common cause.

The legislature of Virginia was in session when intelligence of the Boston port bill reached that province. The house of Burgesses set apart the first of June, the day on which the bill was to go into operation, for fasting, prayer, and humiliation, to implore the divine interposition to avert the heavy calamity which threatened the destruction of their civil rights, and the evils of a civil war; and to give one heart and one mind to the people, firmly to oppose every invasion of their liberties. Similar resolutions were adopted in almost every province; and the first of June became, throughout the colonies, a day of fasting, humiliation, and prayer, in the course of which sermons were preached to the people, well calculated to inspire them with horror, against the authors of the unjust sufferings of their fellow subjects in Boston.

A general congress proposed.

This measure occasioned the dissolution of the assembly. The members, before separation, entered into an association, in which they declared that an attack on one colony to compel submission to arbitrary taxes, is an attack on all British America, and threatens ruin to the rights of all, unless the united wisdom of the whole be applied in prevention. They, therefore, recommended to the committee of correspondence, to communicate with the several committees of the other provinces, on the expediency of appointing deputies from the different colonies to meet annually in congress, and to deliberate on the common interests of America. This measure had already been proposed in town meetings, both in New York and Boston.

While the people of Boston were engaged in the first consultations respecting the bill directed particularly against themselves, general Gage arrived in town. He was received, notwithstanding the deep gloom of the moment, with those external marks of respect which had been usual, and which were supposed to belong to his station.

The general court convened by the governor at Salem, passed resolutions, declaring the expediency of a meeting of committees from the several colonies; and appointed five gentlemen as a committee on the part of Massachusetts. The colonies from New Hampshire to South Carolina inclusive, adopted this measure; and, where the legislatures were not in session, elections were made by the people. The legislature of Massachusetts also passed declaratory resolutions expressing their opinion on the state of public affairs, and recommending to the inhabitants of that province to renounce, totally, the consumption of East India teas, and to discontinue the use of all goods imported from the East Indies and Great Britain, until the grievances of America should be completely redressed.

The governor, having obtained intelligence of the manner in which the house was employed, sent his secretary with directions to dissolve the assembly. Finding the doors shut, and being refused admittance,

CHAP XIV. 1774.

he read the order of dissolution aloud on the staircase. The next day, the governor received an address from the principal inhabitants of Salem, at that time the metropolis of the province, which marks the deep impression made by a sense of common danger. No longer considering themselves as the inhabitants of Salem, but as Americans, and spurning advantages to be derived to themselves from the distress inflicted on a sister town, for its zeal in a cause common to all, they expressed their deep affliction for the calamities of Boston.

About this time rough drafts of the two remaining bills relative to the province of Massachusetts, as well as of that for quartering troops in America, were received in Boston, and circulated through the continent. They served to confirm the wavering, to render the moderate indignant, and to inflame the violent.

An agreement was framed by the committee of correspondence in Boston, entitled "a solemn league and covenant," whereby the subscribers bound themselves, "in the presence of God," to suspend all commercial intercourse with Great Britain, from the last day of the ensuing month of August, until the Boston port bill, and the other late obnoxious laws should be repealed. They also bound themselves, in the same manner, not to consume, or purchase from any other, any goods whatever which should arrive after the specified time; and to break off all dealings with the purchasers as well as with the importers of such goods. They renounced, also all intercourse and connexion with those who should refuse to subscribe to that covenant, or to bind themselves by some similar agreement; and annexed to the renunciation of intercourse, the dangerous penalty of publishing to the world, the names of all who refused to give this evidence of attachment to the rights of their country.

General Gage issued a proclamation in which he termed this covenant "an unlawful, hostile, and traiterous combination, contrary to the allegiance due to the King, destructive of the legal authority of parliament, and of the peace, good order, and safety of the community." All persons were warned against incurring the pains and penalties due to such dangerous offences; and all magistrates were charged to apprehend and secure for trial such as should be guilty of them. But the time when the proclamations of governors could command attention had passed away; and the penalties in the power of the committee of correspondence were much more dreaded than those which could be inflicted by the civil magistrate.*

Resolutions were passed in every colony in which legislatures were convened, or delegates assembled in convention, manifesting different degrees of resentment, but concurring in the same great principles. All declared that the cause of Boston was the cause of British America; that the late acts respecting that devoted town were tyrannical and unconstitutional; that the opposition to this ministerial system of oppression ought to be universally and perseveringly

* Belsham. Minot.

CHAP. XIV
1774.

maintained; that all intercourse with the parent state ought to be suspended, and domestic manufactures encouraged; and that a general congress should be formed for the purpose of uniting and guiding the councils, and directing the efforts, of North America.

The committees of correspondence selected Philadelphia for the place, and the beginning of September as the time, for the meeting of this important council.

Congress assembles.

On the fourth of September, the delegates from eleven* provinces appeared at the place appointed; and, the next day, they assembled at Carpenter's Hall, when Peyton Randolph, late speaker of the house of Burgesses of Virginia, was unanimously chosen president. The respective credentials of the members were then read and approved; and this august assembly, having determined that each colony should have only one vote; that their deliberations should be conducted with closed doors; and that their proceedings, except such as they might determine to publish, should be kept inviolably secret; entered on the solemn and important duties assigned to them.†

Committees were appointed to state the rights claimed by the colonies, which had been infringed by acts of parliament passed since the year 1763; to prepare a petition to the King, and addresses to the people of Great Britain, to the inhabitants of the province

---

* Those of North Carolina arrived on the fourteenth.
† See note No. 7, at the end of the volume.

AMERICAN COLONIES. 411

of Quebec, and to the twelve colonies represented in congress.

Certain resolutions* of the county of Suffolk in Massachusetts, having been taken into consideration, it was unanimously resolved "'that this assembly deeply feels the suffering of their countrymen in Massachusetts Bay, under the operation of the late unjust, cruel, and oppressive acts of the British parliament; that they most thoroughly approve the wisdom and fortitude with which opposition to these wicked ministerial measures has hitherto been conducted; and they earnestly recommend to their brethren, a perseverance in the same firm and temperate conduct, as expressed in the resolutions determined upon, at a meeting of the delegates for the county of Suffolk, on Tuesday the sixth instant; trusting that the effect of the united efforts of North America in their behalf, will carry such conviction to the British nation of the unwise, unjust, and ruinous policy of the present administration, as quickly to introduce better men, and wiser measures."

It was resolved, unanimously, " that contributions from all the colonies, for supplying the necessities, and alleviating the distresses of our brethren in Boston, ought to be continued, in such manner, and so long, as their occasions may require."

The merchants of the several colonies were requested not to send to Great Britain any orders for goods, and to direct the execution of those already

* See note No. 8, at the end of the volume.

sent to be suspended, until the sense of congress on the means to be taken for preserving the liberties of America, be made public. In a few days, resolutions were passed, suspending the importation of goods from Great Britain, or Ireland, or any of their dependencies, and of their manufactures from any place whatever, after the first day of the succeeding December; and against the purchase or use of such goods. It was also determined that all exports to Great Britain, Ireland, and the West Indies, should cease on the 10th of September, 1775, unless American grievances should be redressed before that time. An association, corresponding with these resolutions, was then framed, and signed by every member present. Never were laws more faithfully observed, than were these resolutions of congress; and their association was, of consequence, universally adopted.

Early in the session, a declaration* of rights was made in the shape of resolutions. This paper merits particular attention, because it states precisely the ground then taken by America. It is observable that it asserted rights which were not generally maintained, at the commencement of the contest; but the exclusive right of legislation in the colonial assemblies, with the exception of acts of the British parliament *bona fide* made to regulate external commerce, was not averred unanimously.

The addresses prepared, the various papers drawn up, and the measures recommended by this congress,

* See note No. 9, at the end of the volume.

form the best eulogy of the members who composed it. Affection to the mother country, an exalted admiration of her national character, unwillingness to separate from her, a knowledge of the hazards and difficulties of the approaching contest, mingled with enthusiastic patriotism, and a conviction that all which can make life valuable was at stake, characterise their proceedings.

"When," they say in the address to the people of Great Britain, "a nation led to greatness by the hand of liberty, and possessed of all the glory that heroism, munificence, and humanity, can bestow, descends to the ungrateful task of forging chains for her friends and children, and, instead of giving support to freedom turns advocate for slavery and oppression, there is reason to suspect she has either ceased to be virtuous, or been extremely negligent in the appointment of her rulers.

"In almost every age, in repeated conflicts, in long and bloody wars, as well civil as foreign, against many and powerful nations, against the open assaults of enemies, and the more dangerous treachery of friends, have the inhabitants of your island, your great and glorious ancestors, maintained their independence, and transmitted the rights of men and the blessings of liberty to you their posterity.

"Be not surprised therefore that we, who are descended from the same common ancestors, that we, whose forefathers participated in all the rights, the liberties, and the constitution, you so justly boast of, and who have carefully conveyed the same fair inheritance to us, guaranteed by the plighted faith of government, and the most solemn compacts with British sovereigns, should refuse to surrender them to men, who found their claims on no principles of reason, and who prosecute them with a design, that by having *our* lives and property in their power, they may with the greater facility enslave *you*."

After stating the serious condition of American affairs, and the oppressions, and misrepresentations of their conduct, which had induced the address; and their claim to be as free as their fellow subjects in Britain; they say, " are not the proprietors of the soil of Great Britain lords of their own property? Can it be taken from them without their consent? Will they yield it to the arbitrary disposal of any men, or number of men whatever? You know they will not.

" Why then are the proprietors of the soil of America less lords of their property than you are of yours, or why should they submit it to the disposal of your parliament, or any other parliament or council in the world, not of their election? Can the intervention of the sea that divides us cause disparity of rights, or can any reason be given why English subjects, who live three thousand miles from the royal palace, should enjoy less liberty than those who are three hundred miles distant from it?

" Reason looks with indignation on such distinctions, and freemen can never perceive their propriety."

After expatiating on the resources which the conquest of America would place in the hands of the crown for the subjugation of Britain, the address proceeds, " we believe there is yet much virtue, much justice, and much public spirit in the English nation. To that justice we now appeal. You have been told that we are seditious, impatient of government, and desirous of independency. Be assured that these are not facts but calumnies. Permit us to be as free as yourselves, and we shall ever esteem a union with you to be our greatest glory, and our greatest happiness;—we shall ever be ready to contribute all in our power to the welfare of the empire;—we shall consider your enemies as our enemies, and your interest as our own.

"But if you are determined that your ministers shall wantonly sport with the rights of mankind;—if neither the voice of justice, the dictates of the law, the principles of the constitution, nor the suggestions of humanity, can restrain your hands from shedding human blood in such an impious cause, we must then tell you that we will never submit to be hewers of wood or drawers of water for any ministry or nation in the world.

" Place us in the same situation that we were at the close of the late war, and our former harmony will be restored."*

* The committee which prepared this eloquent and manly address, were Mr Lee, Mr. Livingston, and Mr. Jay. The composition has been generally attributed to Mr. Jay.

CHAP. XIV
1774.
Petition to the King.

The petition to the King states succinctly the grievances complained of, and then proceeds to say,

"Had our creator been pleased to give us existence in a land of slavery, the sense of our condition might have been mitigated by ignorance and habit. But thanks be to his adorable goodness, we were born the heirs of freedom, and ever enjoyed our right under the auspices of your royal ancestors, whose family was seated on the British throne, to rescue and secure a pious and gallant nation from the popery and despotism of a superstitious and inexorable tyrant. Your majesty, we are confident, justly rejoices that your title to the crown is thus founded on the title of your people to liberty; and, therefore, we doubt not but your royal wisdom must approve the sensibility that teaches your subjects anxiously to guard the blessing they received from divine providence, and thereby to prove the performance of that compact, which elevated the illustrious house of Brunswick to the imperial dignity it now possesses.

"The apprehensions of being degraded into a state of servitude, from the pre-eminent rank of English freemen, while our minds retain the strongest love of liberty, and clearly foresee the miseries preparing for us and for our posterity, excites emotions in our breasts, which, though we cannot describe, we should not wish to conceal. Feeling as men, and thinking as subjects, in the manner we do, silence would be disloyalty. By giving this faithful information, we do all in our power to promote the great objects of your royal cares—the tranquillity of your government, and the welfare of your people.

"Duty to your majesty and regard for the preservation of ourselves and our posterity,—the primary obligations of nature and society, command us to entreat your royal attention; and as your majesty enjoys the signal distinction of reigning over freemen, we apprehend the language of freemen cannot be displeasing. Your royal indignation, we hope, will rather fall on those designing and dangerous men, who, daringly interposing themselves between your royal person and your faithful subjects, and for several years past incessantly employed to dissolve the bonds of society, by abusing your majesty's authority, misrepresenting your American subjects, and prosecuting the most desperate and irritating projects of oppression, have at length compelled us, by the force of accumulated injuries, too severe to be any longer tolerable, to disturb your majesty's repose by our complaints.

"These sentiments are extorted from hearts that much more willingly would bleed in your majesty's service. Yet so greatly have we been misrepresented, that a necessity has been alleged of taking our property from us without our consent, to defray the charge of the administration of justice, the support of civil government, and the defence, protection, and security of the colonies."

After assuring his majesty of the untruth of these allegations, they say, "yielding to no British subjects in affectionate attachment to your majesty's person, family, and government, we too dearly prize the privilege of expressing that attachment, by those proofs that are honourable to the prince that receives them, and to the people who give them, ever to resign it to any body of men upon earth.

" We ask but for peace, liberty, and safety. We wish not a diminution of the prerogative, nor do we solicit the grant of any new right in our favour. Your royal authority over us, and our connexion with Great Britain, we shall always carefully and zealously endeavour to support and maintain."

After re-stating in a very affecting manner the most essential grievances of which they complain, and professing that their future conduct, if their apprehensions should be removed, would prove them worthy of the regard they had been accustomed, in their happier days to enjoy, they add,

" Permit us then most gracious sovereign, in the name of all your faithful people in America, with the utmost humility to implore you, for the honour of Almighty God, whose pure religion our enemies are undermining; for your glory which can be advanced only by rendering your subjects happy, and keeping them united; for the interest of your family, depending on an adherence to the principles that enthroned it; for the safety and welfare of your kingdom and dominions, threatened with almost unavoidable dangers and distresses; that your majesty, as the loving father of your whole people, connected by the same bonds of law, loyalty, faith, and blood, though dwelling in various countries, will not suffer the transcendent relation formed by these ties, to be farther violated, in uncertain expectation of effects that, if attained, never can compensate for the calamities, through which they must be gained.*

The address to their constituents is replete with serious and temperate argument. In this paper, the several causes which had led to the existing state of things, were detailed more at large; and much labour was used to convince their judgments that their liberties must be destroyed, and the security of their property and persons annihilated, by submission to the pretensions of Great Britain. The first object of congress being to unite the people of America, by demonstrating the sincerity with which their leaders had sought for reconciliation on terms compatible with liberty, great earnestness was used in proving that the conduct of the colonists had been uniformly moderate and blameless. After declaring their confidence in the efficacy of the mode of commercial resistance which had been recommended, the address concludes with saying, " your own salvation, and that of your posterity, now depends upon yourselves. You have already shown that you entertain a proper sense of the blessings you are striving to retain. Against the temporary inconveniences you may suffer from a stoppage of trade, you will weigh in the opposite balance, the

Address to the American people.

---

* The committee which brought in this admirably well drawn, and truly conciliatory address, were Mr. Lee, Mr. John Adams, Mr. Johnson, Mr. Henry, Mr. Rutledge, and Mr. Dickinson. The original composition has been generally attributed to Mr. Dickinson.

endless miseries you and your descendants must endure, from an established arbitrary power. You will not forget the honour of your country, that must, from your behaviour, take its title in the estimation of the world to glory or to shame; and you will, with the deepest attention, reflect, that if the peaceable mode of opposition recommended by us, be broken and rendered ineffectual, as your cruel and haughty ministerial enemies, from a contemptuous opinion of your firmness, insolently predict will be the case, you must inevitably be reduced to choose, either a more dangerous contest, or a final, ruinous, and infamous submission.

" Motives thus cogent, arising from the emergency of your unhappy condition, must excite your utmost diligence and zeal, to give all possible strength and energy to the pacific measures calculated for your relief. But we think ourselves bound in duty to observe to you, that the schemes agitated against the colonies have been so conducted, as to render it prudent that you should extend your views to mournful events, and be in all respects prepared for every contingency. Above all things, we earnestly entreat you, with devotion of spirit, penitence of heart, and amendment of life, to humble yourselves, and implore the favour of Almighty God; and we fervently beseech his divine goodness to take you into his gracious protection."*

* Mr. Lee, Mr. Livingston, and Mr. Jay, were also the committee who brought in this address.

The letter to the people of Canada required no inconsiderable degree of address. The extent of that province was not so alarming to its inhabitants as to their neighbours; and it was not easy to persuade the French settlers, who were far the most numerous, that the establishment of their religion, and the partial toleration of their ancient jurisprudence, were acts of oppression which ought to be resisted. This delicate subject was managed with considerable dexterity, and the prejudices of the Canadians were assailed with some success.

Letters were also addressed to the colonies of St. Johns, Nova Scotia, Georgia, and the Floridas, inviting them to unite with their brethren in a cause common to all British America*.

After completing the business before them, and recommending that another Congress should be held at the same place on the tenth of the succeeding May, the House dissolved itself.

The proceedings of Congress were read throughout America, with enthusiastic admiration. Their recommendations were revered as revelations, and obeyed as laws of the strongest obligation. Absolute unanimity could not be expected to exist; but seldom has a whole people been more united; and never did a more sincere and perfect conviction of the justice of a cause animate the human bosom, than was felt by the great body of the Americans. The people, gene-

---

* These letters, as well as that to the inhabitants of the province of Quebec, were prepared by Mr. Cushing, Mr. Lee, and Mr. Dickinson

rally, made great exertions to arm and discipline themselves. Independent companies of gentlemen were formed in all the colonies; and the whole face of the country exhibited the aspect of approaching war. Yet the measures of Congress demonstrate that, although resistance by force was contemplated as a possible event, the hope was fondly cherished that the non-importation of British goods would induce a repeal of the late odious acts. It is impossible to account for the non-importation agreement itself. Had war been considered as inevitable, every principle of sound policy required that imports should be encouraged, and the largest possible stock of supplies for an army be obtained.

New counsellors and judges.

With the laws relative to the province, governor Gage received a list of thirty two new counsellors, a sufficient number of whom, to carry on the business of the government, accepted the office, and entered on its duties.

All those who accepted offices under the new system, were denounced as enemies to their country. The new judges were unable to proceed in the administration of justice. When the court houses were opened, the people crowded into them in such numbers that the judges could not obtain admittance; and, on being ordered by the officers to make way for the court, they answered that they knew no court, independent of the ancient laws and usages of their country, and to no other would they submit.* The

* Minot.

houses of the new counsellors were surrounded by great bodies of people, whose threats announced to them that they must resign their offices, or be exposed to the fury of an enraged populace. The first part of the alternative was generally embraced.

CHAP XIV
1774.
Obliged to resign.

In this irritable state of the public mind, and critical situation of public affairs, it was to be expected that every day would furnish new matter of discontent and jealousy. General Gage deemed it a necessary measure of security, to fortify Boston neck; and this circumstance induced the inhabitants to contemplate seriously an evacuation of the town, and removal into the country. Congress was consulted on this proposition; but was deterred from recommending it, by the difficulties attending the measure. It was however referred to the provincial congress, with the declaration that, if the removal should be deemed necessary, the expense attending it ought to be borne by all the colonies.

Boston neck fortified.

The fortification of Boston neck was followed by a measure which excited still greater alarm. The time for the general muster of the militia approached. Under real or pretended apprehensions from their violence, the ammunition and stores which were lodged in the provincial arsenal at Cambridge, and the powder in the magazines at Charlestown, and some other places which was partly private and partly provincial property, were seized, by order of the governor, and conveyed to Boston.

Military stores seized by general Gage

Under the ferment excited by this measure, the people assembled in great numbers, and were with

CHAP XIV. difficulty dissuaded from marching to Boston, and
1774. demanding a re-delivery of the stores. Not long afterwards, the fort at Portsmouth in New Hampshire was stormed by an armed body of provincials; and the powder it contained was transported to a place of safety. A similar measure was adopted in Rhode Island.

About the same time a report reached Connecticut that the ships and troops had attacked Boston, and were actually firing on the town. Several thousand men immediately assembled in arms, and marched with great expedition a considerable distance, before they were undeceived.

It was in the midst of these ferments, and while these indications of an opinion that hostilities might be expected daily were multiplying on every side, that the people of Suffolk assembled in convention, and passed the resolutions already mentioned, which in boldness surpass any that had been adopted.

Before the general agitation had risen to its present alarming height, governor Gage had issued writs for the election of members to a general assembly. These writs were afterwards countermanded by proclamation; but the proclamation was disregarded; the elections were held; and the delegates, who assembled and voted themselves a provincial congress,

Provincial congress in Massachusetts. conducted the affairs of the colony as if they had been regularly invested with all the powers of government; and their recommendations were respected as sacred laws.

They drew up a plan for the defence of the pro-

vince; provided magazines, ammunition and stores CHAP. XIV
for twelve thousand militia; and enrolled a number 1774.
of minute men, a term designating a select part of the Prepares for defence.
militia, who engaged to appear in arms at a minutes
warning.

On the approach of winter, the general had ordered temporary barracks to be erected for the troops, partly for their security, and partly to prevent the disorders which would unavoidably result from quartering them in the town. Such however was the detestation in which they were held, that the select men and committees obliged the workmen to desist from the work, although they were paid for their labour by the crown, and although employment could, at that time, be seldom obtained. He was not much more successful in his endeavours to obtain carpenters in New York; and it was with considerable difficulty that these temporary lodgments could be erected.

The agency for purchasing winter covering for the troops was offered to almost every merchant in New York; but such was the danger of engaging in this odious employment, that not only those who were attached to the party resisting the views of administration, but those also who were in secret friendly to those views, refused undertaking it, and declared "that they never would supply any article for the benefit of men who were sent as enemies to their country."

In Great Britain, a new parliament was assembled; King's speech to parliament.
and the King, in his opening speech, informed them,

CHAP XIV.
1774.

"that a most daring spirit of resistance and disobedience still prevailed in Massachusetts, and had broken forth in fresh violences of a very criminal nature; that the most proper and effectual measures had been taken to prevent these mischiefs; and that they might depend upon a firm resolution to withstand every attempt to weaken or impair the supreme authority of this legislature over all the dominions of the crown."

Proceedings of that body.

The addresses re-echoed the sentiments of the speech; all amendments to which were rejected in both houses by cons derable majorities.* Yet the business respecting America was not promptly introduced. Administration seems to have hesitated on the course to be adopted; and the cabinet is said to have been divided respecting future measures. The few friends of conciliation availed themselves of this delay, to bring forward propositions which might restore harmony to the empire. Lord Chatham was not yet dead. "This splendid orb," to use the bold metaphor of Mr. Burke, "was not yet entirely set. The western horizon was still in a blaze with his descending glory;" and the evening of a life which had exhibited one bright unchequered course of elevated patriotism, was devoted to the service of that country whose aggrandisement seemed to have swallowed up every other passion of his soul. Taking a prophetic view of the future, he demonstrated the impossibility of subjugating America, and urged, with all the

1775.

* Belsham.

powers of his vast mind, the immediate removal of the troops from Boston, as a measure indispensably necessary, to open the way for an adjustment of the existing differences with the colonies. Not discouraged by the great majority against this motion, he brought forward a bill for settling the troubles in America, which was rejected by sixty-one to thirty-two voices.

The day after the rejection of this bill, lord North moved, in the house of commons, an address to his Majesty, declaring that, from a serious consideration of the American papers, " they find a rebellion actually exists in the province of Massachusetts Bay." In the course of the debate on this address, several professional gentlemen spoke with the utmost contempt of the military character of the Americans; and general Grant, who ought to have known better, declared that " at the head of five regiments of infantry, he would undertake to traverse the whole country, and drive the inhabitants from one end of the continent to the other."

The address was carried by 288 to 106 ; and on a conference, the house of lords agreed to join in it. Lord North, soon after, moved a bill for restraining the trade and commerce of the New England provinces, and prohibiting them from carrying on the fisheries on the banks of Newfoundland.*

While this bill was depending, and only vengeance was breathed by the majority, his lordship, to the as-

* Belsham.

tonishment of all, suddenly moved, what he termed, his conciliatory proposition. Its amount was, that parliament would forbear to tax any colony, which should tax itself in such a sum as would be perfectly satisfactory. Apparent as it must have been that this proposition would not be accepted in America, it was received with indignation by the majority of the house; and ministers found some difficulty in showing that it was in maintenance of the right to tax the colonies. Before it could be adopted lord North condescended to make the dangerous, and not very reputable acknowledgment, that it was a proposition designed to divide America, and to unite Great Britain. It was transmitted to the governors of the several colonies, in a circular letter from lord Dartmouth, with directions to use their utmost influence to prevail on the legislatures to accede to the proposed compromise. These endeavours were not successful. The colonists were universally impressed with too strong a conviction of the importance of union, and understood too well the real principle of the contest, to suffer themselves to be divided or deceived by a proposition, conciliatory only in name.

After the passage of the bill for restraining the trade of New England, information was received that the inhabitants of the middle and southern colonies, were supporting their northern brethren in every measure of opposition. In consequence of this intelligence, a second bill was passed for imposing similar restrictions on East and West Jersey, Pennsylvania, Maryland, Virginia, South Carolina, and the counties on the Delaware. The favourite colonies of New York and North Carolina were omitted, as being less disaffected than the others. Fortunately, some time afterwards, the house of commons refused to hear a petition from the legislature of New York, which alone had declined acceding to the resolutions of congress, on the suggestion of the minister that it contained claims incompatible with the supremacy of parliament. This haughty rejection had some tendency to convince the advocates of milder measures than had been adopted in their sister colonies, that there was no medium between resistance and absolute submission.

The King's speech, and the proceedings of parliament, served only to convince the leaders of opposition in America, that they must indeed prepare to meet "mournful events." They had flattered themselves that the union of the colonies, the petition of congress to the King, and the address to the people of Great Britain, would produce happy effects. But these measures removed the delusion. The provincial congress of Massachusetts published a resolution informing the people that there was real cause to fear that the reasonable and just applications of that continent to Great Britain for peace, liberty, and safety, would not meet with a favourable reception; that, on the contrary, the tenor of their intelligence, and general appearances, furnished just cause for the apprehension that the sudden destruction of that colony, at least, was intended. They therefore urged the militia in general, and the minute men in particular, to spare neither time, pains, nor expense, to perfect themselves in military discipline; and also passed resolutions for procuring and making fire arms and bayonets.*

In the mean time, delegates were elected for the ensuing congress. Even in New York, where the influence of administration in the legislature had been sufficient to prevent an adoption of the recommendations of congress, a convention was chosen for the purpose of electing members to represent that province in the grand council of the colonies.

In New England, although a determination not to commence hostility appears to have been maintained, an expectation of it, and a settled purpose to repel it, universally prevailed.

It was not long before the firmness of this resolution was put to the test.

On the night preceding the 19th of April, General Gage detached lieutenant colonel Smith, and major Pitcairn, with the grenadiers and light infantry of the army, amounting to eight or nine hundred men, with orders to destroy some military stores which had been collected at Concord, about eighteen miles from Boston, notwithstanding the secrecy and dispatch which were used, the country was alarmed by messengers sent out by Doctor Warren; and, on the arrival of the British troops at Lexington, about five in the morn-

* Prior documents. Minot.

ing, part of the company of militia belonging to the town, was found on the parade, under arms. Major Pitcairn, who led the van, galloped up, calling out, "disperse rebels, disperse." He was followed close by his soldiers, who rushed upon the militia with loud huzzas. Some scattering guns were fired, which were immediately followed by a general discharge, and the firing was continued as long as any of the militia appeared. Eight men were killed, and several wounded.

After dispatching six companies of light infantry to guard two bridges which lay at some distance beyond the town, lieutenant colonel Smith proceeded to Concord. While the main body of the detachment was employed in destroying the stores in the town, some minute men and militia, who were collected from that place and its neighbourhood, having orders not to give the first fire, approached one of the bridges, as if to pass it in the character of common travellers. They were fired on, and two of them were killed. The fire was instantly returned, and a skirmish ensued, in which the regulars were worsted, and compelled to retreat with some loss. The alarm now becoming general, the people rushed to the scene of action, and attacked the King's troops on all sides. Skirmish succeeded skirmish, and they were driven, from post to post, into Lexington. Fortunately for the British, general Gage did not entertain precisely the opinion of the military character of the Americans, which had been expressed in the house of commons.

CHAP XIV 1775. Apprehending the expedition to be not entirely without hazard, he had, in the morning, detached lord Percy with sixteen companies of foot, a corps of marines, and two companies of artillery, to support lieutenant colonel Smith. This seasonable reinforcement, happening to reach Lexington about the time of his arrival at that place, kept the provincials at a distance with their field pieces, and gave the grenadiers and light infantry time to breathe. But as soon as they resumed their march, the attack was re-commenced; and an irregular but galling fire was kept up on each flank, as well as in front and rear, until they arrived, on the common of Charlestown. Without delay, they passed over the neck to Bunker's hill, where they remained secure for the night, under the protection of their ships of war; and, early next morning, crossed over to Boston.

In this action, the loss of the British in killed, wounded, and prisoners, was two hundred and seventy-three; while that of the provincials did not exceed ninety. This affair, however trivial in itself, was of great importance in its consequences. It was the commencement of a long and obstinate war, and had no inconsiderable influence on that war, by increasing the confidence which the Americans felt in themselves, and by encouraging opposition, with the hope of being successful. It supported the opinion which the colonists had taken up with some doubt, that courage and patriotism were ample substitutes for the knowledge of tactics; and that their skill in the use of fire arms, gave them a great superiority over their adversaries.

Although the previous state of things was such as to render the commencement of hostilities unavoidable, each party seemed anxious to throw the blame on its opponent. The British officers alleged that they were fired on from a stone wall, before they attacked the militia at Lexington; while the Americans proved, by numerous depositions, that at Lexington, as well as at the bridge near Concord, the first fire was received by them. The statement made by the Americans is supported, not only by the testimony adduced, but by other circumstances. In numbers, the militia at Lexington did not exceed one ninth of the British; and it is not probable that their friends would have provoked their fate while in that perilous situation, by commencing a fire on an enraged soldiery. It is also worthy of attention, that the Americans uniformly sought to cover their proceedings with the letter of the law; and, even after the affair at Lexington, made a point of receiving the first fire at the bridge beyond Concord.

The provincial congress, desirous of manifesting the necessity under which the militia had acted, sent to their agents, the depositions which had been taken relative to the late action, with a letter to the inhabitants of Great Britain, stating that hostilities had been commenced against them, and detailing the circumstances attending that event.

CHAP XIV
1775
Massachusetts raises men.

But they did not confine themselves to addresses. They immediately passed a resolution for raising thirteen thousand six hundred men in Massachusetts, to be commanded by general Ward; and called on New Hampshire, Rhode Island, and Connecticut, for their respective quotas, to complete an army of thirty thousand men for the common defence. They also authorised the receiver general to borrow one hundred thousand pounds on the credit of the colony, and to issue securities for the re-payment thereof, bearing an interest of six per centum per annum.

The neighbouring colonies complied promptly with this requisition; and, in the mean time, such numbers assembled voluntarily, that many were dismissed in consequence of the defect of means to subsist them in the field; and the King's troops were themselves blocked up in the peninsula of Boston.

About the same time, that enterprising spirit, which pervaded New England, manifested itself in an expedition of considerable merit.

The possession of Ticonderoga and Crown Point, and the command of lakes George and Champlain, were objects of importance in the approaching conflict. It was known that these posts were weakly defended; and it was believed that the feeble garrisons remaining in them were the less to be dreaded, because they thought themselves perfectly secure. Under these impressions, some gentlemen of Connecticut, at the head of whom were Messrs. Deane, Wooster, and Parsons, formed the design of seizing these fortresses by surprise; and borrowed a small sum of money from the legislature of the colony, to enable them to carry on the expedition. About forty volunteers marched from Connecticut towards Bennington, where they expected to meet with colonel Ethan Allen, and to engage him to conduct the enterprise, and to raise an additional number of men.

CHAP XIV.
1775.

Colonel Allen readily entered into their views, and engaged to meet them at Castleton. Two hundred and seventy men assembled at that place, where they were joined by colonel Arnold, who was associated with colonel Allen in the command. They reached lake Champlain in the night of the ninth of May. Both Allen and Arnold embarked with the first division consisting of eighty-three men, who effected a landing without being discovered, and immediately marched against the fort, which, being completely surprised, surrendered without firing a gun. The garrison consisted of only forty-four rank and file, commanded by a captain and one lieutenant. From Ticonderoga, colonel Seth Warren was detached to take possession of Crown Point, which was garrisoned only by a serjeant and twelve men. This service was immediately executed, and the fort was taken without opposition.

Ticonderoga surprised.

Crown Point surrenders.

At both these places, military stores of considerable value fell into the hands of the Americans. The pass at Skeensborough was seized about the same time by a body of volunteers from Connecticut.

To complete the objects of the expedition, it was

CHAP XIV. necessary to obtain the command of the lakes, which
1775. could be accomplished only by seizing a sloop of war lying at St. Johns. This service was effected by Arnold, who, having manned and armed a schooner found in South bay, surprised the sloop, and took possession of her without opposition.

Thus, by the enterprise of a few individuals, and without the loss of a single man, the important posts of Ticonderoga and Crown Point were acquired, with the command of the lakes on which they stand.

Meeting of congress. Intelligence of the capture of Ticonderoga was immediately transmitted to congress, then just assembled at Philadelphia. The resolutions passed on the occasion, furnish strong evidence of the solicitude felt by that body, to exonerate the government, in the opinion of the people, from all suspicion of provoking a continuance of the war, by transcending the

Proceedings of that body. limits of self defence. Indubitable evidence, it was asserted, had been received of a design for a cruel invasion of the colonies from Canada, for the purpose of destroying their lives and liberties; and it was averred that some steps had actually been taken towards carrying this design into execution. To a justifiable desire of securing themselves from so heavy a calamity, was attributed the seizure of the posts on the lakes by the neighbouring inhabitants; and it was recommended to the committees of New York and Albany to take immediate measures for the removal of the cannon and military stores to some place on the south end of lake George, there to be preserved in safety.

An exact inventory of the stores was directed to be taken, " in order that they might be safely returned, when the restoration of the former harmony between Great Britain and the colonies, so ardently wished for by the latter, should render it prudent, and consistent with the over-ruling law of self preservation."

Measures, however, were adopted to maintain the posts; but, to quiet the apprehensions of their neighbours, congress resolved that, having nothing more in view than self defence, " no expedition or incursion ought to be undertaken or made by any colony, or body of colonists, against, or into, Canada."

This resolution was translated into the French language, and transmitted to the people of that province, in a letter in which all their feelings, and particularly their known attachment to France, were dexterously assailed; and the effort was earnestly made to kindle in their bosoms, that enthusiastic love of liberty which was felt too strongly by the authors of the letter, to permit the belief that it could be inoperative with others.

During these transactions, generals Howe, Bourgoyne, and Clinton, arrived at Boston, soon after which general Gage issued a proclamation declaring martial law to be in force, and offering pardon to those who would lay down their arms and submit to the King, with the exception of Samuel Adams, and John Hancock.

On receiving intelligence of the battle of Lexington, New York appeared to hesitate no longer. In that place also, the spirit which animated the colonies generally, obtained the ascendancy. Yet the royal party remained formidable; and it was thought advisable to march a body of Connecticut troops into the neighbourhood, professedly to protect the town against some British regiments expected from Ireland, but really with the design of protecting the patriotic party.

The middle and southern colonies, though not so forward as those of the north, laid aside the established government, and prepared for hostilities.

Transactions in Virginia.

In Virginia, the governor, lord Dunmore, had just returned from a successful expedition against the Indians, in which he had acquired considerable popularity. Presuming too much on the favour of the moment, and dissatisfied with some recommendations concerning the militia and independent companies made by the colonial convention which had assembled in Richmond, he employed the captain of an armed vessel then lying in James river, a few miles from Williamsburg, to convey to his ship by night, a part of the powder in the magazine, belonging to the colony.

This measure, though conducted with great secrecy, was discovered; and the people of the town assembled next morning in arms, for the purpose of demanding restitution of the property which had been taken. The magistrates, having prevailed on them to disperse, presented an address to the governor, remonstrating against the removal of the powder, which they alleged to be the more injurious, because it was necessary for their defence in the event of an insurrection among their slaves.

The governor acknowledged that the powder had been removed by his order, but gave assurances that he would restore it, if an insurrection of the slaves should render the measure necessary. Unsatisfactory as this answer was, no farther means were used in Williamsburg for its recovery.

This transaction excited a strong sensation in the interior of the country. Meetings were held in several counties, and the conduct of the governor was greatly condemned. The independent companies of Hanover and King William, at the instance of Mr. Patrick Henry, a member of congress, assembled, and marched for Williamsburg, with the avowed design of compelling restitution of the powder, or of obtaining its value. Their march was stopped by the active interposition of Mr. Braxton, who obtained from the King's receiver general, a bill for the value of the property that had been removed, with which he returned to the companies, and prevailed on them to relinquish a farther prosecution of the enterprise.*

The alarm occasioned by this movement induced lady Dunmore, to retire with her family on board the Fowey man of war, lying in James river; whilst his

---

* The independent companies of the upper part of the northern neck, also assembled to the number of about six hundred men, and proceeded on horseback as far as Fredericksburg, when a council was held in which Richard Henry Lee, then on his way to congress, presided, which advised their return to their respective homes.

CHAP XIV lordship fortified his palace, which he garrisoned with
1775. a corps of marines; and published a proclamation in
which he charged those who had procured the bill
from the receiver general, with rebellious practices.

During this state of irritation, lord North's conciliatory proposition was received; and an assembly was suddenly called, to whose consideration it was submitted. The governor used all his address to procure its acceptance; but, in Virginia, as in the other colonies, it was rejected, because it obviously involved a surrender of the whole subject in contest.

One of the first measures of the assembly was to inquire into the causes of the late disturbances, and particularly to examine the state of the magazine. Although this building belonged to the colony, it was in the custody of the governor; and, before admittance could be obtained, some persons of the neighbourhood broke into it, one of whom was wounded by a spring gun, and it was found that the powder which remained had been buried, and that the guns were deprived of their locks. These circumstances excited so great a

Governor Dunmore retires to the Fowey ship of war. ferment that the governor thought proper to withdraw to the Fowey man of war. Several letters passed between him and the legislature containing reciprocal complaints of each other, in the course of which they pressed his return to the seat of government, while he insisted on their coming on board the Fowey. They were content that he should, even there, give his assent to some bills that were prepared, but he refused so to do, and the assembly dissolved itself; the members being generally elected to a convention then about to meet in Richmond.

Thus terminated for ever, the regal government in Virginia.

In South Carolina, so soon as intelligence of the battle of Lexington was received, a provincial congress was called by the committee of correspondence. An association was formed, the members of which pledged themselves to each other to repel force by force, whenever the continental or provincial congress should determine it to be necessary; and declared that they would hold all those inimical to the colonies, who should refuse to subscribe it. The congress also determined to put the town and province in a posture of defence, and agreed to raise two regiments of infantry, and one of rangers.

While the congress was in session, lord William Campbell, who had been appointed governor, arrived in the province, and was received with those demonstrations of joy which had been usual on such occasions. The congress waited on him with an address expressing the causes of their proceedings; in which they declared that no love of innovation, no desire of altering the constitution of government, no lust of independence, had the least influence on their councils; but that they had been compelled to associate and take up arms, solely for the preservation, and in defence, of their lives, liberties, and property. They entreated his excellency to make such a representation of the state of the colony, and of their true mo-

3 K

tives, as to assure his majesty that he had no subjects who more sincerely desired to testify their loyalty and affection, or would be more willing to devote their lives and fortunes to his real service. His lordship returned a mild and prudent answer.*

For some time lord William Campbell conducted himself with such apparent moderation, as to remain on good terms with the leaders of the opposition; but he was secretly exerting all the influence of his station to defeat their views; and was, at length, detected in carrying on negotiations with the Indians, and with the disaffected in the interior. These people had been induced to believe that the inhabitants of the sea coast, in order to exempt their tea from a trifling tax, were about to engage them in a contest, which would deprive them of their salt, osnaburgs, and other imported articles of absolute necessity. The detection of these intrigues excited such a ferment that the governor was compelled to fly from Charleston, and take refuge on board a ship of war in the river. The government was then, as elsewhere, taken entirely into the hands of men chosen by the people; and a body of provincial troops was ordered into that part of the country which adhered to the royal cause, where many individuals, contrary to the advice of governor Campbell, had risen in arms. The leaders were seized, and their followers dispersed.

In North Carolina also, governor Martin was charg-

* Gordon.

ed with fomenting a civil war, and exciting an insurrection among the negroes. Relying on the aid he expected from the disaffected, especially from some highland emigrants, he made preparations for the defence of his palace; but the people taking the alarm before his troops were raised, he was compelled to seek safety on board a sloop of war in Cape Fear river; soon after which, the committee resolved "that no person or persons whatsoever should have any correspondence with him, on pain of being deemed enemies to the liberties of America, and dealt with accordingly."

CHAP XIV
1775.

As soon as congress was organised, Mr. Hancock laid before that body the depositions showing that, in the battle of Lexington, the King's troops were the aggressors; together with the proceedings of the provincial congress of Massachusetts on that subject.

The affairs of America were now arrived at a crisis to which they had been, for some time, rapidly tending; and it had become necessary for the delegates of the other provinces finally to determine, either to embark with New England in war, or, by separating from her, to surrender the object for which they had jointly contended, and submit to that unlimited supremacy which was claimed by parliament.

Even among the well informed, the opinion that the contest would ultimately be determined by the sword, had not become general. The hope had been indulged by many of the popular leaders, that the union of the colonies, the extent and serious aspect of the opposition, and the distress which their non-importation agreements would produce among the merchants and manufacturers of the parent state, would induce administration to recede from its high pretensions, and restore harmony and free intercourse. This opinion had derived strength from the communications made them by their zealous friends in England. The divisions and discontents of that country, had been represented as much greater than the fact would justify; and the exhortations transmitted to them to persevere in the honourable course which had been commenced with so much glory, had generally been accompanied with assurances that success would yet crown their patriotic labours. Many had engaged with zeal in the resistance made by America, and had acted on a full conviction of the correctness of the principles for which they contended, who would have felt some reluctance in supporting the measures which had been adopted, had they believed that those measures would produce war. But each party counted too much on the divisions of the other; and each seems to have taken step after step, in the hope that its adversary would yield the point in contest, without resorting to open force. Thus, on both sides, the public feeling had been gradually conducted to a point, which would, in the first instance, have been viewed with horror, and had been prepared for events, which, in the beginning of the controversy, would have alarmed the most intrepid. The prevailing sentiment in the middle and southern colonies still was, that a reconciliation, on the terms proposed by America, was not even yet impracticable, and was devoutly to be wished; but that war was to be preferred to a surrender of those rights, for which they had contended, and to which they believed every British subject, wherever placed, to be unquestionably entitled. They did not hesitate therefore which part of the alternative to embrace; and their delegates united cordially with those of the north, in such measures as the exigency required. The resolution was unanimous that, as hostilities had actually commenced, and as large reinforcements to the British army were expected, these colonies should be immediately put in a state of defence, and the militia of New York be armed and trained, and kept in readiness to act at a moments warning. Congress also determined to embody a number of men, without delay, for the protection of the inhabitants of that place, but did not authorise opposition to the landing of any troops which might be ordered to that station by the crown. The convention of New York had already consulted congress on this subject, and had been advised to permit the soldiers to take possession of the barracks, and to remain there so long as they conducted themselves peaceably; but, if they should commit hostilities, or invade private property, to repel force by force. Thus anxious was congress even after a battle had been fought, not to widen the breach between the two countries. In addition to the real wish for reconciliation, sound policy directed that the people of America should engage in the arduous conflict which was approaching, with a perfect conviction that it was forced upon them, and not invited by the intemperate conduct of their leaders. The divisions existing in several of the States suggested the propriety of this conduct, even to those who despaired of deriving any other benefit from it, than a greater degree of union among their own countrymen. In this spirit, congress mingled with the resolutions for putting the country in a state of defence, others expressing the most earnest wish for reconciliation with the mother country, to effect which, that body determined to address, once more, an humble and dutiful petition to the King, and to adopt measures for opening a negotiation in order " to accommodate the unhappy disputes subsisting between Great Britain and the colonies."

As no great confidence could be placed in the success of pacific propositions, the resolution for putting the country in a state of defence was accompanied with others rendered necessary by that undetermined state between war and peace, in which America was placed. All exports to those colonies, which had not deputed members to congress, were stopped; and all supplies of provisions, and other necessaries, to the British fisheries, or to the army or navy in Masachusetts Bay, or to any vessels employed in transporting British troops to America, or from one colony to another, were prohibited. Though this resolution was only an extension of the system of commercial resistance which had been adopted before the commencement of hostilities, and was evidently provoked by the late act of parliament, it seems to have been entirely unexpected, and certainly produced great distress.

Massachusetts having stated the embarrassments resulting from being without a regular government, " at a time when an army was to be raised to defend themselves against the butcheries and devastations of their implacable enemies," and having declared a readiness to conform to such general plan as congress might recommend to the colonies, it was resolved " that no obedience is due to the act of parliament for altering the charter of that colony, nor to officers who, instead of observing that charter, seek its subversion." The governor and lieutenant governor, therefore, were to be considered as absent, and their offices vacant. To avoid the intolerable inconveniences arising from a total suspension of government, " especially at a time when general Gage had actually levied war, and was carrying on hostilities against his majesty's peaceable and loyal subjects in that colony," it was " recommended to the convention to write letters to the inhabitants of the several places which are entitled to representation in the assembly, requesting them to choose such representatives; and that such assembly or council exercise the powers of government until a governor of his majesty's appointment will consent to govern the colony, according to its charter."*

These resolutions were quickly followed by others

* Journals of congress

of greater vigour, denoting more decidedly, a determination to prepare for the last resort of nations.

It was earnestly recommended to the conventions of all the colonies to provide the means of making gun powder, and to obtain the largest possible supplies of ammunition. Even the non-importation agreement was relaxed in favour of vessels importing these precious materials. The conventions were also urged to arm and discipline the militia; and so to class them, that one-fourth should be minute men. They were also requested to raise several regular corps for the service of the continent; and a general resolution was entered into, authorising any province thinking itself in danger, to raise a body of regulars not exceeding one thousand men, to be paid by the united colonies.

Congress also proceeded to organise the higher departments of the army, of which, colonel George Washington of Virginia was appointed commander in chief.*

Bills of credit to the amount of three millions of dollars were emitted for the purpose of defraying the expenses of the war, and the faith of the twelve confederated colonies was pledged for their redemption. Articles of war for the government of the continental army were formed; though the troops were raised

---

* Artemus Ward of Massachusetts, then commanding the troops before Boston; colonel Charles Lee, late-ly an officer in the British service; and Israel Putnam of Connecticut, were appointed major generals; Horatio Gates, who had held the rank of major in the British service, was appointed adjutant general

under the authority of the respective colonies, without even a requisition from congress, except in a few instances. A solemn dignified declaration, in form of a manifesto, was prepared, to be published to the army in orders, and to the people from the pulpit. After detailing the causes of their opposition to the mother country, with all the energy of men feeling the injuries of which they complain, the manifesto exclaims " but why should we enumerate our injuries in detail? By one statute, it is declared that parliament can, of right, make laws to bind us in all cases whatsoever! What is to defend us against so enormous, so unlimited a power? Not a single man of those who assume it, is chosen by us, or is subject to our control or influence: but, on the contrary, they are, all of them, exempt from the operation of such laws; and an American revenue, if not diverted from the ostensible purposes for which it is raised, would actually lighten their own burdens in proportion as they increase ours. We saw the misery to which such despotism would reduce us. We, for ten years, incessantly and ineffectually, besieged the throne as supplicants; we reasoned, we remonstrated with parliament in the most mild and decent language."

The manifesto next enumerates the measures adopted by administration to enforce the claims of Great Britain, and then adds,—" we are reduced to the alternative of choosing an unconstitutional submission to the tyranny of irritated ministers, or resistance by force.—The latter is our choice. We have counted the cost of this contest, and find nothing so dreadful as voluntary slavery. Honour, justice, and humanity, forbid us tamely to surrender that freedom which we received from our gallant ancestors, and which our innocent posterity have a right to receive from us. We cannot endure the infamy and guilt of resigning succeeding generations to that wretchedness which inevitably awaits them, if we basely entail hereditary bondage upon them.

"Our cause is just. Our union is perfect. Our internal resources are great; and, if necessary, foreign assistance is undoubtedly attainable. We gratefully acknowledge, as signal instances of the divine favour towards us, that his providence would not permit us to be called into this severe controversy, until we were grown up to our present strength, had been previously exercised in warlike operation, and possessed of the means of defending ourselves. With hearts fortified with these animating reflections, we most solemnly, before God and the world, DECLARE that, exerting the utmost energy of those powers which our beneficent creator hath graciously bestowed upon us, the arms we have been compelled by our enemies to assume, we will, in defiance of every hazard, with unabating firmness and perseverance, employ for the preservation of our liberties; being with one mind resolved to die freemen, rather than to live slaves.

"Lest this declaration should disquiet the minds of our friends and fellow subjects in any part of the empire, we assure them that we mean not to dissolve that union which has so long and so happily subsisted between us, and which we sincerely wish to see restored. Necessity has not yet driven us to that desperate measure, or induced us to excite any other nation to war against them. We have not raised armies with ambitious designs of separating from Great Britain, and establishing independent states. We fight not for glory, or for conquest. We exhibit to mankind the remarkable spectacle of a people attacked by unprovoked enemies, without any imputation or even suspicion of offence. *They* boast of their privileges and civilization, and yet proffer no milder conditions than servitude or death.

"In our own native land in defence of the freedom that is our birth right, and which we ever enjoyed until the late violation of it, for the protection of our property, acquired solely by the honest industry of our forefathers, and ourselves, against violence actually offered, we have taken up arms. We shall lay them down when hostilities shall cease on the part of the aggressors, and all danger of their being renewed shall be removed, and not before."

Some intelligence respecting the movements of the British army having excited a suspicion that general Gage intended to penetrate into the country, the provincial congress recommended it to the council of war to take measures for the defence of Dorchester neck, and to occupy Bunker's hill, a commanding piece of ground just within the peninsula on which Charlestown stands. In observance of these instructions, a detachment of one thousand men; commanded by colonel Prescot, was ordered to take possession of this ground; but, by some mistake, Breed's hill, situate nearer to Boston, was marked out, instead of Bunker's hill, for the proposed intrenchments.

The party sent on this service worked with so much deligence and secrecy that, by the dawn of day, they had thrown up a small square redoubt, without alarming some ships of war which lay in the river at no great distance. As soon as the returning light discovered this work to the ships, a heavy cannonade was commenced upon it, which the provincials sustained with firmness. They continued to labour until they had thrown up a small breast work stretching from the east side of the redoubt to the bottom of the hill, so as to extend considerably their line of defence.

As this eminence overlooked Boston, general Gage determined to drive the provincials from it; and for this purpose, detached major general Howe, and brigadier general Pigot, at the head of ten companies of grenadiers, and the same number of light infantry, with a proper proportion of field artillery. These troops landed at Moreton's point; but, perceiving that the Americans waited for them with firmness, they remained on their ground until the arrival of a reinforcement from Boston, for which general Howe had applied. During this interval, the Americans also were reinforced by a detachment under the command of generals Warren and Pommeroy; and they availed themselves of this delay to strengthen their defences with some adjoining posts and rails which they pulled up and arranged in two parallel lines at a small distance from each other; filling the space between with hay, so as to form a complete cover from the musketry of the assailants.

CHAP. XIV
1775.

The British troops, on being joined by their second detachment, advanced slowly, in two lines, under cover of a heavy discharge of cannon and howitzers, frequently halting in order to allow their artillery time to demolish the works. While they were advancing, orders were given to set fire to Charlestown, a handsome village, which flanked their line of march, and which was soon consumed.

It is not easy to conceive a spectacle more grand and more awful than was now exhibited, nor a moment of more anxious expectation. The scene of action was in full view of the heights of Boston and of its neighbourhood, which were covered with spectators taking deep and opposite interests in the events passing before them. The soldiers of the hostile armies not on duty, the citizens of Boston, and the inhabitants of the adjacent country; all feeling emotions which set description at defiance, were witnesses of the majestic and tremendous scene.

The provincials permitted the English to approach unmolested, within less than one hundred yards of the works, and then poured in upon them so deadly a fire that their line was broken, and they fell back with precipitation towards the landing place. By the great exertions of their officers, they were rallied

Battle of Breed's hill.

and brought up to the charge; but were again driven back in confusion by the heavy and incessant fire from the works. General Howe is said to have been left, at one time, almost alone; and it is certain that few officers about his person escaped unhurt.

The impression to be made by victory or defeat in this early stage of the war, was deemed so important that extraordinary exertions were used once more to rally the English. With difficulty, they were led a third time to the works. The redoubt was attacked on three sides, while some pieces of artillery raked the breast work from end to end. At the same time, a cross fire from the ships, and floating batteries lying on both sides of the isthmus by which the peninsula is connected with the continent, not only annoyed the works on Breed's hill, but deterred any considerable reinforcements from entering the peninsula. The ammunition of the Americans being nearly exhausted, they were no longer able to keep up the same incessant stream of fire which had twice repulsed the assailants; and the redoubt, which the English mounted with ease, was carried at the point of the bayonet. Yet the Americans, many of whom were without bayonets, are said to have maintained the contest with clubbed muskets, until the redoubt was half filled with the King's troops.

The redoubt being lost, the breast work was abandoned; and the hazardous movement was accomplished, of retreating in the face of a victorious enemy over Charlestown neck; exposed to the same cross fire, which had deterred the reinforcements from coming to their assistance.

The detachment employed on this enterprise consisted of about three thousand men, composing the flower of the British army; and high encomiums were bestowed on the resolution they displayed. According to the returns, their killed and wounded amounted to one thousand and fifty four,—an immense proportion of the number engaged in the action. Notwithstanding the danger of the retreat over Charlestown neck, the loss of the Americans was stated at only four hundred and fifty men. Among the killed was Doctor Warren, a gentleman greatly beloved and regretted, who fell just after the provincials began their retreat from the breast work.

At the time, the colonial force on the peninsula was generally stated at fifteen hundred men. It has been since estimated at four thousand.

Although the Americans lost the ground, they claimed the victory. Many of the advantages of victory were certainly gained. Their confidence in themselves was greatly increased; and it was asked, universally, how many more such triumphs the invaders of their country could afford?

The British army had been treated too roughly, to attempt farther offensive operations. They contented themselves with seizing and fortifying Bunker's hill, which secured the peninsula of Charlestown; in which, however, they remained as closely blockaded as in that of Boston.

CHAP. XIV
1775.

The Americans were much elated by the intrepidity their raw troops had displayed, and the execution they had done, in this engagement. They fondly cherished the belief that courage, and dexterity in the use of fire arms, would bestow advantages amply compensating the want of discipline. Unfortunately for the colonies, this course of thinking was not confined to the mass of the people. It seems to have extended to those who guided the public councils, and to have contributed to the adoption of a system, which, more than once, brought their cause to the brink of ruin. They did not distinguish sufficiently between the momentary efforts of a few brave men, brought together by a high sense of the injuries which threatened their country, and carried into action under the influence of keen resentments; and those steady persevering exertions under continued suffering, which must be necessary to bring an important war to a happy termination. Nor did they examine, with sufficient accuracy, several striking circumstances attending the battle which had been fought. It is not easy to read the accounts given of the action without being persuaded, that, had the Americans on Breed's hill been supplied with ammunition, and been properly supported; had the reinforcements ordered to their assistance entered the peninsula, as soldiers in habits of obedience would have done, and there displayed the heroic courage which was exhibited by their countrymen engaged in defence of the works; the assailants must have been defeated, and the flower of the British army cut to pieces. It ought also to have been remarked that, while the few who were endowed with more than a common portion of bravery, encountered the danger of executing the orders they had received, the many were deterred by the magnitude of that danger. But it is not by the few that great victories are to be gained, or a country to be saved.

Amidst these hostile operations, the voice of peace was yet heard. Allegiance to the King was still acknowledged; and a lingering hope remained that an accommodation was not impossible. Congress voted a petition to his majesty, replete with professions of duty and attachment; and addressed a letter to the people of England, conjuring them by the endearing appellations of " friends, countrymen, and brethren," to prevent the dissolution of " that connexion which the remembrance of former friendships, pride in the glorious achievements of common ancestors, and affection for the heirs of their virtues, had heretofore maintained." They uniformly disclaimed any idea of independence, and professed themselves to consider union with England on constitutional principles, as the greatest blessing which could be bestowed on them.

But Britain had determined to maintain, by force, the legislative supremacy of parliament; and America was equally determined, by force, to repel the claim.

APPENDIX.

NOTE—No. I.

The annals of Massachusetts, for this period, exhibit one of those wonderful cases of popular delusion, which infecting every class of society, and gaining strength from its very extravagance; triumphing over human reason, and cruelly sporting with human life; reveal to man his deplorable imbecility, and would teach him, if the experience of others could teach, never to countenance a departure from that moderation, and those safe and sure principles of moral rectitude which have stood the test of time, and have received the approbation of the wise and good in all ages. A very detailed and interesting account of the humiliating and affecting events here alluded to has been given by Mr. Hutchinson, but is too long to be inserted entire in this work: they were, however, of too much magnitude while passing, to be entirely unnoticed even at this day.

In Great Britain, as well as in America, the opinion had long prevailed that, by the aid of malignant spirits, certain persons possessed supernatural powers, which were usually exercised in the mischievous employment of tormenting others; and the criminal code of both countries was disgraced with laws for the punishment of witchcraft. With considerable intervals between them, some few instances had occurred in New England of putting this sanguinary law in force; but in the year 1692, this weakness was converted into frenzy; and after exercising successfully its destructive rage on those miserable objects whose wayward dispositions had excited the ill opinion, or whose age and wretchedness ought to have secured them the pity of their neighbours, its baneful activity was extended to persons in every situation of life, and many of the most reputable members of society became its victims.

The first scene of this distressing tragedy was laid in Salem. The public mind had been prepared for its exhibition by some publications, stating the evidence adduced in former trials for witchcraft both in Old and New England, in which full proof was supposed to have been given of the guilt of the accused. Soon after this, some young girls in Boston had accustomed themselves to fall into fits, and had affected to be struck dead on the production of certain popular books, such as the *assembly's catechism*, and *Cotton's milk for babes*, while they could read Oxford's jests, or popish and quaker books, with many others, which were deemed profane, without being in any manner affected by them. These pretences, instead of exposing the fraud to instant detection, seem to have promoted the cheat; and they were supposed to be possessed by demons who were utterly confounded at the production of those holy books. "Sometimes," says Mr. Hutchinson, "they were deaf, then dumb, then blind; and sometimes, all these disorders together would come upon them. Their tongues would be drawn down their throats, then pulled out upon their chins. Their jaws, necks, shoulders, elbows, and all their joints would appear to be dislocated, and they would make most piteous outcries of burnings, of being cut with knives, beat, &c. and the marks of wounds were afterwards to be seen." At length an old Irish woman, not of good character, who had given one of those girls some harsh language, and to whom all this diabolical mischief was attributed, was apprehended by the magistracy; and neither confessing nor denying the fact, was, on the certificate of physicians that she was *compos mentis*, condemned and executed.

Sir William Phipps, the governor, on his arrival from England, brought with him opinions which could not fail to strengthen the popular prejudice, and the lieutenant governor supported one which was well calculated to render it sanguinary. He maintained that though the devil might appear in the shape of a guilty person, he could never be permitted to assume that of an innocent one. Consequently, when those who affected to perceive the form which tormented them designated any particular person as guilty, the guilt of that person was established, because he could not, if innocent, be personated by an evil spirit.

The public mind being thus predisposed, four girls in Salem, complained of being afflicted in the same manner with those in Boston. The physicians, unable to account for the disorder, attributed it to witchcraft, and an old Indian woman in the neighbourhood was selected as the witch. The attention bestowed on these girls gave them great importance; and not only confirmed them in the imposture, but produced other competitors who were ambitious of the same distinction. Several other persons were now bewitched; and not only the old Indian, but two other old women, the one bedridden, and the other subject to melancholy and distraction, were accused as witches. It was necessary to keep up the agitation already excited, by furnishing fresh subjects for astonishment; and in a short time, the accusations extended to persons who were in respectable situations. The manner in which these accusations were received, evidenced such a degree of public credulity, that the impostors seem to have been convinced of their power to assail with impunity, all whom caprice or malignity might select for their victims. Such was the prevailing infatuation, that in one instance, a child of five years old was charged as an accomplice in these pretended crimes; and if the nearest relatives of the accused manifested either tenderness for their situation, or resentment at the injury done their friends, they drew upon themselves the vengeance of these profligate impostors, and were involved in the dangers from which they were desirous of rescuing those with whom they were most intimately connected. For going out of church when allusions were made from the pulpit to a person of fair fame, a sister was charged as a witch; and for accompanying on her examination a wife who had been apprehended, the husband was involved in the same prosecution, and was condemned and executed. In the presence of the magistrates these flagitious accusers affected extreme agony, and attributed to those whom they accused, the power of torturing them by a look. The examinations were all taken in writing, and several of them are detailed at full length in Mr. Hutchinson's history of Massachusetts. They exhibit a deplorable degree of blind infatuation on one side, and of atrocious profligacy on the other, which if not well attested, could scarcely be supposed to have existed.

Many persons of sober lives, and unblemished characters, were committed to prison; and the public prejudices had already pronounced their doom. Against charges of this nature, thus conducted, no defence could possibly be made. To be accused was to be found guilty. The very grossness of the imposition seemed to secure its success, and the absurdity of the accusation to establish the verity of the charge.

The consternation became almost universal. It was soon perceived that all attempts to establish innocence must be ineffectual; and the person accused could only hope to obtain safety, by confessing the truth of the charge, and criminating others. The extent of crime introduced by such a state of things almost surpasses belief. Every feeling of humanity is shocked when we learn that to save themselves, children accused their parents; in some instances, parents their children; and in one case, sentence of death was pronounced against a husband on the testimony of his wife.

There were examples of persons who under the terrors of examination confessed themselves guilty, and accused others; but unable afterwards to support the reproaches of conscience, retracted their confessions under the persuasion that death would be the consequence of doing so.

During this reign of popular frenzy, the bounds of probability were so far transcended, that we scarcely know how to give credit to the well attested fact, that among those who were permitted to save themselves by confessing that they were witches, and joining in the accusation of their parents, were to be found children from seven to ten years of age! Among the numbers who were accused, only one person was acquitted. For this he was indebted to one of the girls who would not join the others in criminating him.

APPENDIX.

The examination had commenced in February, and the list of commitments had swelled to a lamentable bulk by June, when the new charter having arrived, commissioners of oyer and terminer were appointed for the trial of persons charged with witchcraft. By this court, a considerable number were condemned, of whom nineteen, protesting their innocence, were executed. It is observed by Mr. Hutchinson, that those who were condemned and not executed had most probably saved themselves by a confession of their guilt.

Fortunately for those who were still to be tried, the legislature, convened under the new charter, created a regular tribunal for the trial of criminal as well as civil cases, and the court of commissioners rose to sit no more. The first session of the regular court for the trial of criminal cases was to be held in January, and this delay was favourable to reflection and to the recovery of the public reason. Other causes contributed to this event. There remained yet in the various prisons of the colony, a vast number of women, many of whom were of the most reputable families in the towns in which they had resided. Allusion had been made to many others of the first rank, and some had been expressly named by the bewitched and confessing witches. A Mr. Bradstreet, who had been appointed one of the council, and was son to the old governor of that name; but who as a justice of the peace was suspected of not prosecuting with sufficient rigour, was named by the witnesses as a confederate, and found it necessary to abscond. The governor's lady it is said, and the wife of one of the ministers who had favoured this persecution, were among the accused; and a charge was also brought against the secretary of the colony of Connecticut.

Although the violence of the torrent of prejudice was beginning to abate, yet the grand jury in January, found a true bill against fifty persons, but of those brought to trial, only three were condemned, and they were not executed. All those who were not tried in January, were discharged by order of the governor, "and never," says Mr. Hutchinson, "has such a jail delivery been known in New England. And never was there given a more melancholy proof of the degree of depravity of which man is capable when the public passions countenance crime.

APPENDIX.

NOTE—No. II.

The PLAN of the Union was as follows, viz.

"It is proposed that humble application be made for an act of parliament of Great Britain, by virtue of which one general government may be formed in America, including all the said colonies: [Massachusetts Bay, New Hampshire, Connecticut, Rhode Island, New York, New Jersey, Pennsylvania, Maryland, Virginia, North Carolina, and South Carolina] within and under which government, each colony may retain its present constitution, except in the particulars wherein a change may be directed by the said act, as hereafter follows:

PRESIDENT GENERAL AND GRAND COUNCIL.

That the said general government be administered by a president general, to be appointed and supported by the crown, and a grand council, to be chosen by the representatives of the people of the several colonies, met in their assemblies.

ELECTION OF MEMBERS.

That within   months after passing such act, the houses of representatives that happen to be sitting within that time, or that shall be especially for that purpose convened, may and shall choose members for the grand council in the following proportion, that is to say:

Massachusetts Bay	7
New Hampshire	2
Connecticut	5
Rhode Island	2
New York	4
New Jersey	3
Pennsylvania	6
Maryland	4
Virginia	7
North Carolina	4
South Carolina	4
	48

PLACE OF FIRST MEETING.

Who shall meet for the first time at the city of Philadelphia, in Pennsylvania, being called by the president general as soon as conveniently may be after his appointment.

NEW ELECTION.

That there shall be a new election of the members of the grand council every three years; and on the death or resignation of any member, his place shall be supplied by a new choice, at the next sitting of the assembly of the colony he represented.

PROPORTION OF THE MEMBERS AFTER THE FIRST THREE YEARS.

That after the first three years, when the proportion of money arising out of each colony to the general treasury can be known, the number of members to be chosen for each colony shall, from time to time, in all ensuing elections, be regulated by that proportion (yet so as that the number to be chosen by any one province be not more than seven, nor less than two.)

MEETINGS OF THE GRAND COUNCIL AND CALL.

That the grand council shall meet once in every year, and oftener, if occasion require, at such time and place as they shall adjourn to at the last preceding meeting, or as they shall be called to meet at by the president general, on any emergency; he having first obtained in writing the consent of seven of the members to such call, and sent due and timely notice to the whole.

CONTINUANCE.

That the grand council have power to choose their speaker: and shall neither be dissolved, prorogued, nor continued sitting longer than six weeks at one time; without their own consent, or the special command of the crown.

MEMBERS ATTENDANCE.

That the members of the grand council shall be allowed for their services, ten shillings sterling per diem, during their session and journey to and from the place of meeting; twenty miles to be reckoned a day's journey.

ASSENT OF PRESIDENT GENERAL AND HIS DUTY.

That the assent of the president general be requisite to all acts of the grand council; and that it be his office and duty to cause them to be carried into execution.

POWER OF PRESIDENT GENERAL AND GRAND COUNCIL, TREATIES OF PEACE AND WAR.

That the president general, with the advice of the grand council, hold or direct all Indian treaties in which the general interest of the colonies may be concerned; and make peace or declare war with Indian nations.

INDIAN TRADE.

That they make such laws as they judge necessary for regulating all Indian trade.

INDIAN PURCHASES.

That they make all purchases from the Indians for the crown, of lands not now within the bounds of particular colonies, or that shall not be within their bounds, when some of them are reduced to more convenient dimensions.

NEW SETTLEMENTS.

That they make new settlements on such purchases by granting lands in the king's name, reserving a quit rent to the crown, for the use of the general treasury.

LAWS TO GOVERN THEM.

That they make laws for regulating and governing such new settlements, until the crown shall think fit to form them into particular governments.

RAISE SOLDIERS AND EQUIP VESSELS, &c.

That they raise and pay soldiers, build forts for the defence of any of the colonies, and equip vessels of force to guard the coasts and protect the trade on the ocean, lakes, or great rivers; but they shall not impress men in any colony, without the consent of the legislature.

POWER TO MAKE LAWS, LAY DUTIES, &c.

That for these purposes they have power to make laws, and lay and levy such general duties, imposts, or taxes, as to them shall appear most equal and just, (considering the ability and other circumstances of the inhabitants in the several colonies) and such as may be collected with the least inconvenience to the people; rather discouraging luxury, than loading industry with unnecessary burdens.

GENERAL TREASURER AND PARTICULAR TREASURER.

That they may appoint a general treasurer and particular treasurer in each government, when necessary; and from time time may order the sums in the treasuries of each government into the general treasury, or draw on them for special payments, as they find most convenient.

MONEY, HOW TO ISSUE.

Yet no money to issue but by joint orders of the president general and grand council, except where sums have been appropriated to particular purposes, and the president general has been previously empowered by an act to draw for such sums.

ACCOUNTS.

That the general accounts shall be yearly settled, and reported to the several assemblies.

QUORUM.

That a quorum of the grand council, empowered to act with the president general, do consist of twenty-five members; among whom there shall be one or more from the majority of the colonies.

LAWS TO BE TRANSMITTED.

That the laws made by them for the purposes aforesaid, shall not be repugnant, but, as near as may be, agreeable to the laws of England, and shall be transmitted to the king in council, for approbation, as soon as may be after their passing; and if not disapproved within three years after presentation, to remain in force.

DEATH OF THE PRESIDENT GENERAL.

That in case of the death of the president general, the speaker of the grand council for the time being shall succeed, and be vested with the same powers and authorities, to continue until the king's pleasure be known.

OFFICERS, HOW APPOINTED.

That all military commission officers, whether for land or sea service, to act under this general constitution, shall be nominated by the president general; but the approbation of the grand council is to be obtained, before they receive their commissions. And all civil officers are to be nominated by the grand council, and to receive the president general's approbation before they officiate.

VACANCIES, HOW SUPPLIED.

But in case of vacancy, by death, or removal of any officer, civil or military, under this constitution, the governor of the province in which such vacancy happens, may appoint until the pleasure of the president general and grand council can be known.

EACH COLONY MAY DEFEND ITSELF ON EMERGENCY, &c.

That the particular military as well as civil establishments in each colony remain in their present state, the general constitution notwithstanding; and that on sudden emergencies any colony may defend itself, and lay the accounts of expense thence arising before the president general and grand council, who may allow and order payment of the same as far as they judge such accounts reasonable.

Minot.

APPENDIX.

NOTE—No. III.

Virginia Resolutions --- 1765

These being the first resolutions of any assembly after the passage of the stamp act, they are inserted.

Whereas, The honourable house of commons in England have of late drawn into question how far the general assembly of this colony hath power to enact laws for laying taxes and imposing duties payable by the people of this his majesty's most ancient colony, for settling and ascertaining the same to all future times, the house of Burgesses of the present general assembly have come to the several following resolutions.

Resolved, That the first adventurers and settlers of this his majesty's colony and dominion of Virginia, brought with them, and transmitted to their posterity, and all others his majesty's subjects since inhabiting in this his majesty's colony, all the privileges and immunities that have at any time been held, enjoyed, and possessed by the people of Great Britain.

Resolved, That by two royal charters granted by King James I. the colonies aforesaid are declared entitled to all the privileges of denizens, and natural born subjects, to all intents and purposes as if they had been abiding and born within the realm of England.

Resolved, That the taxation of the people by themselves, or by persons chosen by themselves, to represent them, who can only know what taxes the people are able to bear, and the easiest mode of raising them, and are equally affected by such taxes themselves, is the distinguished characteristic of British freedom, and without which the ancient constitution cannot subsist.

Resolved, That his majesty's liege people of this most ancient colony have uninterruptedly enjoyed the right of being thus governed by their own assembly in the article of their taxes and internal police, and that the same hath never been forfeited nor any other way yielded up, but hath been constantly recognised by the King and people of Great Britain.

Resolved, Therefore, that the general assembly of this colony have the sole power to lay taxes and impositions upon the inhatants of this colony; and that every attempt to vest such a power in any person or persons whatsoever, other than the general assembly aforesaid, has a manifest tendency to destroy British as well as American freedom.*

NOTE—NO. IV. *p. 361.*

Declaration of Rights. Congress. 176

"The members of this congress, sincerely devoted with the warmest sentiments of affection and duty, to his majesty's person and government, inviolably attached to the present happy establishment of the protestant succession, and with minds deeply impressed by a sense of the present and impending misfortunes of the British colonies on this continent; having considered, as maturely as time will permit, the circumstances of the said colonies, esteem it our indispensable duty to make the following declarations of our humble opinion, respecting the most essential rights and liberties of the colonists, and of the grievances under which they labour, by reason of several late acts of parliament.

I. That his majesty's subjects in these colonies, owe the same allegiance to the crown of Great Britain that is owing from his subjects born within the realm, and all due subordination to that august body the parliament of Great Britain.

II. That his majesty's liege subjects in these colonies, are entitled to all the inherent rights and liberties of his natural born subjects, within the kingdom of Great Britain.

III. That it is inseparably essential to the freedom of a people, and the undoubted right of Englishmen, that no taxes be

---

* These resolutions are in a small degree different from those published in the Introduction to the Life of Washington. They are copied from Mr. Wirt's Life of Patrick Henry. That gentleman having been fortunate enough to obtain a copy of the journals of the house of Burgesses for that session, the resolutions extracted from them by him are supposed to be accurate.

APPENDIX. 471

imposed on them, but with their own consent, given personally, or by their representatives.

IV. That the people of these colonies or not, and, from their local circumstances, cannot be represented in the house of commons of Great Britain.

V. That the only representatives of these colonies are persons chosen therein by themselves, and that no taxes ever have been, or can be constitutionally imposed upon them, but by their respective legislatures.

VI. That all supplies to the crown being free gifts from the people, it is unreasonable, and inconsistent with the principles and spirit of the British constitution, for the people of Great Britain to grant to his majesty the property of the colonists.

VII. That trial by jury is the inherent and invaluable right of every British subject in these colonies.

VIII. That the late act of parliament entitled, 'an act for granting and applying certain stamp duties, and other duties, in the British colonies and plantations in America,' &c by imposing taxes on the inhabitants of these colonies; and the said act, and several other acts, by extending the jurisdiction of the courts of admiralty beyond its ancient limits, have a manifest tendency to subvert the rights and liberties of the colonists.

IX. That the duties imposed by several late acts of parliament, from the peculiar circumstances of these colonies, will be extremely burdensome and grievous; and from the scarcity of specie, the payment of them absolutely impracticable.

X. That as the profits of the trade of these colonies ultimately centre in Great Britain, to pay for the manufactures which they are obliged to take from thence, they eventually contribute very largely to all supplies granted to the crown.

XI. That the restrictions imposed by several late acts of parliament on the trade of these colonies, will render them unable to purchase the manufactures of Great Britain.

XII. That the increase, prosperity, and happiness of these colonies depend on the full and free enjoyment of their rights and liberties, and an intercourse with Great Britain mutually affectionate and advantageous.

XIII. That it is the right of the British subjects in these colonies to petition the king, or either house of parliament.

XIV. That it is the indispensable duty of these colonies, to the best of sovereigns, to the mother country, and to themselves, to endeavour, by a loyal and dutiful address to his majesty, and humble applications to both houses of parliament, to procure the repeal of the act for granting and applying certain stamp duties, of all clauses of any other acts of parliament, whereby the jurisdiction of the admiralty is extended as aforesaid, and of the other late acts for the restriction of American commerce."

*   *Prior Documents.*

NOTE—No. V.

Province of Massachusetts Bay, Feb. 11, 1768.

Sir,

The house of representatives of this province have taken into their consideration the great difficulties that must accrue to themselves and their constituents, by the operation of the several acts of parliament imposing duties and taxes on the American colonies.

As it is a subject in which every colony is deeply interested, they have no reason to doubt but your house is duly impressed with its importance: and that such constitutional measures will be come into as are proper. It seems to be necessary, that all possible care should be taken that the representations of the several assemblies, upon so delicate a point, should harmonise with each other: the house, therefore, hope that this letter will be candidly considered in no other light, than as expressing a disposition freely to communicate their mind to a sister colony, upon a common concern, in the same manner as they would be glad to receive the sentiments of your or any other house of assembly on the continent.

The house have humbly represented to the ministry their own sentiments; that his majesty's high court of parliament is the supreme legislative power over the whole empire: that in all free states the constitution is fixed: and, as the supreme legislative derives its power and authority from the constitution, it cannot overleap the bounds of it, without destroying its foundation; that the constitution ascertains and limits both sovereignty and allegiance; and therefore, his majesty's American subjects who acknowledge themselves bound by the ties of allegiance, have an equitable claim to the full enjoyment of the fundamental rules of the British constitution; that it is an essential unalterable right in nature, ingrafted into the British constitution as a fundamental law, and ever held sacred and irrevocable by the subjects within the realm, that what a man hath honestly acquired is absolutely his own, which he may freely give, but cannot be taken from him without his consent; that the American subjects may therefore, exclusive of any consideration of charter rights, with a decent firmness adapted to the character of freemen and subjects, assert this natural and constitutional right.

It is moreover their humble opinion, which they express with the greatest deference to the wisdom of the parliament, that the acts made there, imposing duties on the people of this province, with the sole and express purpose of raising a revenue, are infringements of their natural and constitutional rights; because as they are not represented in the British parliament, his majesty's commons in Britain by those acts grant their property without their consent.

This house further are of opinion, that their constituents, considering their local circumstances, cannot by any possibility be represented in the parliament; and that it will forever be impracticable that they should be equally represented there, and consequently not at all, being separated by an ocean of a thousand leagues: that his majesty's royal predecessors, for this reason, were graciously pleased to form a subordinate legislative here, that their subjects might enjoy the unalienable right of a representation. Also, that, considering the utter impracticability of their ever being fully and equally represented in parliament, and the great expense that must unavoidably attend even a partial representation there, this house think, that a taxation of their constituents, even without their consent, grievous as it is, would be preferable to any representation that could be admitted for them there.

Upon these principles, and also considering that were the right in the parliament ever so clear, yet for obvious reasons it would be beyond the rule of equity, that their constituents should be taxed on the manufactures of Great Britain here, in addition to the duties they pay for them in England, and other advantages arising to Great Britain from the acts of trade; this house have preferred a humble, dutiful, and loyal petition to our most gracious sovereign, and made such representation to his majesty's ministers, as they apprehend would tend to obtain redress.

They have also submitted to consideration, whether any people can be said to enjoy any degree of freedom, if the crown, in addition to its undoubted authority of constituting a governor, should appoint him such a stipend as it shall judge proper without the consent of the people, and at their expense; and whether, while the judges of the land, and other civil officers, hold not their commissions during good behaviour, their having salaries appointed for them by the crown, independent of the people, hath not a tendency to subvert the principles of equity, and endanger the happiness and security of the subject.

In addition to these measures, the house have written a letter to their agent Mr. de Berdt, the sentiments of which he is directed to lay before the ministry; wherein they take notice of the hardship of the act for preventing mutiny and desertion, which requires the governor and council to provide enumerated articles for the king's marching troops and the people to pay the expense: and also the commission of the gentlemen appointed commissioners of the customs to reside in America, which authorises them to make as many appointments as they think fit, and to pay the appointees what sums they please, for whose mal-conduct they are not accountable: from whence it may happen, that officers of the crown may be multiplied to such a degree, as to become dangerous to the liberties of the people, by virtue of a commission which doth not appear to this house to derive any such advantages to trade as many have been led to expect.

These are the sentiments and proceedings of the house, and as they have too much reason to believe that the enemies of the colonies have represented them to his majesty's ministers and the parliament as factious, disloyal, and having a disposition to make themselves independent of the mother country, they have taken occasion in the most humble terms, to assure his majesty and his ministers, that, with regard to the people of this province, and, as they doubt not, of all the colonies, the charge is unjust.

The house is fully satisfied, that your assembly is too generous and enlarged in sentiment to believe, that this letter proceeds from an ambition of taking the lead, or dictating to the other assemblies; they freely submit their opinion to the judgment of others; and shall take it kind in your house to point out to them any thing further that may be thought necessary.

This house cannot conclude without expressing their firm confidence in the king, our common head and father, that the united and dutiful supplications of his distressed American subjects will meet with his royal and favourable acceptance.

NOTE—No. VI.

An account of the origin of these committees, and of their mode of proceeding, is thus given by Mr. Gordon, and is not unworthy of attention.

"Governor Hutchinson and his adherents having been used to represent the party in opposition, as only an uneasy factious few in Boston, while the body of the people were quite contented; Mr. Samuel Adams was thereby induced to visit Mr. James

Warren, of Plymouth. After conversing upon the subject, the latter proposed to originate and establish committees of correspondence in the several towns of the colony, in order to learn the strength of the friends to the rights of the continent, and to unite and increase their force. Mr. Samuel Adams returned to Boston, pleased with the proposal, and communicated the same to his confidents. Some doubted whether the measure would prosper, and dreaded a disappointment which might injure the cause of liberty. But it was concluded to proceed. The prime managers were about six in number, each of whom, when separate, headed a division; the several individuals of which, collected and led distinct subdivisions. In this manner the political engine has been constructed. The different parts are not equally good and operative. Like other bodies, its composition includes numbers who act mechanically, as they are pressed this way or that way by those who judge for them; and divers of the wicked, fitted for evil practices, when the adoption of them is thought necessary to particular purposes, and a part of whose creed it is, that in political matters the public good is above every other consideration, and that all rules of morality when in competition with it, may be safely dispensed with. When any important transaction is to be brought forward, it is thoroughly considered by the prime managers. If they approve, each communicates it to his own division; from thence, if adopted, it passes to the several subdivisions, which form a general meeting in order to canvass the business. The prime managers being known only by few to be the promoters of it, are desired to be present at the debate, that they may give their opinion when it closes. If they observe that the collected body is in general strongly against the measure they wish to have carried, they declare it to be improper: is it opposed by great numbers, but not warmly, they advise to a re-consideration at another meeting, and prepare for its being then adopted; if the opposition is not considerable, either in number or weight of persons, they give their reasons, and then recommend the adoption of the measure. The principal actors are determined on securing the liberties of their country, or perishing in the attempt.

"The news of his majesty's granting salaries to the justices of the superior court, afforded them a fair opportunity for executing the plan of establishing committees of correspondence through the colony. The most spirited pieces were published, and an alarm spread, that the granting such salaries tended rapidly to complete the system of their slavery.

"A town meeting was called, and a committee of correspondence appointed, to write circular letters to all the towns in the province, and to induce them to unite in measures. The committee made a report, containing several resolutions contradictory to the supremacy of the British legislature. After setting forth, that all men have a right to remain in a state of nature as long as they please, they proceed to a report upon the natural rights of the colonists as men, christians, and subjects; and then form a list of infringements and violations of their rights. They enumerate and dwell upon the British parliament's having assumed the power of legislation for the colonies in all cases whatsoever —the appointment of a number of new officers to superintend the revenues—the granting of salaries out of the American revenue, to the governor, the judges of the superior court, the king's attorney and solicitor general. The report was accepted; copies printed; and six hundred circulated through the towns and districts of the province, with a pathetic letter addressed to the inhabitants, who were called upon not to doze any longer, or sit supinely in indifference, while the iron hand of oppression was daily tearing the choicest fruits from the fair tree of liberty. The circular letter requested of each town a free communication of sentiments on the subjects of the report, and was directed to the select men, who were desired to lay the same before a town meeting, which has been generally practised, and the proceedings of the town upon the business have been transmitted to the committee at Boston. This committee have their particular correspondents in the several towns, who, upon receiving any special information, are ready to spread it with dispatch among the inhabitants. It consists of twenty-one persons of heterogeneous qualities and professions, &c."

Gordon's Hist. Am. War, vol. 1. p. 312.

APPENDIX.

NOTE—NO. VII.

THE FOLLOWING IS A LIST OF THE MEMBERS COMPOSING THE FIRST CONGRESS:

New Hampshire.

John Sullivan,   Nathaniel Fulsom.

Massachusetts Bay.

James Bowdoin,   John Adams,
Thomas Cushing,   Robert Treat Paine.
Samuel Adams,

Rhode Island and Providence Plantations.

Stephen Hopkins,   Samuel Ward.

Connecticut.

Eliphalet Dyer,   Silas Deane.
Roger Sherman,

From the city and county of New York, and other counties in the province of New York.

James Duane,   Philip Livingston,
Henry Wisner,   Isaac Low,
John Jay,   John Alsop.

From the county of Suffolk, in the province of New York.

William Floyd.

New Jersey.

James Kinsey,   Stephen Crane,
William Livingston,   Richard Smith.
John Dehart,

Pennsylvania.

Joseph Galloway,   John Morton,
Charles Humphreys,   Thomas Mifflin,
Samuel Rhoads,   Edward Biddle,
George Ross,   John Dickinson.

APPENDIX. 479

Newcastle, Kent, and Sussex, on Delaware.
Cesar Rodney, George Read.
Thomas M'Kean,

Maryland.
Robert Goldsborough, Samuel Chase,
Thomas Johnson, Matthew Tilghman.
William Paca,

Virginia.
Peyton Randolph, Richard Bland,
Richard Henry Lee, Benjamin Harrison,
George Washington, Edmund Pendleton.
Patrick Henry,

North Carolina.
William Hooper, Richard Caswell.
Joseph Hughes,

South Carolina.
Henry Middleton, Christopher Gadsden,
John Rutledge, Edward Rutledge.
Thomas Lynch,

NOTE—NO. VIII.

These resolutions manifested a degree of irritation which had not before been displayed. They are introduced in the following manner:

" Whereas the power but not the justice, the vengeance but not the wisdom of Great Britain, which of old persecuted, scourged, and exiled our fugitive parents from their native shores, now pursues us their guiltless children, with unrelenting severity; and whereas this, then savage and uncultivated desert, was purchased by the toil and treasure, or acquired by the blood and valour of those our venerable progenitors; to us they bequeathed the dear bought inheritance; to our care and protection they consigned it; and the most sacred obligations are upon us to transmit the glorious purchase, unfettered by power, unclogged with shackles, to our innocent and beloved offspring. On the fortitude, on the wisdom, and on the exertions of this important day, is suspended the fate of this new world, and of unborn millions. If a boundless extent of continent, swarming with millions, will tamely submit to live, move, and have their being at the arbitrary will of a licentious minister, they basely yield to voluntary slavery, and future generations shall load their memories with incessant execrations. On the other hand, if we arrest the hand which would ransack our pockets, if we disarm the parracide which points the dagger to our bosoms, if we nobly defeat that fatal edict which proclaims a power to frame laws for us in all cases whatsoever, thereby entailing the endless and numberless curses of slavery upon us, our heirs, and their heirs for ever; if we successfully resist that unparalleled usurpation of unconstitutional power, whereby our capital is robbed of the means of life; whereby the streets of Boston are thronged with military executioners; whereby our coasts are lined, and harbours crowded with ships of war; whereby the charter of the colony, that sacred barrier against the encroachments of tyranny, is mutilated, and in effect annihilated; whereby a murderous law is framed to shelter villians from the hands of justice; whereby the unalienable and inestimable inheritance, which we derived from nature, the constitution of Britain, and the privileges warranted to us in the charter of the province, is totally wrecked, annulled, and vacated: Posterity will acknowledge that virtue which preserved them free and happy; and while we enjoy the rewards and blessings of the faithful, the torrent of panegyrists will roll our reputations to that latest period, when the streams of time shall be absorbed in the abyss of eternity.

"Therefore resolved," &c. &c. &c.

NOTE—NO. IX.

[handwritten: p. 412 Declaration of Rights— Congress. 1774.]

"Whereas, since the close of the last war, the British parliament, claiming a power, of right, to bind the people of America by statutes in all cases whatsoever, hath in some acts expressly imposed taxes on them; and in others, under various pretences, but in fact for the purpose of raising a revenue, hath imposed rates and duties payable in these colonies, established a board of commissioners with unconstitutional powers, and extended the jurisdiction of courts of admiralty, not only for collecting the said duties, but for the trial of causes merely arising within the body of a county.

"And whereas, in consequence of other statutes, judges, who before held only estates at will in their offices, have been made dependent on the crown alone for their salaries, and standing armies kept in times of peace: And whereas it has lately been resolved in parliament, that by force of a statute, made in the thirty-fifth year of the reign of King Henry VIII. colonists may be transported to England and tried there upon accusations for treasons, and misprisons and concealments of treasons committed in the colonies, and by a late statute, such trials have been directed in cases therein mentioned.

"And whereas, in the last session of parliament, three statutes were made; one entitled, 'An act to discontinue in such manner and for such time as are therein mentioned, the landing and discharging, lading or shipping of goods, wares, and merchandise, at the town, and within the harbour of Boston, in the province of Massachusetts Bay in North America;' another entitled, 'An act for the better regulating the government of the province of Massachusetts Bay in New England;' and another act, entitled, 'An act for the impartial administration of justice, in the cases of persons questioned for any act done by them in the execution of the law, or for the suppression of riots and tumults, in the province of the Massachusetts Bay in New England;' and another statute was then made, 'for making more effectual provision for the government of the province of Quebec," &c. All which statutes are impolitic, unjust, and cruel, as well as unconstitutional, and most dangerous and destructive of American rights.

"And whereas, assemblies have been frequently dissolved, contrary to the rights of the people, when they attempted to deliberate on grievances; and their dutiful, humble, loyal, and reasonable petitions to the crown for redress, have been repeatedly treated with contempt by his majesty's ministers of state; the good people of the several colonies of New Hampshire, Massachusetts Bay, Rhode Island and Providence Plantations, Connecticut, New York, New Jersey, Pennsylvania, New Castle, Kent and Sussex on Delaware, Maryland, Virginia, North Carolina, and South Carolina, justly alarmed at the arbitrary proceedings of parliament and administration, have severally elected, constituted and appointed deputies to meet and sit in general congress, in the city of Philadelphia, in order to obtain such establishment, as that their religion, laws, and liberties, may not be subverted: whereupon the deputies so appointed being now assembled, in a full and free representation of these colonies, taking into their most serious consideration, the best means of attaining the ends aforesaid, do in the first place, as Englishmen their ancestors in like cases have usually done, for asserting and vindicating their rights and liberties, DECLARE, that the inhabitants of the English colonies in North America, by the immutable laws of nature, the principles of the English constitution, and the several charters or compacts, have the following rights.

"Resolved, N. C. D. 1st, that they are entitled to life, liberty, and property; and they have never ceded to any sovereign power whatever, a right to dispose of either without their consent.

"Resolved, N. C. D. 2d, that our ancestors, who first settled these colonies, were, at the time of their emigration from the mother country, entitled to all the rights, liberties, and immunities of free and natural born subjects, within the realm of England.

" Resolved, N. C. D. 3d, that by such emigration they by no means forfeited, surrendered, or lost any of those rights, but that they were, and their descendants now are, entitled to the exercise and enjoyment of all such of them, as their local and other circumstances enabled them to exercise and enjoy.

" Resolved, 4th, that the foundation of English liberty and of all free government, is a right in the people to participate in their legislative council : and as the English colonists are not represented, and from their local and other circumstances cannot properly be represented in the British parliament, they are entitled to a free and exclusive power of legislation in their several provincial legislatures, where their right of representation can alone be preserved, in all cases of taxation and internal polity subject only to the negative of their sovereign, in such manner as has been heretofore used and accustomed : but from the necessity of the case, and a regard to the mutual interest of both countries, we cheerfully consent to the operation of such acts of the British parliament, as are, *bona fide*, restrained to the regulation of our external commerce, for the purpose of securing the commercial advantages of the whole empire to the mother country, and the commercial benefits of its respective members ; excluding every idea of taxation internal or external, for raising a revenue on the subjects in America without their consent.

" Resolved, N. C. D. 5th, that the respective colonies are entitled to the common law of England, and more especially to the great and inestimable privilege of being tried by their peers of the vicinage, according to the course of that law.

" Resolved, 6th, that they are entitled to the benefit of such of the English statutes, as existed at the time of their colonisation ; and which they have, by experience, respectively found to be applicable to their several local and other circumstances.

" Resolved, N. C. D. 7th, that these, his majesty's colonies are likewise entitled to all the immunities and privileges granted and confirmed to them by royal charters, or secured by their several codes of provincial laws.

"Resolved, N. C. D. 8th, that they have a right peaceably to assemble, consider of their grievances, and petition the King; and that all prosecutions, prohibitory proclamations, and commitments for the same, are illegal.

"Resolved, N. C. D. 9th, that the keeping a standing army in these colonies, in times of peace, without the consent of the legislature of that colony in which such army is kept, is against law.

"Resolved, N. C. D. 10th, it is indispensably necessary to good government, and rendered essential by the English constitution, that the constituent branches of the legislature be independent of each other; that, therefore, the exercise of legislative power in several colonies, by a council appointed, during pleasure, by the crown, is unconstitutional, dangerous, and destructive to the freedom of American legislation.

"All and each of which the aforesaid deputies, in behalf of themselves and their constituents, do claim, demand, and insist on, as their indubitable rights and liberties; which cannot be legally taken from them, altered or abridged by any power whatever, without their own consent, by their representatives in their several provincial legislatures.

"In the course of our inquiry, we find many infringements and violations of the foregoing rights, which, from an ardent desire that harmony and mutual intercourse of affection and interest may be restored, we pass over for the present, and proceed to state such acts and measures as have been adopted since the last war, which demonstrate a system formed to enslave America.

"Resolved, N. C. D. that the following acts of parliament are infringements and violations of the rights of the colonists; and that the repeal of them is essentially necessary, in order to restore harmony between Great Britain and the American colonies, viz.

"The several acts of 4 Geo. III. chap. 15, and 34.—5 Geo.

III. chap. 25.—6 Geo. III. chap. 52.—7 Geo. III. chap. 41, and chap. 46.—8 Geo. III. chap. 22; which imposed duties for the purpose of raising a revenue in America; extend the power of the admiralty courts beyond their ancient limits; deprive the American subject of trial by jury; authorise the judge's certificate to indemnify the prosecutor from damages, that he might otherwise be liable to; requiring oppressive security from a claimant of ships and goods seized, before he shall be allowed to defend his property, and are subversive of American rights.

"Also 12 Geo. III. chap. 24 intituled, 'an act for the better securing his majesty's dockyards, magazines, ships, ammunition, and stores,' which declares a new offence in America, and deprives the American subject of a constitutional trial by a jury of the vicinage, by authorising the trial of any person charged with the committing of any offence described in the said act, out of the realm, to be indicted and tried for the same in any shire or county within the realm.

"Also the three acts passed in the last session of parliament, for stopping the port and blocking up the harbour of Boston, for altering the charter and government of Massachusetts Bay, and that which is intitutled, 'an act for the better administration of justice,' &c.

"Also, the act passed in the same session for establishing the Roman catholic religion in the province of Quebec, abolishing the equitable system of English laws, and erecting a tyranny there, to the great danger, (from so total a dissimilarity of religion, law, and government) of the neighbouring British colonies, by the assistance of whose blood and treasure the said country was conquered from France.

"Also, the act passed in the same session for the better providing suitable quarters for officers and soldiers in his majesty's service in North America.

"Also, that the keeping a standing army in several of these colonies, in time of peace, without the consent of the legislature of that colony in which such army is kept, is against law.

"To these grievous acts and measures, Americans cannot submit; but in hopes their fellow subjects in Great Britain will, on

APPENDIX.

a revision of them, restore us to that state, in which both countries found happiness and prosperity, we have for the present only resolved to pursue the following peaceable measures: 1. to enter into a non-importation, non-consumption, and non-exportation agreement or association. 2. To prepare an address to the people of Great Britain, and a memorial to the inhabitants of British America: and, 3. To prepare a loyal address to his majesty, agreeable to resolutions already entered into."

THE END.